Dylan Jones is the Editor of GQ, the most
successful upmarket men's magazine in Britain.

'This book is unputdownable!' Matthew d'Ancona

'Requisite reading for the ambitious, would-be modern
gentleman. Jones' tips will have you looking and acting
the part as you scale the ladders of success.'
David Furnish

'Do everything he says.' Peter York

MR JONES' RULES
FOR THE
MODERN MAN

Dylan Jones

HODDER

Copyright © 2006 by Dylan Jones
Illustrations © 2006 by Richard Holiday

First published in Great Britain in 2006 by Hodder & Stoughton
A division of Hodder Headline

This paperback edition published in 2007

The right of Dylan Jones to be identified as the Author
of the Work has been asserted by him in accordance with the
Copyright, Designs and Patents Act 1988.

A Hodder paperback

1

A CIP catalogue record for this title is available from the British Library

ISBN 978 0 340 92086 2

Hodder Headline's policy is to use papers that are natural, renewable
and recyclable products and made from wood grown in sustainable forests. The
logging and manufacturing processes are expected to conform to the environ-
mental regulations of the country of origin.

Hodder & Stoughton Ltd
A division of Hodder Headline
338 Euston Road
London NW1 3BH

For Audrey Jones

CONTENTS

ETIQUETTE & DECORUM

SEX & SENSIBILITY

STYLE & FASHION

SPORT & LEISURE

HEALTH & EFFICIENCY

ELBOW GREASE & SKYHOOKS

FOOD & DRINK

ACKNOWLEDGEMENTS

I'd first like to thank my employers at Condé Nast, Nicholas Coleridge and Jonathan Newhouse, for all their continued help and encouragement. Thanks also to Nicholas for kindly reading some passages for me, and for making some extremely valuable suggestions (although bizarrely none concerning How to Ask for a Pay Rise or How to Suck Up to Your Boss).

I'd also like to thank Richard Atkinson for originally commissioning the book, Nick Davies for guiding me through the editing and publishing of it, and my wife Sarah Walter for giving me enough time to write it. Thanks also to Michael Jones, Richard Campbell-Breeden, Tony Parsons, Sir Paul Smith, Alex Field, Jamie Bill, Alice Morgan, Pino Guido, David Livingstone, Alasdair Lane, Danielle Radojcin, Simon Kelner, Peter Wright, Gerard Greaves, Robin Derrick and Nick Foulkes, all of whom helped in some way. Some of the material here originally started life as columns in *GQ*, the *Independent* and the *Mail on Sunday*'s *Live* magazine supplement, and I'd like to thank the various section- and sub-editors of those publications for their patience and diligence in improving my work. Thanks also to my PowerBook G4's Word spell-check.

Finally, I'd like to thank Grainne Fox, Hitesh Shah, Cristina Corbalan and everyone else at Ed Victor's agency, as well as the brilliant Ed Victor himself, a man who, had he been so inclined, could have written this book himself.

INTRODUCTION

When I began researching this book, Jamie, a trusted colleague, kept talking about this dog-eared, dust-covered book he had in his attic in Suffolk, an ancient (well, fifty years old, at least) tome that, he said, contained all there was to know about wining, dining, gambling and dealing with the opposite sex.

This was Jamie's own personal Holy Grail, a secular scroll containing a litany of rules and regulations as to how the modern man should conduct himself. He kept taunting me, telling me that if I behaved myself, and didn't keep pointing out his new jacket to his staff (come on – it was covered in cowhide!), and stopped leaving phoney messages for him from the managing director, he would bring it in.

And one afternoon, as I returned from lunch, there on my desk was this oblong, cloth-covered hardback, its cover so weathered, that it looked like a church bible (which, in a way, it was). As I opened it up, the stiff, brittle pages peeling away like municipal lavatory paper, it was as if a whole other world was opening up before me, a world where men all wore dinner jackets and sock garters, drank martinis with impunity and considered cigarette-holders to be a stamp of sophistication, rather than advertising the fact they might be rather light in the loafers.

But oh, how times have changed. These days, men's social standing doesn't live or die by their understanding of which way to pass the port after dinner (clockwise, in case you didn't know). I've always been fairly suspicious of the old rules and regulations regarding how 'us men' are meant to behave – a feeling exemplified by a story I once heard about Claus von Bülow, who was tried in 1982 for the attempted murder of his wealthy wife Sunny (after being found guilty he was acquitted on appeal). Towards the end of a smart cocktail party in London, von Bülow spies a poorly dressed paparazzo, and promptly walks up to him to castigate him for his woeful attire.

'You must never, ever wear a brown belt with black shoes!' screams von Bülow.

To which the photographer replies, 'Well, at least I didn't murder my wife.'

While we still need to know how to tie a bow-tie (page 215), and how to make that martini (page 396), we also need to know how to win an argument, how to suck up to our boss, how to behave at a lap-dancing club, how to get the best room in a hotel, and how to look after our skin without feeling like a girl.

Today there are new international rules of cool.

And so here, in this book, is the complete modern guide to being a man, a proper etiquette guide for real men – not the sort who spend their life imagining they're in a Cary Grant movie. My book aims to give you the best possible platform for advancing in the world; it offers the best advice for a multitude of difficult situations. After all, there's no need to plateau just because of lack of experience.

Hopefully this book has all the experiences for you.

It is a fact that, although we are now all part of the new, shiny, all-singing, all-dancing meritocracy, there are still very definite rules about what you should and shouldn't do. Not only that, there is also a huge list (contained herein) of *new* rules regarding work, gambling, style, the sex-wars and etiquette: just how *do* you ask for a pay rise, or read the financial pages of a newspaper, rebuff an unwanted advance, dress your age, find the G-spot, handle a celebrity or cope with failure?

If I'm honest, I could have done with a bit of guidance myself when I was younger, could have done with a helping hand, a concerned word in my shell-like. Like many young men, I embodied the dictionary definition of gauche: I didn't know what to say, what to do, or what to wear. Even in my early twenties I'd be in an alien social situation and just . . . sort of have to wing it. Sometimes I got by – charm helps a lot in these situations – and sometimes I sank, deep, deep into the murky, glutinous depths of visible, very public embarrassment.

Once, when I was about 22 or 23, and had just started working in the magazine industry, I was taken to Caviar Caspia, the tremendously smart Mayfair restaurant that Princess Diana used to go to. I was new in my job, and was being taken to lunch by the MD of a French luxury goods company, who was all suited and booted in what I assumed to be top-dollar Savile Row. We both ordered gravadlax (smoked salmon to me), and as he waited for me to start eating (the man was nothing if not polite), I carefully took the gauze off the half lemon that had kindly been left on my plate, so I could squeeze the juice over my fish. Having never seen anyone do this before, I naturally thought this was the right thing to do. Until, of course, I saw my host simply squeeze his lemon through the gauze, making me feel like a jumped-up inter-loper (which I was, and most probably still am). You could say that if he'd been truly polite my host would have copied me, but then as he no doubt knew everyone else in the restaurant, he wasn't going to embarrass himself by acting like a rube. That was my job.

So I felt like a fool. But I didn't die, and no legs were broken, and I lived to fight another day.

Around the same time, I was invited to lunch at L'Escargot in Soho by the head of a fantastically important PR agency. At the time – 1984-ish – this was the coolest restaurant in London, and I was almost giddy with excitement. Although not so giddy that I bothered to dress properly. I turned up – what was I thinking! – in a ridiculously trendy black nylon MA-1 flying jacket, the sort worn by American fighter pilots, the sort that used to go down very well at two o'clock in the morning in nauseatingly fashionable nightclubs in Camden, but looked more than ridiculous in the world's smartest eaterie in the middle of the day.

I learned my lesson, though, and the very next day went and bought two suits in Katharine Hamnett. Never again was I going to feel like a boy when I wanted to feel like a man.

Trust me, there will always be the right and the wrong way to conduct yourself in public (and in bed), and this book shows you how. If you look carefully, you'll notice that success in life is determined by small, tell-tale signs, just as it ever was, the sort of sociological and sartorial give-aways that still separate the men from the boys. If society has changed at all in the last few decades it's in the way in which style has replaced class as a signifier of success, while the new pagan gods are more likely to be a flash car or a designer raincoat rather than a private banking account or a golf club membership. And because men are now as sophisticated as women in their shopping habits, and as we've learned to consume in the way our wives and girlfriends have been doing for years, we are now susceptible to the same kind of mistakes. And you don't have to wear a belt made from bailer twine to tell everyone you're from the wrong side of the fence; all you need do is wear square-toed shoes, *diamanté* cufflinks, a fat footballer's tie or a four-button suit.

It pays to be a hungry observer of the world around you, as it will always stand you in good stead. And as you don't want to be overwhelmed by the sheer muchness of the world, you sometimes need a guide.

Hopefully this book is that guide – a compendium of cool, a cathedral of gentlemanliness, and a considerable mass of information leavened by a large dose of personal prejudice.

Enjoy it, please.

WORK
&
MONEY

HOW TO SUCK UP TO YOUR BOSS

'The Chairman thinks, and I agree with him . . .'

One of my all-time favourite cartoons appeared, predictably, in the *New Yorker*. The caption reads, 'Rudolph the brown-nosed reindeer', and it features a generic New York saloon bar, in which Father Christmas and his trusty steed are quietly having a drink. As Santa quietly sips from his tumbler, Rudolph leans over and says, 'By the way, nice choice of coat, Santa, really nice . . .'

Is Rudolph being a sycophant? Perhaps a little, but what he's really doing is what we all need to do every now and then, he's Managing Upwards. There are very few people in business who don't have someone to report to (even the chairmen of plcs have shareholders), so we all need to learn how to do this. Whenever an employee has a problem with their immediate superior I tell them that one of the 'skill sets' they need as an executive (or indeed anyone who runs their own department) is the ability to manage up as well as down. To be able to read their boss's moods and steer his decisions. I don't see it as sucking up, but more as making the relationship function as smoothly as possible. So this chapter should really be called How to Handle Your Boss.

1   If you can't manage upwards, then I tend to think it's probably your fault, not the fault of your manager (who, incidentally, hasn't complained about you).

2   Praise your boss. I've said it before but I'll say it again: everyone has an ego, especially the person you work for. So tell him how good you thought he was at clinching the deal/dealing with a client/coming up with a particular solution.

3   You should find out how he likes to do everything and then make sure things happen that way. It's not underhand, nor expedient, nor is it Machiavellian, just good business practice.

4   I once overheard a Hollywood studio bigwig say that he hated it when one of his staff came into his office for a meeting/chat/whatever and didn't bring a pen and notepad, and ever since then I've felt the same. What, are you so gifted you're going to remember everything I ask you to do?

5   Never outshine the master. Never contradict your boss in public (although contradict him whenever you like in private – as long as he's present!), or show him up in front of people.

6   He wants solutions, not problems. This doesn't mean that you should keep problems from him, but ideally you should also go armed with a solution or two (or three).

7   Never hide things from him. If there's a problem, talk about it immediately (unless you're going to be clever enough to get rid of said problem without him knowing).

8   Give him the opportunity to say yes or no to something, rather than him having to come up with a litany of solutions (i.e. you should do the legwork).

9   Never let your boss make a mistake. If he needs more facts in order to make a decision, do the homework for him. If he has a weak presentation, beef it up. Good bosses train you to take their place so that when they get promoted you can progress.

10 Don't sulk and don't be surly. He will *so* not respect you.

11 Do things with a smile (how difficult is that?).

12 Don't dwell on things, either mistakes or past glories. He's moving on to the next problem, and expects you to be there with him, on the front line, anticipating solutions with him.

13 Check his schedule so that when you walk into his office and launch into a tirade-about something, he isn't about to receive ten representatives from a Chinese trade delegation. You won't get his full attention (or any of it), and he'll be irritated that you have broken his concentration.

14 If a project involves your boss's immediate boss, be aware that he will be taking extra special care with it, and that he will expect to be updated as to its progress at every step of the way.

15 If you screw up, admit it, immediately. He'll think more of you for doing so.

16 Get back to him immediately, too. If I ask somebody to do something, the last thing I want to have to do is to ask them how it's going. I want them to fill me in before I've had a chance to wonder why they didn't get back to me.

17 Don't get involved in things that are of no concern to you.

18 Try not to bring too many issues up with him at any one time. He tends to focus on one thing at a time, and will not take kindly to you trying to solve half a dozen problems in one go.

19 Do not become a dittohead (the next generation of yes men, taking sycophancy to the final frontier). If he thinks you'll say yes to anything, he won't trust you to make decisions (bearing in mind, of course, that the most important phrase you'll ever master is 'You're right').

20 Demonstrate your ability to make things happen (everyone has an opinion, but not everyone can turn these opinions into reality).

21 Never take the credit for something you didn't do, as he'll find out and wonder why you are obviously so insecure.

22 Don't make him wait (don't make anyone wait).

23 Eat your own dog food (a saying invented by software developers to imply they should try products before releasing them). Make sure you try solutions out before suggesting them. Because, if you don't, all your boss will say is, 'Well, have you asked them?'

24 Ideally, when your boss comes up to you in the office and suggests something might be a good idea, you need to be able to turn around and say, 'I've already done it.' He won't think you're a smart-arse, he'll think you're smart, full stop.

25 If he has kids, enquire about them (but not too often).

26 While the opposite regularly appears true, your boss has a lot less time on his hands than you do, so spare him the details when you're briefing him.

27 Similarly, when you're sending him an email, don't turn it into an essay. Give him short pieces of information, preferably the sort that only need short, ideally one-word answers.

28 If your boss doesn't like you, and you've picked this up, the onus is on you to solve the problem. It's not your fault *per se*, but it is your problem. And if the boss plainly doesn't like you – and it's probably not his fault either – you must go out of your way to force him to like you, or else leave (unless you think he's going to).

29 Tell him you like his jacket (just like Rudolph did). If you think he looks a bit daft wearing his new cravat/trainers/fluorescent shell suit, let someone else tell him.

30 Oh, and his jokes are funny. But I bet you knew that already.

HOW TO WIN AN ARGUMENT

'That's a fascinating idea. Have you thought of doing it this way?'

With arguments, as with everything else in life, it's not the destination that's important, it's the journey. Some arguments you will win, others you will lose, and your strike rate will fluctuate according to how much preparation you do. Do at least ten times more preparation than you think is enough. Prepare your opening and closing remarks and keep them clear and positive. It's a fact that people tend to remember what you say at the very beginning and the very end of a meeting.

In a business meeting, the sort you know will result in an argument, it's crucial to find out exactly what your opponent's goals are, what they hope to achieve, and what they'll settle for. (And, trust me, you should always think of them as opponents.) Plan meticulously how you're going to present your case, and think of answers to every possible query ('You think it's too expensive? Well, that's not exactly true, as we've saved £15,000 on promotion and shaved the editorial budget by 30k, so in terms of the bottom line we're actually under budget by six and a half thousand. Of course we're going to spend at least a third of that on ancillary costs but there is absolutely no way this project is going to cost the company a penny. It's a win-win situation.')

Remember this expression: win-win. If you go into a meeting expecting to come away with everything you want then you'll invariably be disappointed. Again, think of certain clever compromises that are going to please your opponent (OK, call them your business partner if it makes you feel happier), while still adhering to your goals. Nobody likes to lose an argument, and nobody likes to lose one in front of other people, so respect your opponent's ego, and try and find a solution that lets him leave the meeting with some dignity. That way you'll find it easier to get what you want.

You win arguments by being quick witted, by coming up with compromises your opponent hasn't thought of.

There is an old business expression that you might want to think about the next time you're planning for a meeting: 'I felt like I was fucked and not kissed.' You do not want anyone leaving your meeting feeling like this, so try and show a little love along the way, especially if they're about to leave the room with a lot less than you are.

Anthony Haycroft, a criminal barrister with twenty years' experience at the Bar, boils his technique down to three basic negotiating skills: 1) Preparation, 2) Communication, and 3) Persuasion. Persuasion is crucial, as you never want to seem as though you're pushing ideas on people. You should never tell them what to think, and while you can be forceful about your own ideas, you shouldn't express horror or disdain that they don't share your point of view. What you have to do is explain why your point of view makes the most sense.

If the room is full of people, try and make eye contact with all of them, as you would a jury if you were a defence attorney, regardless of whether they are 'on message' or not. If you have a personal relationship with someone – and a smile and a nod and some eye contact is a little bit of a relationship – it is harder to disagree with them.

When you're making your point, enunciate properly. Speak clearly, in a measured fashion. Don't repeat yourself, don't patronise and don't use excessive, elaborate language. Never use a word you think might be unknown to more than forty per cent of the room; someone will ask you what it means and slow you down, and when you then explain what it means, everyone else in the room will wonder why you didn't use the other word in the first place.

Don't thump the table with your fist; you'll look as if you're trying to be Al Pacino. And never slap the wall in frustration; the only man who can get away with this is Tom Cruise (and then not all of the time).

Don't forget to make the occasional joke as well, because it will lift the air a little.

And if someone brings up a previous altercation, or mentions the fact that the two principles or the two companies have been in battle before, and that there was an unsavoury outcome, move by quickly. Smile, shrug your shoulders and smile again. 'Big smile, short memory,' is the only thing you need to think.

Don't knock the competition either, as it only serves to publicise them while diminishing you in the process.

Always say, 'Let me finish' – forcefully, brusquely, almost rudely – when someone tries to interrupt you. Then you can go on for as long as you like, as they're unlikely to want to embarrass themselves again by butting in. As Haycroft says, 'Be seen to be fair. Concede what you have to, but always fight your corner. Always be pleasant and polite, even in the toughest arguments.'

If someone else begins talking to someone else in the room, splitting up the group, say – again forcefully, brusquely, almost rudely – 'Can we just have one meeting here, please?' (This is a rhetorical question, by the way.) The same applies if someone's phone rings: 'Do we really have to have mobiles turned on? Thank you.'

Crucially, you should never be swayed by the other person's point of view. If they've done their homework, and done the right amount of preparation, then they're going to be coming up with some plausible ideas – but don't be fooled. Never, ever, question your stance. Keep thinking that the only way you can win this argument is by getting the result you intended (of course you can buckle on a few minor points, but not the big ones). Don't doubt yourself (the Toyota company believes that if two people always agree, then one of them is superfluous). Stay calm, stay quiet, and let the other person rant to their heart's content. Keep saying, 'Yes, I understand,' without obviously implying that you think they're an ignoramus. Have open, engaging, relaxed body language (don't sit with your arms crossed). And while you don't want to appear patronising, a little subtle intimidation is allowed. A wry half-smile should occasionally cross your lips, the sort that could drive your opponent demented – if he thought for one second that you were doing it on purpose, that is.

Be confident, be assured, and look as though you know what you're talking about. You need to give the impression that you've thought about this subject for hours, days, weeks on end, and that the solution you've arrived at is the only alternative. 'OK guys, now how would you feel if you were in this position, if you were in my position?'

Then give a quick, pithy recap of your points, thank them for listening and then shut up. If you've done your job then the immediate discussion will concern the basic principles of your suggestions and the possibilities of making them work. If this starts to happen, don't interrupt and try and help them on their way. It's up to other people to appropriate this now. Because it really doesn't matter whose idea it is, or whose idea it becomes, as long as it gets done.

Capisce?

HOW TO STEER A MEETING

'Hey ho, let's go! Hey ho, let's go!'

Meetings cripple business, and my policy is to have as few as possible. And when I do have them – unless everyone's having fun, and being really creative – I make them as short as possible. Most decisions can get made between two people in a hallway in the space of a few minutes (sometimes even a few seconds), and you don't need to get eight people into a room to thrash them out. People will then also not be so upset about not being invited. Also, not everyone shines in meetings: some like to show off and grandstand, while others feel intimidated. Others – like me – simply get bored.

But some people just like having meetings, and you should watch out for them. They are the worst. Meetings make them feel important. To them, the meeting is the achievement, whereas for People Who Make Things Happen, the meeting is only the beginning. Keep meetings short, encourage people to say what they mean (quickly, simply), and then make sure things are actioned, and that everyone in the meeting comes out of it with clear tasks.

Write down a list of topics you want to cover and cross them off as you go. Do the easy topics first, and save the longer, more problematic topics until later. And keep things moving. After a point has been settled, push on to the next one. Backing and filling is one of the mortal diseases of dinner party conversation, and is even more of a crime in business meetings. *Don't repeat yourself!* And if you're interrupted, and that person is then interrupted by someone else, don't automatically pull the conversation back to your point. If the topic is moving in the right direction, move forward with it.

You need to be flexible without succumbing to peer pressure. Stick to your guns. Victoria Medvec at Kellogg business school says that when we sit down together, there is a tendency for us to seek confirmation of what everyone already knows. To avoid this, she suggests we do two things before we open our mouths:

1 Write down what we think about the items on the agenda.

2 Rate the strength of our views on a scale of, say, one to ten. That way we'll remember what we thought before our views were influenced by others.

Here are some other tips:

1 Don't sit opposite anyone too attractive or choose a seat with a window view (both will be distracting).

2 Never excuse yourself to go to the loo (you'll lose momentum).

3 Never be afraid to ask someone to explain what they mean. The chances are that everyone feels the same, but that they're too embarassed to ask.

4 Don't lose your temper; if you do it too often, no one will take you seriously the next time you do it.

5 Meetings that begin at odd times – 3.15, say, instead of 3.30 – are generally attended with greater punctuality.

6   The more people in a meeting, the less chance you have of reaching a decision.

7   Decide to have meetings where you discuss more subjects than you think you'll have time for. While discussing them you might realise that you can solve a problem very simply, and thus not need the meeting you'd scheduled to discuss it at length.

When you're chairing meetings with people who don't work for or with you, i.e. people from other companies, pay particular attention to those few minutes at the beginning and end of the meeting. These periods are extremely revealing, as people tend to let their guard down a little, and if you're clever it's possible to gauge their real intentions. With meetings like these it is always best to explain, at the outset, what you hope to achieve from the meeting (are we going to work together, and how?).

If someone important is being unduly slow, and deliberately not getting to the point, they're probably winding you up a little, and trying to get you to jump in and force their hand (because, in their eyes, you can't cope with what they're saying). If this appears to be the case, my advice would be to just shut up and let them get on with it. They obviously want to grandstand a little, and if you need them to make a decision, then it's probably best for you to let them waffle on and get to the point in the end (the fact that they're actually in your office means they've already decided to make a decision you'll be pleased with).

If someone is prevaricating with no particular purpose, then I would interrupt and cut to the chase. 'So, we're here because I think both companies are interested in achieving X . . .'

Much has been made these last few years of video conferencing – with the latest equipment giving participants the impression that they are facing a bunch of people sitting round a table – but still the most efficient way to get decisions made is to actually be in the room with them. Meetings should take place in sealed environments and subscribe to the rules on a sign to be found outside a particularly popular swingers' club in San Francisco: 'No alcohol. No drugs. No sleeping. No uproarious or loud laughter. Turn all cell phones off. Condoms obligatory.'

Meeting jargon has never been so pervasive, or so fashionable, and there is now such a culture surrounding it that it's even spawned its own collective term: 'jargonics'. Its increased popularity is obviously due to the Internet, although I think the *GQ* office is at least partly responsible, as the staff seem to devote a large amount of time to discussing and inventing business jargon and acronyms. A while ago, the following was overheard on the features desk, as the team were talking about the perennial war of attrition they have with the art department: 'We have bench', meaning that they had enough supporters to back them up in the field of play, so to speak. They only used it in jest, but unfortunately other expressions have become part of office vernacular.

Some that have come to light recently include 'undertiming' (doing freelance work when you're in the office), 'sham over' (any illness invented between 8 and 9 a.m. due to serious over-indulgence the previous evening), 'boiling the ocean' (as in 'We're not boiling the ocean here, guys', signifying frustration at the inability to effect even small business changes), MBWA (the 'Management By Walking Around' technique employed by uninspiring executives who earn extravagant salaries for aimless wandering) and three euphemisms for being fired: 'de-careered', 'reconfigured', and 'he's had his portfolio shuffled'. One of my favourite buzzwords is 'toejam!', used as an exclamation when spotting more than three people in the office wearing Birkenstocks or sandals. I like this because its insulting nature usually results in the guilty parties leaving their beachwear at home and coming into work the next day in sensible footwear (i.e. a proper pair of heavily polished brogues).

Because as much as I love my Birkys, I fail to see why men in a respectable office would feel they ought to wear them to work. Unless, of course, they feel like being 'de-careered', 'reconfigured' or having their 'portfolio shuffled'.*

---

* Some phrases never to be used in business meetings: 'Going forward' (it doesn't mean anything; why don't you try 'What we should do next . . .'); 'Crackberry' (everyone uses BlackBerrys these days, and we're all addicted to them; but so what?); 'brainstorm' (why don't you come up with your own ideas instead of relying on other people's?); 'It is what it is' (I still say this a lot, but I shouldn't as it's ultimately defeatist); 'outsourcing' (if you're going to get someone else to do it, then just say so); 'tipping point' (yeah yeah, we get it, it's over!); 'candy-striped' (an increasingly popular but pretentious word meaning confidential, from the red-and-white diagonal stripes that run across the covers of classified IBM documents); and my (least) favourite, 'What we need is an idea' (well, why don't you fucking have one, then?).

HOW TO ASK FOR A PAY RISE

'You couldn't improve on that four per cent, could you?'

Rule one: If you don't ask, you don't get. In the twenty years I've been a man manager, I have hardly ever just given someone a pay rise without them asking for one. Why would I? At most places I've worked, everyone gets an annual review, where an increase will be an inflation-aligned 2–5 per cent. Occasionally you'll give more, and often a little less, in consideration of their achievements (or lack of), but you very rarely go up to someone out of the blue, pat them on the back and say, 'Oh, what the hell. Have a fifteen per cent pay rise.' Much as I'd like to give my staff a pay rise every Friday afternoon, the budget won't allow it, it would play havoc with the pay structure, and, I like to think, they're pretty well compensated anyway. Occasionally, when someone has told me they turned down a particular job (and I believe them), or I think they should be rewarded for doing something spectacularly well, or if they're earning a particularly low salary, then I might do it. But then again I might not.

So you have to ask. Often, the best time to do this is when you're actually having your annual review, which is traditionally a time of reflection and commendation (hopefully; either that or deflection and condemnation). This is the one time in the year when you are allowed to ask for more money, and your boss is totally prepared for you to try and twist his arm – he almost expects you to do it. So don't be afraid to. If your boss is feeling generous (or has recently given someone a rather meagre rise, or maybe none at all, and possibly has some money left), he may buckle and give you another one per cent or so, but there's absolutely no guarantee that he will.

And if you are asking for more, actually name a figure or a percentage point, so that he can negotiate, and end up giving you less than you asked for, but more than he was going to give you in the first place. (Heads, you win . . .)

Crucially, there is no point telling your boss how hard you work (and so much harder than everyone else), or what hours you keep, or how much business you've brought to the firm, etc. Don't justify your position. Remember that many bosses are unlikely to give you any extra reward simply for doing your job well – after all, that's what you're paid to do, surely? And if you're doing your job properly then it just shows that the management were right to hire or promote you in the first place. So they'll think it has little to do with you and rather more to do with their good judgement. If he can tell that you're genuinely concerned about your future, though, and are possibly at a crossroads in your career, or that you're unreasonably depressed, then he might – might, I say – throw you a bone to make you feel a little better about yourself. You are, at the end of the day, one of his employees, and if he likes you he'll want to keep you. But you can only do this if you're really feeling despondent; if you're not, and he's moderately good at his job, he'll be able to tell you're spoofing.

Also, never, ever ask for a pay rise in a letter or an email, as this will allow your boss to formulate considered, and seemingly incontrovertible responses to your reasons for wanting more cash. Always, always do it face to face, without giving your boss any warning. Never do it on a Monday morning either. No one is in a good mood at the start of the week, especially those people who have little to look forward to all week other than several dozen people coming into their office and giving them problems. Don't try Friday afternoon either, as this is really the 'last fucking straw' day. And never try after work, or socially. He'll think you're abusing your position (you are), and you'll be pushed to the perimeter of the sphere of influence. The best time will be mid-week, maybe a Tuesday or Wednesday, before everyone gets tired.

You must never go above his head either, as this will sound the death knell of your career, at least at your current company. There are few things your boss hates more than employees attempting to undermine him by leapfrogging their complaints or suggestions to a higher floor. So don't do it.

If your boss turns you down, and refuses to give you any more money, then try asking for additional perks, like a bigger car, a laptop, additional health insurance, or a parking space. You never know: it might be something that's quite easy for your boss to give up, something he doesn't begrudge doing.

And you must never make him unhappy. If he feels you've been too aggressive, too pushy, or naïve in your attempts to squeeze more cash out of him – cash which he clearly doesn't think you deserve – then he will certainly hold it against you, and remember you as being greedy. Which won't help the next time he's giving you a salary review. It will cause a rift between you, and if you're always asking for more money, he will begin to think that money must be your prime motivation, which will make him wonder whether you're actually suited to your job. And he's right. If you are solely driven by financial gain then you are obviously not creatively fulfilled and should probably start looking for alternative employment. One of the key things to remember when asking for a pay rise is that the situation is very much like a job interview, and you will be assessed on performance, presentation and how you actually ask for more money. So do it with a smile, not a belligerent sneer. (Bosses always want solutions, not problems. Remember that the next time you're thinking of asking for a pay rise.)*

Don't bluff either. If you tell him that you've been offered another job then you'd jolly well better take it if he refuses to increase your salary. So you'd better be prepared to leave. Quickly. People have sometimes done this to me, and if I'm in two minds about whether they should stay anyway, I'll quickly shake their hands, implying that I'm accepting their resignation (even though they haven't officially offered it), say it's about time they moved on, wish them well and then usher them out of the office before they realise what's hit them. I actually did this with someone I'd been wanting to get rid of for months, so him telling me he had been offered something else was the best thing that could have happened to me. Unfortunately for him, he hadn't been offered another job at all, and was just trying to get me to treat him a little better and to bump up his salary. More fool him.

The best way to get a raise is to discover that someone else in the company who's doing a similar job to you, with the same responsibilities, is earning more. Then you've really got a story to tell. Often, your boss won't know this, as the person you're talking about probably works for someone else. So he will not only feel aggrieved on your behalf, he may even get a bit sniffy because one of his staff is earning less than someone doing the same job in another part of the building. Your boss will now be totally on your side and will make sure you get what you deserve. He may even get you a little more.

And if anyone in my office is reading this, don't even think about it, because the answer is NO. Categorically.

---

* Never use the word 'gobsmacked' with your boss, as in 'I was gobsmacked not to get that job'. It is unspeakably naff, and is always used by useless people.

HOW TO KNOW YOUR EMAIL

In cyberspace, no one can hear you scream

We've all done it, haven't we? And if you haven't, you will shortly, believe me.

There you are, having a perfectly normal three-way email correspondence with, say, a colleague in the office, and a business associate from another company. Things are going well until the business associate (who shall now be referred to only as 'Moronic Idiot Woman') sends your colleague an email of such profound stupidity that they pass it on to you, just to make you gag. And you, immediately enraged (how dumb is she?!), instantly reply, applying to 'Moronic Idiot Woman' a variety of impressive insults and using an even more impressive litany of profanities.

Though of course you haven't just sent it to your colleague. You (and I think you should now start referring to yourself simply as 'Moronic Idiot Man') have accidentally, and irrevocably, sent it straight to 'Moronic Idiot Woman'. Who, understandably, now wants nothing to do with you. Or the company you work for. In fact she and her company want to start having nothing to do with you immediately.

Happened to you? Happened to me.

Bizarrely, email hasn't quite yet assumed the importance and gravitas it ought to have done. Even though it has outstripped the competition to become the most common form of business communication, we still tend to treat it in a flippant, occasionally dismissive manner. Weird, isn't it – how we can be so casual about a form of communication that will soon replace all others?

There are some people who, rather endearingly, still treat email like regular mail, composing letters containing the full address and title of the recipient as well as the sender, using the same convoluted grammar you find in any nineteenth-century correspondence. I rather like these people, even though their numbers dwindle by the month. And then there are Americans, some of whom treat email with barely disguised contempt. I remember a few years ago when I worked on a Sunday supplement, a member of our features team sending an especially long email to an infamously tacitrn Hollywood agent, requesting an interview and a photo session with one of his more famous charges. If I remember rightly, and I think I do, the request ran to several pages, outlining just what a superb idea it would be if **** ****** were to appear on our cover. Not only did it take the agent over a week to reply, but the response was also inspiringly curt. I'd worked with Hollywood agents for years, and knew how dismissive they could be, but even I was shocked by this new reply. Just four words: 'I don't think so.' Of course it would have taken her a little less time to just write 'No', but somehow 'I don't think so' possessed slightly more malice while also implying the perfect amount of sarcastic disdain (I could almost hear her say it).

Most people, however, lie somewhere between the two – on the one hand treating email like a slightly less formal letter, and on the other using it as they would a phone. Me, I try to condense everything into a perfect paragraph, an all-purpose mini-letter that imparts as much information as possible, while being quick and easy to read. I figure if I can't get everything I need to say into a four-sentence, six-line paragraph then I have no right to be a journalist in the first place.

I just wish other people would do the same, as most of the stuff I get is dashed-off, convoluted and unwieldy, or simply unwanted. Of course everyone hates junk email, or spam, and my least favourite unwanted emails right now are those change of address group emails from people you've never heard of. Really? You're moving? Changing your email address? Fascinating. And who exactly are you? When I get one of these – and they're always accompanied by that annoying little red exclamation mark, just in case I was intending giving it anything but urgent attention – I always feel like pinging back a reply containing the words written on my favourite ever New York T-shirt: 'You must have mistaken me for someone who gives a shit.'

When email started to become ubiquitous, there was a rash of pieces in the press about how our generation would have no record of important correspondence, how electronic communication would eventually kill off the art of formal letter writing. In several ways this is right, because not only does the form encourage most people to be more succinct, but also, who in their right mind actually keeps emails?

Well, I do for one, and for the last eight years have been keeping printed copies of some of the rudest as well as some of the most important or amusing ones. One or two have been from politicians, a few are from rock stars, several of the least amusing ones are from comedians, while most, naturally, are from friends. The best are from journalists, but then I'd expect them to be.

The thing is, almost every email I've kept (and I've kept about two or three hundred of them) contains at least one spelling mistake, even the ones from members of the so-called establishment. Adjectives turn into bracelets of vowels, multisyllabled questions morph into extravagant, if nonsensical insults, and affectionate sign-offs fall at the final hurdle. Yes, I've had my fair share of pip pips, over and outs, and tally hos. I've even had a 'One day you're the cock of the walk, the next you're a feather duster.'

But I've only ever had one 'Pasta la vista, baby'.

1   Beware of flirting. Because with email it's soooo easy.

2   Answer promptly, because if you don't, the person who sent you the email in the first place will have forgotten all about it.

3   Don't write in CAPITALS.

4   Don't leave out the message thread (i.e. include all previous correspondence).

5   Make it personal.

6   Do not attach unnecessary files. In fact if you can help it, don't include any attachments at all (some are still difficult to open, even on powerful, sophisticated machines, and are prone to viruses).

7   Don't overuse the high priority symbol.

8   ALWAYS ALWAYS read your email through before you send it. You'll rarely get it exactly right the first time around, and there's bound to be a spelling mistake or two.

9   Do not overuse REPLY TO ALL. In fact, use this sparingly (no one needs to get any more emails than they do already).

10   Use the bcc (blind carbon copy) facility sparingly too (you need to remember who has been copied on things, and you need to know who knows . . .).

11   Say 'please'.

12   Don't 'flame' someone – i.e. don't be aggressive. If you're aggressive in an email you're only being passive-aggressive. Would you say the same thing to this person's face?

13 Never ask to recall a message as it gives it too much importance.

14 Never forward chain letters.

15 FYI don't use abbreviations.

16 Never refer to someone unless you'd be OK with that person reading the email.

17 Avoid long sentences.

18 Never reply to spam (it just proves you exist).

19 Don't be a novelist.

20 Be careful about your tone. Some people will get your humour, but others won't.

21 Don't fanny around with the formatting.

22 Don't use smileys – :-) etc. They're dumb.

23 Email is not private. Know that.

24 It's called netiquette, stupid.

HOW TO BE A GOOD BOSS

Don't do it like that, do it like this!

You are a very lucky man. Trust me, if you don't know it already, learn this *now*. Not everyone gets to be in charge, not everyone gets to run their own department, or indeed their own life. So if you're the boss, don't slap yourself on the back and think how fabulous you are, just quietly consider how lucky you are. Because it could have been someone else. And at some point in the future it will be. I think of myself as the custodian of a brand, one I intend to leave in exactly the same shape, if not better shape, when I leave. But I was lucky to be given the opportunity to do it. Which is what you are if you're the boss: lucky.

So, having established that, you must learn not to exploit your position, or, what's more important, make sure you don't turn into an arsehole. I have seen so many people turn into self-aggrandising fools when they get a bit of power, and the worst ones are those who take it out on their staff. Don't, because you're only doing it because you can. It's childish, and absolutely no one will respect you for it, least of all the people you're screaming at.

What do people want from a boss? Direction. There are quite a few people in my office who could do my job just as well as me. Some might do it a little worse, some might do it a lot better . . . but they would certainly do it differently. In business, especially where creativity is involved, there is not one solution, no through-line that you have to follow. As an old boss of mine used to say, 'There is more than one way to fuck a pig.' (Believe me, he's a lot more charming in real life.)

So your way is not the only way, but it happens to be the only way right now. So tell people what it is, tell them where they're going, and how they're going to get there. Tell them what to do and then let them get on with it. There'll be plenty of things for you to do after that, believe me: fire fighting, damage limitation, crisis management, and reassuring the picture editor that the art director doesn't hate him (even when he does). Being a boss doesn't just mean being in charge, it means leading; and the best bosses lead from the front. Nothing about your decisions should be ambiguous, unless of course you want them to be (about which more later). You are running a benevolent dictatorship, so tell people what to do, and tell them properly. Your office, you understand, is not a democracy. As Henry Ford said, back in the day, 'If I'd asked the public what they wanted, they would have said faster horses.'

This doesn't mean you have to treat staff badly (the opposite is always true), but there needs to be a grand plan, a grand plan drawn up, principally, by you. Treat people well. Pay them properly. And then set them free. Give them the freedom to express themselves. Make sure they know exactly what they're meant to be doing, and then make sure they do their job *exactly* as you want it done. But give them the space to do it in their own way.

Don't be a perpetrator of banana problems. A banana problem is a snag which develops because of constant tinkering and failure to know when to stick a fork in it and call it done (pronouncing an idea dead, deciding you've done enough research, or going to market). The saying is thought to be derived from the story about the child who said, 'I know how to spell banana, I just don't know when to stop.'

Don't bullshit, don't waffle, and don't prevaricate. Have an opinion at all times. Even saying 'I don't have an opinion on that' is a pro-active opinion. Don't end meetings with the sort of summation that goes, 'OK, Mike, if you call Arcadia, and Nicky, if you call PMK, and Alex, if you sort out the Dubai problem . . .' This not only shows weakness (why are you using 'if'? Are you too embarrassed to tell people what to do?), it is also open to ambiguity. Instead, say, 'Mike, you're going to deal with Arcadia; Nicky, you deal with the PMK thing; and Tim, kick Hobbs up the backside and get a photographer for Friday. OK, thanks everyone, that's it.' Over and out. Never be rude, but never be embarrassed about making decisions.

And never put off difficult or possibly fractious discussions. If someone needs a bollocking, give it to them; if someone has been insubordinate – even if only in a tiny way – or gives you an indication that there might be some trouble coming down the line, have a word now . . . not tomorrow, not next week, but now. If someone deserves praise, don't keep it from them – do it immediately. Everyone thrives on praise. Everyone has an ego and everyone likes knowing that they've done well – so if someone has done well, tell them. Privately sometimes, other times publicly. You may want them to feel special, or you may want the whole office to know how brilliant they've been. Either way, do it.

You should never forget to listen to your staff – you're paying them to have opinions, remember – as it not only empowers them, but also makes it easier for you to make decisions. If what they're suggesting sounds right, and a better solution than your own, then choose it. You're still in charge because you made the decision to go with their idea. What you don't need is an office full of yes-men. You do not know everything, and if you've hired properly, your staff should be able to teach you a lot. So let them do it. If they make mistakes, you can correct them. They will learn and improve, as you will by listening to them.

When you're choosing people to work with – when you're hiring – you look for people with brains, with capabilities, with experience, and with an aptitude for learning. So train people to do everything you want them to do. Nobody knows everything (you certainly don't, as you're probably a Jack of all trades and a master of none; a lot of good bosses are), and there's no reason to expect them to. So train them. And help them to be good. To be great. To be better than you.

Delegate, but do it for the right reasons. Don't just delegate the things you don't like doing, and don't refuse to delegate something because you're afraid not to do it yourself. Many bosses do this, and it's wrong; you should let your staff get to know your contacts too, as it makes the operation stronger. As the great Mark McCormack once wrote, in *What They Don't Teach You at Harvard Business School*, 'It is difficult to let go of a responsibility. Again, it's often a matter of ego. People convince themselves that they can do something better than anyone else, or are afraid that if they give up a task or respon-sibility they will be perceived as being less essential to the company. It takes a very confident person to be a good manager, confidence in the people who work for you and enough confidence in yourself to overcome ego problems.'

People also can't do everything, so don't be disappointed if someone can't do a specific task as well as you or as well as someone else in the office. You'll also have to accept that not everyone in the office will get on, so just accept it and deal with it. That's why you're in a management position.

Of course, there will be times when you do, for whatever reason, want to undermine an individual, or make them get back in their box. And sometimes you'll obfuscate – this tends to happen a lot when two or three staff members have applied for the same job. And every now and again you'll have to apply the brakes simply to let them know who's boss. Because that's what you are. But it doesn't make you a bad person; far from it, it makes you a better leader.

Sometimes you'll have to be overly diplomatic with people – about salaries, about what another staff person said, about what you think about their work, about every damn thing under the sun. But you're never doing it to undermine them – you're doing it to empower them and to make them feel good about themselves.

Be careful what you say to them about other members of staff, too. It may well be flattering (to them) to have you take them into your confidence, but it can also cause them to worry; 'If he's telling me this about Y, then what's to stop him telling Y about me? Or even worse, X!'

There'll also be times when you'll intend being vague about something, usually when someone is pursuing something in the office that you either have private knowledge of yourself, or that you actually want to fail because it clashes with something you're working on. Don't worry about that; part of your remit is looking at the bigger picture, and your staff will expect you to be privy to a lot of stuff that they have no knowledge of (they'd think you were a sad sack if they thought you were being kept out of decisions made above you). Occasionally you will be asked a question you don't want to answer, because it will compromise you; so don't.

Sometimes I'm asked things that I don't want to answer and I just delete the email. There's nothing that says you have to respond to every staff query, and some things just fall by the wayside. It's no big deal.

And don't assume people like you for who you are. They like you because you're their boss, because you are responsible for them getting paid each month. That's why they laugh at your jokes. Don't get me wrong – they don't hate you (not all of them, anyway), but it's an uneven relationship and you should accept that. So enjoy it. Enjoy their company and make as many friends as you can. If you're a good boss you'll know who you can really trust. Whether you socialise with them is up to you – Manchester United manager Alex Ferguson has never socialised with any of his team, though plenty of other managers do – but I wouldn't sit near them in the office if I were you. They will feel intimidated and under scrutiny, and won't be able to do their jobs properly.

And remember: people leave, so don't hold it against them. Loyalty is one of the most important qualities there is in business, and nobody likes to see a great employee leave. But everyone leaves eventually. So smile, wish them luck, and give them a huge leaving party. But not before you've tried to make them stay by offering them a higher salary, a promotion, a blow-job or use of the executive washroom.

What the hell, maybe even a blow-job *in* the executive washroom.

HOW TO HIRE SOMEONE

Be smart: hire people smarter than you

In one of my first jobs, the editor of the magazine I was working for asked my opinion about a particular article that had been sent in by someone far better known and much more talented than me. Slightly scared, insecure, and worried that if this person started contributing to the magazine it might affect my own position, I gave it the thumbs down, and the piece was never published. Dumb move. All I succeeded in doing was letting the journalist wander off to another magazine. So hire the best, even if they're better than you.

You should also try to hire people you like. You don't have to be best buddies with everyone you hire, but it helps if you quite like them, especially if you're in a relatively small office of fifty people or less. If you're hiring someone who won't be spending too much time in the office, then this is obviously less important, but life is too short to work closely with people you actively don't like. Some managers don't think this way – they simply hire the best person for the job – although it really depends what industry you're in.

Equally, never hire people just because you like them, or want to like them more. Do not hire your friends. If you get to like the people around you, then fabulous, but any boss will tell you that you don't have to fall in love with the people who work for you. They don't even have to like you, just as long as they respect you and do a good job. (Many years ago a friend of mine left London for a job in Milan. During the final negotiations, the editor of the magazine he was joining began describing what his social life might be like once he had moved to Italy. She said that every two weeks she would be inviting him down to her holiday home in Portofino. 'It will be great,' she said. 'And enough.')

And don't hire loose cannons, or those who are highly strung. For years I'd hire people – usually designers or art directors – who were highly creative, even though they may have had slightly unstable personalities. But never again. Eventually I just got sick of the arguments. I would rather forgo the extra five per cent of creativity for the sake of an easy life. Also, in my experience, truly maverick people only have a limited working life, as their personalities are not suited to office life.

Here are some things you should be careful about when you're actually interviewing people:

1   Don't give them too much information about what is expected of them; rather allow them to ask questions and to suggest how they might fill the role.

2   *Listen.* If you listen more and talk less you'll learn far more, and be able to size up your potential employee a hell of a lot easier.

3   When you ask questions, don't butt in and answer them yourself.

4   Don't show off. *They're* the ones meant to be showing off.

5   Never ask questions to which the answers are yes or no.

6   The most important follow-up question you can ever ask is, 'Why?'

7   Always ask, 'Do you have any questions for me/us?' If they don't, beware.

8   Be wary of potential employees who ask what their salary will be too early in the interview.

9   If you ask a question and you don't get a satisfactory answer, don't start begging for it. Just sit there in silence and see if the interviewee comes up with the goods.

10   If they don't, then you can ask again.

11   Look for people who you think you're going to be able to trust, the sort who seem like they'll be loyal in the long run.

12   If you're trying to ingratiate yourself with someone, and trying to get them to join your company when they're perhaps being resistant, then the easiest way to put people at ease is to make them laugh. If you get them laughing then you're half-way home.

13   Don't tell too many jokes, as you'll look like a fool.

14   I don't especially warm to people who don't look me in the eye when they're talking to me, although it doesn't necessarily mean they're being shifty. Some people get incredibly nervous in interviews, while others just find it hard to look other people in the eye for very long. But it is indicative of a certain shyness, a certain reluctance to engage with people, and should make you at least a little suspicious.

15   And if someone rubs their eye when they're saying something, it usually means they're feeling self-conscious, and possibly not telling you the complete truth. Either that, or they're embarrassed about their version of events. It's a dead give-away, and motorway service stations are signposted with more subtlety.

16   Once you've got someone to agree to something, move on, and don't bring it up again. If you do bring it up there's always the possibility that they'll renege on the deal or alter their terms, or simply change their mind. Also, when I've mentally completed something, I don't want people banging on about it. When a contributor has called up to pitch a story, and I've commissioned it, the last thing I want is for the journalist to keep going on about what a great story it is. I know that! You've just convinced me! What does he expect, for me to commission it twice? Go away and write it!

17 Socrates used maieutics (the science of asking people the right questions so they can arrive at the right answers), and this is precisely what you have to do.

Remember: you'll never interview someone who says, 'I've never read a book.' They're going to be putting top-spin on everything, so pay attention to the detail. What you have to do is to estimate how much of their character you like, how much aptitude they have for the job, and how easy it might be to change them. If you've ever been involved in a focus group – on either side of the glass – you'll know that people say what they think you want to hear, rather than how they actually feel. They will also want to create a good impression, and consequently will be less honest.

If you get immediate follow-up to a request, then that's a big plus in my book. There are few things that impress so significantly, and if I've asked someone to send me a full CV, or a copy of something they might have been involved with (a magazine, a newspaper or a video or something), then I really want to receive it the very next day, ideally delivered by hand with a personal note. Certainly not two weeks later, when I've forgotten all about it and given the job to someone else.

HOW TO FIRE SOMEONE

'Tony, could you pop into my office for a minute . . .'

As a boss, this is something you need to be able to do without blinking. If you worry about firing people then you shouldn't be in charge. Obviously you should try not to fire anyone, and to nurture, support and empower your team – but if the axe has to fall, make sure you do it quickly and effectively.

I've fired enough people to know that I should have got rid of most of them sooner. You usually have a gut instinct about someone (especially when you arrive at a job), and whenever I've given someone the benefit of the doubt, I've been proved wrong. In the creative industries you often have to deal with emotionally unwieldy people, and you have to judge whether or not someone's creativity, and their ability to make magic, is worth all the grief you get because of their character. Creatives can be sensationally high maintenance, and you may decide that it's worth the trade-off. Not me.

If you're sure you want to get rid of someone, the first thing you need to do is make yourself aware of the European legislation governing employment law. Years ago it was relatively easy getting rid of useless people – they were, er, fired. Unceremoniously. These days, the power lies with the employee, and you, as an employer, have to jump through hoops in order to get them to leave.

Essentially you need to learn the term 'transparency', and liaise closely with your personnel director or HR department. And remember to write everything down. The procedure is as follows:

1　Have a quiet word with your problem child, and tell him he has to pull his socks up (in *GQ*, I've often meant this literally).

2　If he is still proving to be a problem, and does something tangibly wrong, give him a verbal warning in the presence of a witness of his choosing (i.e. someone else in the office), and then tell him that the next time there's a problem, he'll be getting a written warning.

3　When this happens, draft a letter with your HR department and have it delivered either by the internal mail, or send it to his home. The letter should explain *exactly* what he's done wrong, and how you expect him to improve his work ethic/attitude/aptitude/ timekeeping etc, and over what time period. Never imply that it's only a matter of time before he's fired.

4　If, after all this, the employee continues malfunctioning, then call him into your office and talk to him. The talk will have one of two outcomes: if you actually want him to stay, and are prepared to put in the work, then give him an almighty bollocking, swiftly followed by a pep talk. If you actually want him to leave – and by this stage I'll wager that you'll want him out of the door as soon as possible – then tell him you're giving him a month to buck his ideas up, or else it's curtains.

5　Then, four weeks later, when it – thankfully – hasn't worked out, call him into your office and fire him.

Make it short. Tell him why he's going and when he's going (now would be preferable, but if he wants to work out his notice you should ask him to go and sort it out with HR). Don't apologise, and don't repeat yourself. If you're sitting down, stand up, open the door and usher him out. Then close the door and immediately call HR and fill them in.

You may have been advised to give him a month's notice, in which case you should try and fire him on a Friday, because if he's angry after being let go – and you'd be surprised by the number of people who think they're going to somehow escape the cull – he'll have calmed down by the time he comes to work on Monday. Also, if your problem child is a bit unstable, and likely to break down (or up – i.e. become violent), and he has his own office, then fire him there. Then you can walk out after you're done.

Sometimes you have to get rid of people simply because things change. And in business, things change all the time. A department may have been merged into another, or even folded, or maybe a job description has had to change because of a change in technology. Or maybe you've just worked out that someone isn't good enough at what they do. Some people are let go just because it's time for them to go, and not because they've turned into a monster, or started stealing or taking drugs in the boardroom. In these instances, the meetings don't always need to be so abrupt or attritional. If this is the case, then you should apologise as you're getting rid of them. Having explained just why they have to go, you will offer them whatever redundancy package you think is fair (and in accordance with their contract), and then talk through whatever it is that this person might do next. Sometimes it is possible to still be friends with the people you fire, and it helps if you can part on good terms. If there is a good reason for them to go – and there had better be, if you don't want legal action – then there should be little resistance on their part.

One of the few things you can summarily fire someone for, other than violence or taking drugs in the office, is insubordination. If someone swears at you, then get rid of them immediately, and worry about it later. Only a (fucking) lunatic is going to take you to a tribunal. While a good argument or discussion can be healthy for the creative process, insubordination only leads to a parting of the ways. I've rarely had any problems with this, and on the one occasion when I did, I simply called the person into my office and said, 'When my boss says, "Jump," I say, "How high?" – and that's what I expect from you. You don't like it, you get out. Now.' In any work relationship, trust and loyalty are crucial, and when that trust has been broken, it's very difficult to get it back. The one thing I have learned is that offices are not democracies; there can only ever be one person in charge. You.*

---

* Celebrity chef Anthony Bourdain has a particular way of dealing with overly creative people. He doesn't hire them. 'When a job applicant starts telling me how Pacific Rim cuisine turns him on and inspires him, I see trouble coming,' he says. 'Send me another Mexican dishwasher anytime. I can teach *him* to cook. I *can't* teach character. Show up at work on time six months in a row and we'll talk about red curry paste and lemongrass. Until then, I have four words for you: "Shut the fuck up."'

HOW TO HANDLE THE BUSINESS LUNCH

The most convivial meeting of the day. Maybe . . .

Arriving

• Be on time, exactly five minutes early. No less, no more.

• If you see people you know when you enter the restaurant, and your guest has already arrived, just nod and smile; don't go over and chat for five minutes. Remember, this is not their lunch.

• If your guest has already ordered a drink, then match him.

• If you arrive before your host, and there is obviously a good seat (the one facing the restaurant, rather than the wall), don't take it.

• Turn your phone off. Can I say that again? Turn your phone off.

• If your guest is twenty minutes late, when they arrive just smile and listen attentively while they fill you in on the car/tube/takeover deal that's detained them. It's no big deal, and happens to everyone. Just ask for a newspaper while you wait.

• If they're more than half an hour late and haven't called the restaurant, chances are there's a bigger problem, and you should probably leave. The best way to do this is to pay cash for your drink, pick up your phone, clasp it to your ear and walk out.

Greeting

• Your handshake should involve a firm, full-handed grip, a steady quick squeeze, and then an understated downward snap. Don't pump up and down, and release quickly.

• If you're kissing, then kiss twice, first on the left, then on the right cheek. It's totally OK to kiss a man in this way.

• If you know the maître d', have a few brief words when he comes over, even share a joke, but don't launch into a conversation, even if he's a friend, as this could intimidate or annoy your guest. On the other hand, if the object of your lunch is to impress your guest, then try to keep the maître d' at your table for as long as possible.

Ordering

• If you're being taken to lunch by your boss, never have the same as him (show some individuality, you toad), unless he encourages you to have something – 'If you haven't had the iced berries you really should, you know.'

• Never announce that you're on a diet, or try to encourage your guest – or indeed your host – to eat less than they want to.

• If you're lunching with the boss, try and undercut him by at least two pounds per dish.

• Never order two starters in place of a main course. Unless your host suggests you do. Or unless of course you're a girl, and girls shouldn't really be reading this book.

Eating

• Never order anything that's difficult to eat, because the contract isn't going to the guy with the linguine doing a slalom down his tie. Food to be avoided is spaghetti, soup, lobster, snails, oysters, shrimp, noodles, spare ribs (you were thinking of ordering spare ribs?), dishes containing a lot of liquid, and anything that involves you using your hands.

• You only order dessert if your host wants to. If you're the host, ask if your guest would like dessert, and act as though you mean it. Unless, of course, you are men of the world and both immediately fold the dessert menu down when it's presented by the waiter, and bark, 'A single espresso and the bill, please,' regardless of whose lunch it is.

Drinking

• Drink if your host/guest/boss drinks. You shouldn't drink alone or allow your guest to. Who cares if you don't actually want a drink? It's not going to kill you.

• If you're lunching with someone who likes to booze and you need, for whatever reason, to stay sober, then just allow the waiter to fill your glasses and sip occasionally. After a while, your guest/host will think you're drinking properly and then forget about it (if you're drinking you usually assume other people are too). When Stalin entertained the Politburo he would pour them vodka but only drink water himself, keeping a note of indiscretions and perceived dissatisfaction. The bastard.

• Never, under any circumstances, order a white wine spritzer. Or a pint of Stella. Or a Red Bull. With anything . . .

• You can, of course, order a Coke. This shows you don't stand on ceremony, and has the added benefit of really pissing off stroppy French waiters (and we all need to tick that box on a regular basis).

• If your guest isn't drinking, then you could allow yourself an aperitif (a glass of champagne, a Bullshot), but nothing more.

• If it's your lunch then order the wine with confidence. Never order the most expensive.

Etiquette

• Never tuck your napkin into your collar like they do on *The Sopranos*. Because you're not in *The Sopranos*. If you do this you will look (a) Uncouth, (b) As though you're about to make one hell of a mess, (c) Really really old.

• Don't use the table hardwear – ashtray, cutlery, condiments – to make a point.

• Never hold your knife or your fork like a biro; it's common. And don't use either as a shovel; that's common too.

• Don't look over people's shoulders when you're talking to them.

• If the waiter's brought an implement or side dish you're not familiar with, then for God's sake leave it alone (we don't want you taking the lemon for your gravadlax out of its linen pouch).

• Don't smoke until after the coffee, and then only if you really have to (you loser).

• At some restaurants the waiter will take the napkin off the table for you, but if not you should lay it across your lap as soon as you sit down. Don't call it a serviette, not even jokingly. Leave it on your seat if you have to get up for any reason, and never on the table.

• If you're in a restaurant for the first time, and you've gone for a pee, when you run the tap stand well back from the sink. You have no way of knowing how ferocious it is, and the last thing you need is to walk back into the dining-room with a map of Belgium (or, worse, Australia) on your trousers.

- If you're lunching with a woman, never lunge. Ever.

Conversation

- Don't give advice when it's not asked for.

- Don't assume you are charming.

- Have anecdotes ready, tailored to your guest's interests: political gossip, industry gossip, sexual gossip.

- Try not to go to the loo half-way through lunch as it will break the flow of conversation.

- Don't name-drop.

- Never discuss the cost of anything on the bill.

- Laugh at other people's jokes, and never say, 'Oh, I've heard it,' when you have, a dozen times before.

- Tell self-deprecating stories.

- Be modest, but flatter your guest. Don't bombard them with compliments, but find something about their appearance you like (his tie, her watch, his suit, her nails, etc, but never *his* nails).

- Thoroughly research your victims (sorry, lunch guests'

- Let others talk about themselves.

- Let them finish their sentences and anecdotes.

Paying

- If you're paying, do it quietly.

- If it's not your lunch, and your host pays with something outlandish like a Centurian Amex, comment upon it. People don't use

Centurians unless they want other people to notice, so be suitably impressed.

• Always have a pound for the coat check girl, and another in case your guest doesn't have cash. If you only have notes, get the waiter to break one when you're paying the bill.

• If by chance your meal is being comped, and there is no charge, leave a more than generous tip for the waiter.

The Clincher

• Never take an important client you have never met before to a fancy restaurant you haven't been to before. No one will know you, the service won't be up to much, you won't get a good table and they won't take you seriously. Take them to a fancy restaurant you go to all the time, so all you have to worry about is the meeting, not the food or the service or the table or where the loos are (or even the restaurant, come to that). One of the irritating things about going to a new restaurant for the first time is having the waiter gesticulate wildly with his hands when you ask where the loo is – and we don't want that, now do we? And if you don't have a fancy restaurant you go to all the time, start doing so immediately. In business this is invaluable.

HOW TO READ THE FINANCIAL PAGES

What the investment bankers never tell you

If you're an investment banker, or in business yourself, then the *Financial Times* will still be your first port of call, and in particular the Lex and Lombard columns. These are generally read for the commentary and to see how deals are playing out in the market. In fact, from a banker's point of view, the comment columns are the only things really worth reading, as they probably already know everything else that's in the paper. Columnists are as important to the financial pages as they are to the op-ed pages, and – until she became editor of the *Sunday Telegraph* – if you wanted to read someone as influential and as well-connected as the *Observer*'s Andrew Rawnsley is in the political world, then you looked no further than Patience Wheatcroft in *The Times*. Bankers also recommend the Breaking News website, which publishes around eight notable stories every lunchtime. However, if you're looking for breaking news, then both Reuters' and Bloomberg's on-line presence has diminished the necessity of reading a newspaper for this purpose.

These columns are also good for leaking stories, or for steering deals in particular ways. If some stock isn't moving quickly enough, or if a private equity group is taking too long to close a deal, and a rival bank wants to force the issue, then a quiet word in a columnist's ear might encourage them to mention the fact that another company could be interested in buying the commodity. In this respect financial columnists are used in exactly the same way that sports journalists are by football agents, often 'suggesting' that Real Madrid are thinking of making an offer for Gary Footballer, when in fact the only interest has come from a Conference side languishing near the bottom of the table.

If someone from a public company is being unreasonable about an aspect of a purchase or sale, investment bankers will take them to task through a columnist. If they're trying to close a deal, and the bank's client is offering £3m, say, while the company is holding out for £10m, some adroitly placed words in the *FT* might suggest that the company should maybe think about accepting £4m or £5m. Where public companies are concerned, in our modern culture of transparency, there is an enormous pressure to respond to criticism, so a columnist can start a public conversation (or slanging match) simply by a line or two of playful conjecture. If it's in the press, then you have to talk about it.

To understand how the business pages work, you only have to look at the way the rest of a paper works. In defence of their shrinking circulation and readership, broadsheet editors say that readers increasingly want context and opinion and comment rather than just news. Which is just as well because most people will have already got their daily fix from the TV or radio before they leave home. Increasingly, these days, people at work are logging on to a news service as soon as they get to work, rather than plough through a newspaper.

Readers, say editors, want viewspapers, not newspapers. Which is why there are now so many columnists, and so many of them who get away with murder. Columnists tend to be enormously pleased with themselves, both the ones you despise, and the ones you admire. In fact if you actually despise a columnist, then the paper is really doing its job. Columnists are hired to irritate regular readers as much as to confirm their beliefs, and all papers have plenty who do both. Writers and their papers have a symbiotic relationship, although some fit their surroundings better than others. Papers are now full of columnists, and it's usually possible to find someone you like (and someone you like to hate) in every one. In the *Independent*, for instance, you can find Deborah Ross – one of the funniest writers in the English language – and also Stephen Glover, the paper's almost unbearably pompous media critic. On the *Daily Telegraph* you have truly great right-wing polemicists such as Simon Heffer and Boris Johnson, and a seemingly inexhaustible supply of rather lily-livered lifestyle journalists.

And if you're skimming, and want to know if a piece is worth reading, check out the second paragraph, and look for quote marks. 'Surprisingly often, the key fact is not in the first paragraph, which is general and designed to grab attention,' says former BBC political editor and *Independent* editor Andrew Marr in his memoir *My Trade*. 'Look for the hard fact in the next paragraph. If it seems soft and contentless, there is probably very little in the story. Similarly, always look for direct quotation. If a reporter has actually done the work, and talked to people who know things, the evidence will usually be there. Who are the sources? Are they speaking themselves? Are they named? Generic descriptions, such as "senior backbencher" or "one industry analyst" (my mate on the other side of the desk) or "observers" (nobody at all), should be treated sceptically.' Conversely, one should also note that when you read 'a source close to the Government', it usually means a source *in* the Government.

If the headline asks a question, try answering 'No.' Andrew Marr again: 'Is This the True Face of Britain's Young? (Sensible reader: No.) Have We Found the Cure for AIDS? (No; or you wouldn't have put the question mark in.) Does This Map Provide the Key for Peace? (Probably not.) A headline with a question mark at the end means,

in the vast majority of cases, that the story is tenden-
tious or over-sold. It is often a scare story, or an
attempt to elevate some run-of-the-mill piece of
reporting into a national controversy and, preferably, a national panic. To a busy journalist hunting for real
information a question mark means "don't bother reading this bit".'

To get the measure of what is actually exclusive to a paper, buy three
or four on one day and see how much is repeated in each – same
news stories, same poll results, same first nights, movie reviews etc.
Also, those 'exclusive' quotes from José Mourinho will turn out to
be simply from a post- or pre-match press conference. Just check the
other papers – the quotes are often identical.

Apart from the *FT* and *The Times*, the only other paper that's important for business is the *Daily Telegraph*, which is read by a lot of
private, influential stockholders (those responsible for public insti-
tutional stock will read the *FT*). Few bankers at Goldman Sachs or
Morgan Stanley are going to bother reading the *Guardian*'s business
pages. The European edition of the *Wall Street Journal* is worth a
glance, although not the *International Herald Tribune*, which is good
on politics, OK on economics, and weak on finance. The other paper
bankers read is the *Sun*, not necessarily for the editorial (well, maybe
the nipples), but to see who is advertising. It costs more to place ads
in the *Sun* than in any other paper, so if Dixons or Carphone
Warehouse are splashing out on spreads, then you get a view of what's
happening in the market.

On this topic, some British newspapers have started using Eyetrack
to see how effective their advertising sites are. Eyetrack is a form of
mobile eye technology that owes its development largely to the air-
defence industry. It arrived at the start of the 1990s and uses a head-
mounted camera to record eye movements over fractions of a second,
in this case seeing which parts of a newspaper the consumer tends
to linger over. The findings have underscored what the industry
thought it knew already, mainly that the higher up the page, the

more likely the eye is to process the information; that the eyes tend to follow the following sequence: image, largest headline, content; and that the right-hand page gets noticed more than the left. Unless – and this is crucial – you are reading from the back of the paper (which a lot of bankers tend to do, as the City pages are usually near the sports section); consequently, if you are placing an ad in the sports section, left seems to be best.

To truly keep abreast of the market you should also have a glance at the business pages in the *Sunday Times* (good gossip), the *Observer* (good for media news) and, of course, the *Economist*. It might surprise you to know that the best obituary of the legendary punk rocker Johnny Ramone wasn't in *Mojo*, wasn't in *The Word*, wasn't even in the *Daily Telegraph* (which traditionally does these things better than anyone, or at least they do if the deceased was in the RAF). No, the best obit of the Ramones' lead guitarist appeared in, of all places, the *Economist*. Funny, erudite and pedantically accurate, it read as if it had come straight from the pages of the *New Yorker*.

The *Economist* is also frighteningly good on cool-hunting, TV wars, luxury branding, the Internet, socio-economic trends, digital harmonisation and pop culture in general. Its 2004 article on Giorgio Armani's succession plans – an incredibly detailed piece – told me more about the company than practically any other piece I'd ever read (and I speak as someone who has also written his fair share of pieces about Armani). Just a few weeks later, the magazine carried an investigative piece on the accelerating war of attrition between record companies and the new breed of subscription-only download services, featuring the sort of in-depth reporting and pin-sharp analysis that you'd never find in *Music Week* or *Variety*.

Most impressively, the *Economist* endorsed John Kerry for the 2004 presidency, a decision that the magazine's then editor, Bill Emmott, went on record saying he had no regrets about. 'Election endorsements aren't about backing the winner,' he said after Kerry lost.

'They're about taking a reasoned position. We backed Bush in 2000, and also the war in Iraq. But he's handled it incompetently.'

Magazines tend to reach critical mass at the most unlikely moments, and there is no quantifiable reason why the *Economist* should have become so well regarded recently – unless, of course, it is simply due to the fact that a lot more people have finally realised how good it is.

For years, the British magazine that media folk would express a particular fondness for was *The Week*. No media questionnaire was complete without a hearty plug for this weekly news magazine, liberally sprinkled with business stories (example: 'I only scan the papers during the week. I catch up with everything at the weekend with *The Week*'). But the *Economist* appears to have replaced it in people's affections. It's become like a badge of cool, like acknowledging an interest in Prada, the Arctic Monkeys or Bob Dylan's *Chronicles* (which, as the *Economist* can tell you, is probably the best book ever published about pop music). In fact it has almost become a status symbol (it's even recommended by *Vogue*).

The magazine's worldwide ABC is just over a million, including around 500,000 in North America and 150,000 in the UK. There are currently six different editions, covering the UK, mainland Europe, the US, Latin America, Asia Pacific and the Middle East and Africa, and it is one of the few magazines (or newspapers) to offer genuine global reach. Its circulation figures are equally impressive abroad, with all five markets showing a minimum 50 per cent growth since 1994. The editors claim it's the only magazine that is taken seriously by the global ruling classes, and although they're unlikely to say otherwise, when you peruse the readership demographics, it's easy to see why: they claim 94 per cent of the UK readership went to university, 50 per cent took a postgraduate course, and 15 per cent completed an MBA.

Analysts are making much of the fact that the magazine's impressive global sales figures are due to its keen-eyed interest in world affairs rather than the more domestic agenda of a paper like the *FT*. However, I tend to think its success has more to do with the fact that its international editions are not only brilliantly put together, but also well marketed. (And, of course, there's that obituary of Johnny Ramone.)

But remember, while news magazines like the *Economist* are refreshingly free from bias, when you're reading the business pages in the nationals, take everything with a generous pinch of salt; not just because of the relentless lobbying by Machiavellian bankers in double-breasted suits and stripy shirts, but also because of the papers' owners. It always helps to know who the proprietor is. After all, as Reuven Frank, the former head of NBC news, used to say, 'News is what someone, somewhere wants to suppress. Everything else is advertising.'

HOW TO BUILD AN EQUITY PORTFOLIO

Because it's better than sticking your money in a bank

Can you sniff the altering breeze? Can you make a gesture at once definitive and prophetic? Can you take a tip and turn it into gold?

The massive privatisations of the mid 1980s tried to turn us all into speculators. Then the talk was of creating a shareholder democracy, one where ownership of previously nationalised industries – British Telecom, British Airways, British Petroleum, British Gas, etc – would encourage millions of private investors to build their own share portfolios.

And it worked. In 1980 there were just 2.5 million individual shareholders, whereas five years later there were over six million. And I was one of those investors, buying up stock the way I had previously bought beer. I didn't make a lot of money, but I made some, as many other people did. Fundamentally it freed up the way I was investing my money, and – via a stockbroker – encouraged me to start buying and selling stocks and shares with impunity. I didn't exactly become obsessed, but began to sense that investment was the only sensible way to begin making money. Because, as Pink Floyd's David Gilmour once so eloquently said, 'Money can't buy you love, sure. But it'll let you park your yacht right next to it.'

These days, investing in the stock market is very different from what it used to be, as you can now trade shares through your bank, over the phone or via the Internet.

The aims, however, remain the same: to generate capital gain and dividends. And of course the trick to successful stocks and shares acquisition is knowing what you're going to do with them afterwards (be aware of the old City maxim 'Something well bought is half sold').

The first thing you should do is decide what type of broker you want. If you want help with your investments you might be best suited to a Full Advisory Service, where the broker will look at your individual circumstances and devise a strategy to suit your needs, monitor your investments and make suggestions on buying and selling. Some may even buy and sell shares for you without asking for your approval first. This service, known as discretionary broking, is highly tailored and, unsurprisingly, can prove to be quite expensive. You should beware of the layers of fees levied by advisors, brokers, fund managers and the other professional intermediaries whose avowed objective is to help you beat the market.

A lot of people these days are prepared to do their own research, and if you're in this camp you need to look for an 'execution only' stockbroker. This means the broker will simply take your order and execute it for you. These brokers can't legally offer you advice on your decisions and, to keep costs down, usually operate over the phone or through the Internet.

Finding the right broker will depend on your individual requirements but there are four factors you should look for: (1) Quality of information, (2) Speed, (3) Access to the right markets, and (4) Cost. And generally speaking, the more you pay, the better the information. One of the best ways to find a broker is through the London Stock Exchange's 'Locate a broker' service.

You should know that while telephone and Internet services may give you access to instant dealing, completing your deal takes slightly longer. By law all share deals have to be 'settled' three days from when they were struck, known in the trade as T+3.

Deals can be settled so quickly because shares can now be held electronically rather than in paper form. But this form of ownership has its downsides. Your shares are held in a nominee account managed by your broker and the name of the ultimate owner is not known to the company. This means there can be no direct communication between you and the company and you must rely on the broker to pass on annual reports and dividends. You can still get the certificate if you really want it, but you might have to pay an extra fee when you trade and settling your deal might take longer (perhaps ten days). You can get the best of both worlds by becoming a personal member of CREST (http://www.crestco.co.uk/). This enables you to maintain a direct link with the company whose shares you own and lets you settle your deals in three days. To become a personal member of CREST you need to be sponsored by a corporate user.

Until recently, buying overseas shares directly was both difficult and costly for private investors, but not any more. Investors can get a ton of information on overseas shares over the Internet, and access to the London Stock Exchange's International Retail Exchange has made it cheaper to trade on overseas markets. You can get access to companies listed on European and US exchanges through UK brokers, although you will pay more to trade than if you were buying UK shares. Alternatively you can buy CREST Depository Interests (CDIs) on the International Retail Service (IRS). It offers access to more than two hundred international stocks such as Coca-Cola and Microsoft.

As with any London Stock Exchange listed stock, you can trade in sterling during London market hours and settle trades with the same ease and at the same cost as UK shares. You can also save on tax as few international shares are subject to stamp duty.

But what do you buy? Experts stipulate that in terms of asset allocation you should really have 10 per cent of your money in cash, 40 per cent in bonds, 20 per cent in property, and 30 per cent in equities. But which companies do you now invest in, having learned how to manipulate and exploit the markets? Unless you have a hot tip (and a tip on a company is really no different from a tip on a horse), then it's safer to take advice, and invest in companies that have a history of successful trading. The FTSE 100 (the 'Footsie') is made up of the hundred largest quoted UK companies by market capitalisation. Usually they are companies over £2 billion in value. The FTSE 100 index is calculated every minute so that changes in the prices of the constituent companies are reflected 'instantly'. When you hear on the news that FTSE climbed fifty or a hundred points, it refers to this index. The composition of the FTSE 100 is revised quarterly, with new companies coming in to replace old ones as their market capitalisations change. Membership of the index has real commercial significance, because if a company slips into the FTSE 250 many tracker funds will be unable to invest in it, depressing the share price.

According to financier Warren Buffett, one of the world's richest people – and the man who managed to turn every $10,000 his original investors provided him with in 1957 into more than an astonishing $400 million today – the basic principles of seriously sound investment for the irregular non-professional investor (i.e. you and I) are simple. They can be summed up as follows: (1) Buy low, sell high. (2) Bet big only when you know something others don't. (3) Avoid popular fads. (4) Trade only when you have to (as the transaction costs will damage your returns).

However, as a banker friend of mine said to me when I asked him the best way to build a portfolio: 'You need a page in the *FT*, a monkey and a dart. The received wisdom used to be that you gave the dart to the monkey and then waited for it to throw it at the paper. But more scientific research shows that you should really just stick the dart in the monkey's backside and see what happens. That's about as scientific as it gets.'

Some notes:

• Investment institutions look for controlled growth: companies that deliver what they forecast; management teams with a good track record and relevant skills. Above all, a board must be seen to be in control – to have the ability to drive the business forward and the vision to grow.

• A Covered Warrant is a financial instrument that bestows on the holder the right, but not an obligation, to buy or sell an asset at a specified strike price during, or at the end of, a specified time period.

• The 'price/earnings ratio' is a measurement of a company's rating. It is calculated by dividing the share price by the annual earnings per share. A high P/E ratio means the company is highly rated by the stock market, suggesting that investors think its prospects are good.

• Liquidity is a measure of the tradability of a company's shares.

• AIM (Alternative Investment Market) gives companies from all countries and sectors access to the market at an earlier stage of their development by combining the benefits of a public quotation with a more flexible regulatory approach.

• The Share Monitoring Service allows you to track specific companies' shares.

• To find a historic price on a company, use the Historic Price Service, as it provides end-of-day Daily Official List quotations for securities traded on the London Stock Exchange.

- Price-sensitive information is any information that could lead to substantial movement in the price of a company's shares. Companies have an obligation to notify the market of any such information.

- Corporate governance is the way a company conducts itself and structures its senior management.

- In a rights issue, a company which has already been listed invites existing shareholders to buy additional new shares in the company for a set price. Shareholders can either 'take up' their rights or 'pass' them.

- You can buy government-issued bonds, known as 'gilts', simply through the Post Office or a stockbroker. Corporate bonds can only be bought through a stockbroker. If you don't want to buy bonds directly, you can choose from a variety of bond funds run by investment companies. These funds pool your money with that of other investors and invest in a number of bonds. A professional money manager is appointed to manage the fund, for which you pay a fee. You can buy bond funds investing in different types of bonds, including investment grade, high-yield and overseas bonds. Some funds also specialise in investing in emerging market bonds.

HOW TO SURVIVE THE OFFICE PARTY

Don't sit under the mistletoe with anyone but yourself

As anyone who has ever been to one knows – usually to their cost – the office party can often be the scariest day of the whole year. Yes, your annual review might be sobering, but then at least you have a fairly concrete and black-and-white idea of what's going to happen (either you've had a good year and get a bonus, or, like me when I worked for Rupert Murdoch back in the 1980s, you get a voucher for a free turkey from Iceland). And yes, the annual awayday to Goodwood or Kempton has the potential to be eventful (who knew the girl in promotions could juggle ping-pong balls like that?). But nothing beats the Christmas party. Maybe it's the sense of celebration, maybe it's the official, traditional marking of time, or maybe it's just the fact that you haven't got to spend the next six months worrying about your behaviour. After all, office parties might be scary, but at least you get special dispensation for attending them (i.e. what happens on the photocopier stays on the photocopier).

I've been to more Christmas parties than I care to remember, many of which turned out disastrously. However, I've probably been to just as many that ended up like *The Office* Christmas special – long, arduous damp squibs.

Every year we have a Christmas lunch in the boardroom at Vogue House, our offices in Hanover Square. It's a staff event to which we invite a selection of friends and contributors – Tony Parsons, Boris Johnson, Peter Mandelson, Piers Morgan, Lauren Booth, Rod Liddle, Abi Titmus, Tracey Emin, James Nesbitt, etc. (We once invited Pamela Anderson, although somewhat less successfully – she didn't come.) In 2001 we invited the disgraced Tory MP Neil Hamilton and his bubbly wife Christine, largely because we'd just photographed them naked for the magazine, posing as Adam and Eve (a joy to organise, let me tell you, although not necessarily to behold), and thought it would be a wheeze to ask them along. We couldn't have wished for better sports, and while Neil stripped down to his boxers in order for one of our girls to shave his chest hair (having failed to get him to shave his head), Christine, emboldened by seven or eight glasses of vintage champagne, leapt on to the boardroom table and played the most enthusiastic air guitar I've ever seen, belting out Townshend-esque windmill chords to Rod Stewart's 'Maggie May' without a care.

When I woke up the next day, I couldn't quite believe it, but I suppose that's the point of office parties. You never know what's going to happen, and considering what can and does it's probably best this way.

And even though you probably don't consider it such a big deal, most people in your office have been talking about it for ages. And there's this nagging voice at the back of your mind suggesting that you really ought to be taking it a little more seriously. So my advice is simple: be prepared. You don't need the guilt, the embarrassment, the recriminations, the shame, the indignity, or indeed the ad hoc cold sweat of instant recall.

So here is what you have to do:

1   Eat before you arrive. It doesn't matter that Alain Ducasse is preparing an eight-course lunch; a few hastily prepared Marmite sandwiches will never go amiss.

2 Ban mistletoe, and if you inadvertently come across some, hide it immediately.

3 Don't wear your new shoes. You will be dancing later, even if you've sworn not to this year, and you don't want to be crippled with ankle pain as you're trying to throw a crazy shape to 'You're Beautiful' or 'Wake Me Up Before You Go Go'.

4 On no account wear a red velvet smoking jacket. People will laugh at you.

5 Feign illness and don't go.

Oh, and one final thing. Admit nothing. It may have looked like you, but it wasn't, was it? Not only have you never worn women's panties, but you've certainly never worn a pair belonging to Pamela Anderson.

Not this year, anyway.

HOW TO GIVE A BOLLOCKING

'What is your major malfunction, numb nuts?'*

The most effective bollocking is the one you don't give at all. If the threat of a bollocking is enough to keep someone in line, then you'll never have to raise your voice. Because, let's face it, unless you're a national newspaper editor (for whom being able to bollock on an hourly basis is a contractual requirement), no one *likes* having to give bollockings. You do, however, have to be able to give them occasionally, and when you do, they should be exemplary, and you should bollock like fury. The culprit should leave your office wilting. As the Fonz once said in *Happy Days*, you don't have to go round hitting people, but at some point in your life you should have hit someone so hard that only a psychopath would ever pick a fight with you.

So. Someone has done something to warrant a bollocking. And so you call them into your office. Personally, I don't think it matters much whether you do it standing up or sitting down, it's the ferocity

---

* R. Lee Ermey as Sgt. Hartman in Stanley Kubrick's *Full Metal Jacket* (1987).

of the attack that's important. First and foremost you need to explain to the person *exactly* what they have done that has displeased you so. If you just start shouting at them they won't properly take in what you have to say because they'll be too busy trying to interrupt, as they won't know what you're referring to.

So explain what they've done, then explain why you are so unhappy about it, and then tell them that if they ever, *ever* do it again they will be toast. Then ask them if they understand. And then dismiss them, turning your eyes away as they walk towards the door.

Some tips:

1   Your bollocking should be conclusive, but not demotivational.

2   Don't get over-emotional. Remember: this is business.

3   Don't get into a discussion: this is a one-sided argument.

4   Swear, but sparingly, and carefully. The *Guardian*'s Guy Browning describes swearing as the way humans bark, and he's right. He breaks swear words down into three grades, with Grade 1 (the worst) usually containing a 'k' sound, Grade 2 usually containing a hard 't', and Grade 3 containing the sort of vowels and consonants you hear in everyday conversation. 'Triptyches are very popular in swearing,' he says. 'A fairly innocuous triptych would be "great steaming idiot". However, most follow the usual pattern of "stupid" + Grade 1 + Grade 1, with the middle word being the f-word.' No bollocking should really contain more than two, perfectly delivered triptyches.

5   The bollockee will no doubt now write you a letter or send you an email outlining just how sorry they are, and explaining in greater detail why they screwed up. It might be fiction, but take the olive branch. They mean well and are obviously worried about their future at the company.

A good piece of advice from Dick Best, the ex-England rugby coach, is to begin the bollocking by telling the guilty party that his misdemeanour was brought to your attention by his team-mates. That way, you appear to be acting on behalf of the team/the office etc. Psychologically this works fantastically well because it makes the culprit feel belittled. It also stops you from looking as though you're victimising them.

Essentially, a bollocking only really works if the recipient is suitably shocked. They can be shocked by it happening in the first place, but it's far more important for them to be shocked by its intensity. Bollockings should be properly scary, and they should be remembered by those on the receiving end for ever. So learn to do it well (if you're going to bollock, then Bollock Like Fury) and learn to give them sparingly.

ETIQUETTE
&
DECORUM

HOW TO REMEMBER SOMEONE'S NAME AND WHAT TO DO IF YOU CAN'T

She's walking towards you, smiling, and your mind's gone blank

Oh dear. You've just seen her, over by the door. She's just picked up a glass of champagne and, armed only with a smile and bold-case bag, she's determinedly, possibly even aggressively, heading your way. She's staring at you intently, and you know that unless someone rugby tackles her – which doesn't often happen at this type of event, not in my experience, anyway – she is going to be with you in approximately five seconds. You know you know her – of course you do, you fool – but right now you just can't place her. What the hell is her name? Did you have a meeting with her in your office last week? Was she one of the women from the weird marketing company you met at that conference three weeks ago? Did you once make a pass at her (if you did she's making no bones about coming back for more)? Or does she work for your own company, one of those blonde women you bump into in the lift and have never really got to the bottom of (so to speak).

No, you're fairly sure she doesn't work for your company, and having frantically scrolled through the ailing Rolodex of your mind, you're pretty sure she's someone important – and judging by her bag and her outfit (head-to-toe top-line navy Armani), she is. But who the hell is she?

In situations like this, if you're by yourself, then you can easily get away with it, as a few obvious questions will identify your quarry immediately (and while you won't have remembered her name, at least you'll know what she does). But what if you're standing at a cocktail reception, talking to your boss, and a top-line navy Armani woman who obviously knows you is going to be wanting some serious face time by the time you've taken the next sip of your vintage Krug? What do you do then? Your boss will not take too kindly to being embarrassed, and if this woman knows you as well as you think she might, she's not going to be leaping through the air doing backward somersaults once she's realised that you have absolutely no idea who she is, that she has singularly failed to make an impression on your life.

You are, not to put too fine a point on it, screwed.

Unless you handle things carefully.

The first trick is to kiss her warmly on both cheeks (always the left, then the right), so she feels welcome. (And if it's a man then shake his hand emphatically.) Then simply ask her how she's doing with the sort of enthusiasm that implies you know she's doing brilliantly, and then immediately introduce her to your boss, or whoever's standing next to you ('You know Charlie Trotter, don't you?'). If you're lucky (and the odds are a clear-cut fifty-fifty) then your navy babe will respond with, 'A pleasure to meet you. Christine Keeler from Blackwood Publishing.' And you're home free, a slam-dunk. If she says, 'Of course,' and she obviously does know him, then move out of the way as quickly as possible, wipe the sweat from your forehead, and walk briskly to the other side of the room, and let them get on with it.

If she doesn't introduce herself, then the only thing to do is brazen it out and begin bombarding her with questions about anything and everything. She will either think you're being slightly rude, or assume that both you and your boss think she's so well-known or so damn important and such a regular fixture on the giddy social circuit that no introduction is necessary (you'll be amazed at how many people believe this). Your boss – because he is your boss and therefore probably smarter than you – will hopefully have worked out that you have absolutely no idea who this bloody woman is and steer the conversation accordingly.

And if the introduction falters, and it's painfully obvious that neither of you know who she is, then quickly interject with a 'Where did we last meet?' in a charming-but-befuddled-Hugh-Grant-sort-of-way. You'll soon work out who she is, and if you smile long and hard enough you might even get away with it.

A worst-case scenario involves you talking to someone who thinks you should know who they are (they're right: you ought to), only to be joined by someone else who feels the same way. Then the only possible thing to do is to say, 'Damn! Sorry, I'll be back . . .' and actually run away. Rude, yes, but forgivably so, and at least your two acquaintances (you know the ones: they're probably quite important but not so important that you're going to bother to remember their names) will be intrigued, and at least when you bump into them again, you can dispense with worrying about what their names are and instead invent a plausible story explaining why you left them in the lurch last time you met.

I am terrible with names, and occasionally, when I'm going out somewhere with my wife, I will remind her that if I don't introduce her to certain people, it's not because I'm being rude, it's just that I can't remember who they are. She has got used to this now, and when I turn and introduce her to a navy Armani babe or a grey Versace bloke, she leaps right in with, 'And how do you know my lovely husband?' (although I've noticed the 'lovely' is being used rather sparingly these days).

If you are of a similar disposition, you'll know that meeting large groups of people at once can be a nightmare. If I'm attending a conference, or chairing a large meeting or a boardroom lunch, I actually write everyone's name on a piece of paper, with an exact diagram of where they'll be sitting. Another easy trick, if you're the host, is to write your guests' names on both sides of the placement cards, so their names can clearly be seen from wherever you are.

Everyone has an ego, and it is crucial to remember this. In fact, remembering this is as important as remembering people's names. We all like hearing our own name, so if you know a person's name, use it, always at the beginning of a question. We warm to people who do this, and as long as you don't do it too much – making us think you're nothing but a two-bit, low-rent, scum-sucking lowlife, or an estate agent, or both – then we'll think the world of you. If we can remember who you are, that is.

HOW TO MAKE A SPEECH

Heartfelt, short and funny (and that's just the groom!)

Many years ago, a friend asked me to give her away at her wedding reception, at the Chelsea Physic Garden in London. Her father was almost pathologically shy, and didn't feel he was up to the task. So I obviously said yes. This was the first time I had been asked to do anything remotely like this, and I was incredibly, almost unbearably nervous. Having had a terrible stammer as a boy, I loathed public speaking and tended to go out of my way to avoid it. But if a friend asks you to do something like this, then you do it, don't you?

So I spent a good month collating material, and building a speech around anecdotes and personal observations. In hindsight I don't think the speech was that wonderful, but it was completely, thoroughly researched, so I certainly knew what I was talking about.

When I was actually called upon to say my words – sober, sweating, clutching my speech as though it were the deeds to my house – I took a deep breath, started e-x-t-r-e-m-e-l-y slowly and took extra care to enunciate. And everything was going fine – and then I told my first joke. It wasn't an especially funny joke (I had tailored the material to the crowd) but as I delivered the punchline, the entire crowd fell about laughing. This not only gave me the confidence to finish the speech, but also taught me a fundamental lesson about captive audiences: they want to enjoy themselves, and they want to laugh. If they haven't paid to see you, and your job is to entertain them, then you're more than half-way home. The guests at Lucy's wedding weren't going to stand on ceremony and deliberately try not to laugh. They were already in a fabulous mood, and only needed a slight nudge to start laughing. Would they have laughed at anything? Probably, but then that's the point. Whether you're talking at a wedding, a leaving party, a dinner party or a roast, you have to understand that everyone watching you wants to have a good time. They want to laugh. So don't be scared. An audience can smell fear as soon as you step up to the podium, so smile, appear confident, and talk slowly.

At a wedding it is traditional for three men to speak – first the bride's father, or a friend of the family, then the groom, and finally the best man. The first proposes a toast to the bride and groom; the second, a toast to the bridesmaids; the third replies on behalf of the brides-maids. Often the bride wants to talk herself, and if she does she can really talk at any point during the speeches.

The bride's father will usually refer to amusing family incidents, and mention his son-in-law and his parents (welcome addition to the family etc). The groom's response will acknowledge his father-in-law's remarks, and thank him for laying on the reception (and paying for everything). He should mention the bride's mother, his own parents ('Thank you for having me' is a common joke), and then lavish praise, compliments and adoration on his new wife.

When in doubt, thank everyone. No one minds being thanked twice, while everyone remembers if they haven't been thanked at all.

The best man's speech is the most important of the day, and is usually considered to be the part of the ceremony when everyone knows they can relax. Best man speeches should be funny and heartfelt but should never attempt to tell the truth. This is not a time for disclosure. As far as content is concerned, begin by making a list of everyone you have to thank, and then work backwards.

The first thing you need to understand is that there is no substitute for research and rehearsals: know your subject, and hone your speech as many times as you can bear to. Write it out, read it out, and record it if you can. Stand in front of a mirror, and try to make sure that you're actually going to be looking at the guests when you're making a point . . . unless by looking at your shoes you're actually making the joke funnier. You should practise your speech until your reflection is bored to tears by the sight of you. Trust me: the harder you prepare, the easier it will come across.

And look smart. Look as if you've just been dry-cleaned. Don't shuffle your feet, and don't loosen your tie (you'll look drunk). Don't use in-jokes, don't swear, and don't be unnecessarily rude. Jokes at the groom's expense are expected, but don't be overly cruel.

Print your speech out from your computer, and format it so that it fits on to prompt cards that will easily fit in your pocket. Break anecdotes down so that they fit on one card; the last thing you want to do is to have to turn a card in order to deliver a punchline. You should not read the speech verbatim, either, and you should use what you've written as a guide – the more conversational you are, the better. Also, number your cards. This will not only help keep them in the right order, but if you number them thus: 7/20 (page seven out of a total of twenty), it will give you an indication of how many you have left. (It is also a good idea to have a printed A4 copy of the speech in your inside pocket, just in case.)

And as you reach the end of your speech, and you're gradually beginning to enjoy it, don't try to prolong it by adding new material. Trust me, this has been great and enough, so don't ruin it.

Harold Macmillan used to say that you should always know what you're going to say but never how you're going to say it. If you're adept at public speaking, and actually look forward to it, then this is a good policy. For everyone else in the world (i.e. you and me), I would reiterate the importance of practice, timing and the arc of narrative. If something occurs to you while you're speaking – and the location and the event are both cheap material – then so be it. But always have a structure to fall back on.

Instead of showing off, instead of giving them the benefit of your wit and wisdom, try painting a picture instead. As advertising bigwig Paul Arden says, 'In a song, we remember firstly the melody and then we learn the words. The more strikingly visual your presentation is, the more people will remember it. And more importantly, they will remember you.'

It's crucial to know your audience. If you're remotely unsure about anything or anyone, then tread carefully and avoid jokes that involve politics, race, religion, ethnic groups or sex. Gentle ribaldry is fine, but avoid personal digs, which will make you seem bitter and make your audience uncomfortable. If you're going to go for someone, then make it funny. I've mentioned a Chinese joke in the appendix at the end of this piece, but be careful how and where you use it – this is a bachelor party gag, not one for an international sales conference.

The audience will want to laugh and they want to laugh with you, so you must try to remember that you have a captive audience. Take them with you – make them feel complicit in the exercise. Personalise all your jokes, and make them specific to the person you're roasting/toasting etc. No one will care whether it's true or not, and as long as it's passably funny, they'll laugh.

If it's a roast, or a leaving speech, then you'll need to mention one person's name over and over again. One way of avoiding this is by using the 'elegant variation'. This is the thing sports reporters do when they've just mentioned someone by name and don't want to do it again, so Wayne Rooney becomes 'the Manchester United and England striker', 'the temperamental boy wonder', etc.

The host of the event is always the first to make a toast, which is generally directed towards the guest of honour. Toasts can be made at the beginning, in the middle, or at the end of an event. However, if it's a stand-up affair, then you should speak in the middle of the event, when most people are in the room. You should make sure everyone's glass has been refreshed, and then go for it.

You, on the other hand, should make sure you only have one drink beforehand. I usually only drink water before I'm due to talk, and then, about ten minutes before approaching the podium, I have one glass of champagne just to jolly myself up.

Talk about things that are relevant to you and to your audience. Sportsmen are not always the best motivational or after-dinner speakers because they're talking about something none of the audience could ever accomplish. The best speakers refer to their own business or your own business, and give trade secrets that are funny. And don't put anything sappy in the middle – if you're going to be nice about someone, put it right at the end. Everyone knows you like the person, because otherwise you wouldn't be making the speech.

Every man should be able to recite a poem, so you should learn one. My friend Robin's favourite poem is Edgar Allan Poe's 'Annabel Lee', an ambitious 300-word eulogy that I have, every now and then, attempted to learn myself. Personally I would recommend something a little shorter (100 words, say), and something rather more upbeat – not jokey, you understand, and never coarse.

Speeches should never be more than five minutes long, although one minute can easily suffice. When you need to actually make the toast, make eye contact with the guest of honour, raise your glass, and say, 'To Jerry.'

If you are the recipient of the toast, don't raise your glass or drink anything (it's bad form). After people have drunk your health, you simply stand up, offer a swift return toast – *Skol, Salud* – say thank you, and then sit down.

Finally, just remember this: There is no speech that was ever given that would not have been improved by being shortened by five minutes. Strike that: ten minutes.

Twenty Infallible Jokes

Let me tell you a story about Jerry. A while ago Jerry was out hunting in the woods with an old friend from school when his friend trips and cracks his head on a tree branch. He doesn't appear to be breathing so Jerry pulls out his mobile and calls 999.

He gasps to the operator, as only Jerry can, 'I think my friend is dead! What can I do?' The operator calmly reassures Jerry and says in a soothing voice, 'Just take it easy. First, let's make sure he's dead.' There is silence, then a shot is heard. Jerry's voice comes back on the line. He says, 'OK, now what?'

Years ago, while driving home from the pub one night, Jerry is stopped by the police. The police officer says to Jerry, 'Excuse me, sir, have you been drinking at all?'

'Why?' says Jerry. 'Is there an ugly woman in the car?'

Jerry's going to New York on what can loosely be called business and he boards his British Airways flight at Terminal One. He takes his seat, opens his copy of *GQ*, and starts reading. As he settles in, he glances up and sees a beautiful woman heading straight towards him.

Jerry was never as experienced with women as he liked to make out, and a wave of nervousness washes over him as she takes the seat next to his.

Eager to start chatting, he blurts out, 'Business, or pleasure?'

'Advanced aggressive sexuality convention in Brooklyn,' she replies.

Jerry swallows hard and is obviously instantly crazed with excitement. And if you've ever seen Jerry after he's just come back from a meeting at *Vogue*, you'll know what I mean. Struggling to maintain his cool, he asks, 'What's your role at this convention?'

'I'm a lecturer,' she says, matter-of-factly. 'I use my experiences to debunk some of the popular myths about sexuality.'

'Really,' says Jerry, swallowing hard, 'what myths are those?'

'Well,' the woman explains, 'one popular myth is that African-American men are the most well-endowed when, in fact, it is the Native American men who are most likely to possess such a trait. Another myth is that French men are the best lovers, when actually Greek men are the best.'

Suddenly the woman becomes very embarrassed and starts to blush. 'I'm so sorry,' she says, 'I really shouldn't be discussing this with you, I don't even know your name.'

'Tonto,' says Jerry as he extends his hand. 'My name is Tonto Papadopoulos.'

There was the time Jerry was caught wandering drunk and naked in London Zoo, after a party at Ed Victor's. An elephant bumps into him, looks him up and down and says, 'How do you eat with that thing?'

Jerry, as I was coming into the church this morning, one of your aunts asked if she could have a word. She wanted to offer you some advice, but felt that it would be better coming from the best man. If you're in a long-term relationship, your aunt suggests you try the following to spice up your love life: Get your lover, blindfold them, get some ropes and chains and then tie them very tightly to the bed. Now go and have sex with someone else.

I also gave Jerry some advice about how to woo Samantha. I told him that the easiest way to impress a woman was to compliment her, cuddle her, kiss her, caress her, love her, idolise her, tease her, comfort her, protect her, hug her, hold her, shower her with gifts, wine and dine her, care for her, stand by her, support her, and go to the ends of the Earth for her. I gave some similar advice to Samantha: I said that the easiest way to impress Jerry would be to turn up naked with beer.

I must tell you a joke that Samantha told me when we first met, all those years ago. A man and a woman are sitting beside each other on a flight to Barcelona. The woman sneezes, takes out a tissue, gently wipes her nose and then visibly shudders for about ten seconds. A few minutes later, the woman sneezes again. Once more she takes a tissue, wipes her nose and then shudders. A few more minutes pass before the woman sneezes and violently shudders again.

Curious, the man says, 'I can't help noticing that you keep sneezing and shuddering. Are you OK?'

'I'm so sorry if I disturbed you,' says the woman. 'I'm suffering from a very rare medical condition. Whenever I sneeze, I have an orgasm.'

'Are you taking anything for it?' asks the man.

'Oh yes,' says the woman. 'Pepper.'

Many men say that women can't tell jokes, but this is another one from Samantha's repertoire. A woman accompanies her husband to the doctor's office.

After his check-up, the doctor calls the wife into his office alone. 'Your husband is suffering from a very severe stress disorder,' he says. 'If you don't do the following, your husband will die.

'Each morning, fix him a healthy breakfast. Be pleasant to him at all times. For lunch, make him a nutritious meal. In the evening, prepare something exceptional for him, because it's important that he eats as varied a diet as possible. Don't burden him with chores. Don't discuss your problems with him, as it will only make his stress worse. No nagging. Make all his calls for him, and learn to use his BlackBerry. And most importantly, make love to him at least six or seven times a week. If you can do this for the next ten months to a year, I think your husband will regain his health completely.'

On the way home, the husband asks his wife, 'What did the doctor say?'

'He said you're going to die.'

The funniest story I know involving Jerry was when he was staying in LA about fifteen years ago. He'd been staying at the Château Marmont for about three weeks working for Paramount, and was feeling a bit lonely. So one night he calls up an escort number he finds in the phone book.

He gets through and says, 'Good evening, I'm looking for a girl in about an hour. I'd like a tall, young blonde with large breasts and a sunny disposition. I'd like her for about an hour and I'd like her to bring plenty of sex toys, including a strap-on. Is that OK?'

'I'm sure it will be fine,' says the girl on the other end of the phone. 'But you might want to dial nine for an outside line first.'

A priest who has to spend the night in a hotel asks the girl on reception to come up to his room for dinner. The receptionist thinks this is a little odd, but as the priest says he's come a long way, and could really do with some company, and after all, he is a priest, she kindly agrees.

Anyway, after a while he makes a pass at her, knocking over a bottle of Tuscan red in the process. The receptionist is obviously a bit shocked by this, and reminds the priest that he is in fact a holy man.

'It's OK,' says the priest, 'it's written in the bible.'

So, being the gullible sort, she believes him, and ends up staying the night – a night of wild, exuberant sex. In the morning she asks to see his bible, and especially the part where it says it's OK for priests to behave badly.

The priest rolls over, takes the Gideon out of the bedside cabinet and shows her the first page. On it, in large handwriting, was the following: 'The girl on reception will shag anyone.'

A woman hasn't had sex for quite some time and, eventually, she decides to seek professional help. She sees her GP, a psychotherapist, a sex therapist, all kinds of experts. But to no avail.

Then one of her friends recommends a Chinese herbalist who she says she should go and see.

So she makes an appointment, and duly turns up. She sits in the waiting room, and eventually is called through to see the doctor. The doctor, who has an incredibly strong Cantonese accent, asks her what her problem is. After explaining that she hasn't had sex for quite some time, the doctor says, 'OK, fank you. Vot I vant you to do now is to take off all of-a your clothes and then crawl up and down the floor in-a front of me.'

The woman thinks this is a little odd, but as she hasn't had sex in such a long time, she figures it might be worth it. So she takes off her clothes, gets on her hands and knees and begins crawling in front of the doctor, first up, and then down the floor.

After she has done this for some time, the doctor says, 'OK, I understand your problem, so please, put on your clothes and go and sit outside.'

So after a while, the woman is called back into the surgery, and the doctor starts his diagnosis.

'I have ah correctly diagnosed your problem,' he says. 'You have Zachary disease, maybe the worst case of Zachary disease I ever, ever see. And this is why you get absourtery no sex.'

The woman, looking confused, says, 'But, doctor, I'm delighted that you have diagnosed the problem, but I confess I have never heard of Zachary disease. What is it?'

'Zachary disease? How to exprain,' says the doctor. 'OK, Zachary disease is when your face look Zachary rike your arse.'

It's nice to see that so many of our French brethren have made the trip today. I'm not sure if you know this, but the

French have just launched their own version of Google, called Quaero. You just type in the subject you're interested in, and Quaero refuses to look it up for you.

An old Italian is talking to a young man in a bar. 'Lad, look out there to the field. See the wall? Look how well it's made. I built that wall stone by stone with my own two hands. Piled it for months. But do they call me Giuseppe the Wall Builder? No they don't,' sighs the old-timer.

Then the man gestures towards the bar. 'Look here at the bar. See how flat and smooth it is? I planed that surface down and carved that wood with my own hard labour for eight days. But do they call me Giuseppe the Bar Builder? Nooo,' says the old man.

Then he points out the window. 'Look out to sea. Do you see that pier that stretches out as far as the eye can see? I built that pier with the sweat off my own back. I nailed it board by board. But do they call me Giuseppe the Pier Builder? Nooo,' says the old man. He pauses, takes a sip of his beer and sighs. 'But you fuck one lousy sheep . . .'

A man comes home from work one day and as he gets closer to his house he notices his wife sitting on the front porch with all her bags packed. With a bit of surprise in his voice, he asks her where she thinks she's going.

She says she's on her way to Vegas, because she's just found out that she can get paid £400 a night for what she's been doing with him for years for free.

The man is obviously a bit taken aback by this, but says nothing and goes upstairs. A few minutes later, he's back at the front door, coat on, bags packed and ready to go.

His wife is flabbergasted and says, 'What are you doing?'

'What am I doing?' he says. 'Easy. I'm coming with you. I want to find out how you can live on £800 a year.'

A blonde goes into a library and says, 'Hello, I'm here to see the doctor.'

The librarian says, 'Sorry, madam, but this is a library.'

'Oh, sorry,' says the blonde, taking her voice down to a whisper: 'I'm here to see the doctor.'

A police officer comes across a terrible car crash where the driver and passenger have both been killed. As he looks upon the scene, a little monkey emerges from the wreckage and hops around the car.

The policeman looks down at the monkey and says, 'I wish you could talk.'

The monkey looks at the officer and nods his head.

'You can understand me?' asks the policeman.

Again the monkey nods his head up and down.

'Well, did you see this?'

'Yes,' motions the monkey.

'OK, so what happened?'

The monkey pretends to have a can of beer in his hand and turns it up by his mouth.

'They were drinking?' asks the policeman.

The monkey nods his head.

'What else?'

The monkey pinches his fingers together and holds them to his mouth.

'They were smoking marijuana?'

The monkey nods his head.

'What else?'

The monkey puckers his lips.

'They were kissing too?' asks the policeman.

The monkey nods his head.

'Now wait, you're saying your owners were drinking, smoking and kissing before they crashed?'

The monkey nods his head.

'What were you doing during all of this?' asks the policeman.

'Driving,' says the monkey.

An old farmer and his wife are lying in bed. He leans over one night, touches her breast, and says, 'If this thing could still give milk, we could get rid of the cow.' His wife leans over and grabs his member. 'And if this thing could still get hard,' she says, 'we could get rid of the dog.'

The CIA are interviewing three potential agents – two men and a woman. For the final test, they bring one of the male candidates to a door and hand him a revolver. 'We must know that you will follow instructions, no matter what,' says the interviewer. 'Inside this room you will find your wife sitting in a chair. Kill her.'

'You can't be serious,' says the man. 'I could never shoot my wife.'

'Then you're not the right man for the job,' says the CIA chap.

The second man is given the same instructions. Five minutes later, he emerges with tears in his eyes and says, 'I can't.'

Finally, the woman is given the test, but with her husband. She takes the gun and enters the room. Shots are heard, then screaming, crashing and a lot of banging. After a few minutes, she comes out and wipes the sweat from her brow. 'You didn't tell me the gun was loaded with blanks,' she says. 'I had to beat him to death with the chair.'

One Friday afternoon, two secretaries are having a chat in the office.

'Veronica, I just don't know what to do,' Danielle says to her friend. 'That good-looking Bill in Accounts has asked me out on a date tomorrow. Do you think I should go?'

'Oh my God!' shrieks Veronica. 'He'll wine you, dine you and then use any ruse to get you up to his flat. Then he'll rip your dress off and have sex with you all night.'

'What should I do?' asks Danielle.

To which Veronica says, 'Wear an old dress.'

An old drunk is trying to cross a busy road, but every time he steps out into the street, a car comes round the corner and pushes him back on to the kerb.

He does this for a while, until a kind young man comes up to him. 'I couldn't help noticing that you're having trouble crossing the road,' he says, with some concern in his voice. 'You know there's a zebra crossing just down the street.'

'Really?' says the drunk. 'I hope he's having more luck than I am.'

HOW TO CIRCULATE AT A PARTY

Pleasing your host, the guest of honour and yourself

If you're pitching up at a party where you will probably not know too many people, you have two options re your arrival time. Either arrive when the party is packed (allow 45 minutes from kick-off), or really early. Be punctual and there will be so few people there that you will be forced to talk to a few people, maybe even your host. You will meet people you haven't met before, allowing you to go and talk to them again later in the evening when the room is full and you don't know anyone else. However, you never want to be the first person to arrive at a party, or the last person to leave, and never, *ever* both.

My advice would be to stay sober. Carry a glass (if you haven't met them before, you don't want people to think you're a stick-in-the-mud), but don't drink from it. When people are drunk they never notice how much other people drink, or whether you're drunk or not. So when you walk up to people and introduce yourself, or go up and loiter around a small group of people (which is totally acceptable behaviour in a situation like this), they'll all assume that you're as drunk as they are (and trust me: they will be drunk). If you look charming – i.e. you're smiling, and looking eager – then you'll be brought into the conversation. You could also wear something extrav agant; not a fluorescent kilt (no one will talk to you then), but an interesting tie or shirt or a buttonhole (call it a silk ice-breaker).

And if you really don't know anyone at all, then head straight for the women, especially women over a certain age. Women over fifty will have less men around them, and will be willing accomplices. They will appreciate the attention, and think kindly of you later on (when you still don't know anyone). This will give you the confidence – if you needed any – to then move on to the babes, and to start chatting up the cuties (see How to Seduce a Woman). You should remember that it is no crime to be an innocent abroad, and that we are always looking for new people to talk to – why shouldn't one of those people be you?

It is also no crime to stand in one place. There is an assumption that one has to keep moving at parties, but I've found that if you stand still, then everyone comes by you eventually anyway. It's also safer, as you don't really want to give up a good spot, or a half-decent conversation, in the hope that the room next door is where all the action is . . . only to find that it's (a) empty, (b) full of another eighty braying drunks you don't know, or (c) the holding pen for two deaf dowagers who know as many people as you do (none), and who are about to leap on you like two bald men fighting over a comb.

You should have done some homework before you arrive. You should always, always come with at least two jokes in your arsenal, and it bodes well to have something witty to say about the latest developments in the news. For this you will need an opinion about (a) whatever's happening in the war (and there's always a war somewhere), (b) the latest celebrity marriage, and (c) a Big Book that's just been comprehensively reviewed by what we still laughingly call the broadsheets. If you're asked if you've read a Big Book and you haven't, bounce back with, 'Yes, of course I have. Not personally, obviously . . .' Your levity will hopefully make up for the fact you've had your nose in the tabloids for the last month. You should also have some nugget regarding a news item that could have come from you and from you only – a friend in the army, someone you know in PR etc. It sounds silly to bone up for a cocktail party, but trust me, it helps. And if you find no common ground whatsoever with the person you're talking to, simply ask, 'So, what's the gossip?'

Contrary to popular opinion, if you're trapped, and the chap you're with is boring the pants off you, just smile, mutter something about 'fascinating' and wander off. Frankly, life is too short.

If this is more of a duty visit, or the sort of event you'd gladly eat your own eyes rather than attend, and you want to make an impression without hanging around, then you should do the following. Arrive 30–45 minutes after the start time (if the invitation says 6.30, rock up at 7.15), as the room will be full by then. If you're wearing an overcoat, don't take it off as you'll never get it out of the cloakroom. (Cloakrooms are dangerous places, because it's here that you undo a lot of the artfully produced small-talk you've used earlier on. Remember that cleverly delivered putdown of a colleague you whispered in your boss's ear as you breezed past him, pushed by the force of the crowd? Well, he's now standing behind you, and you've got to summon up at least three minutes' worth of tittle-tattle in order not to embarrass yourself. You better be armed.) Pick up a glass of champagne as you enter but don't touch it: take a sip and you could be there all night; after all, if you've had one glass, why not have two – or eight! Some suggest walking round holding three drinks – by inference, refreshers for others – although this can prove rather difficult. You should immediately identify your host and the guest of honour (in either order), and then walk right up, thank them, congratulate them, and continue talking until you get interrupted by someone else. When that happens, take a circuitous route back to the door and leave. Never say goodbye. To anyone. And never give a reason why you're leaving – no one will believe it anyway.

HOW TO WRITE A THANK-YOU LETTER

'What a night. I think we took Stuart's wife home with us. But I'm not exactly sure . . .'

According to lore, formal invitations to a couple are traditionally addressed on the envelope just to the lady, and to both parties on the actual hard card. You should RSVP as promptly as possible. Most people I know are terrible at this, and seem to assume that as they've received the invitation, then it's to be assumed that they're coming. Alternatively, it allows them to see if anything better comes along.

Wake up, guys. You must reply, and afterwards you must write to thank your host. Thank-you letters are tremendously classy, and mark you out as someone with standards. I'm not kidding – people these days (especially in the creative industries) are so blasé about corporate entertaining and free gifts/dinners/trips/treats etc that they take them for granted. Wrong. If someone's been kind enough, for whatever reason, to invite you to something, or to feed you, or to send a gift, then the least you can do is thank them in the appropriate manner. Which, it has to be said, is not by email (not yet anyway, although this will no doubt change). Some think that you only have to write a thank-you letter if you've had a knife and fork in your hand . . . again, wrong.

Thank-you cards should be written, in long hand, with a fountain pen (using black or navy ink) on your own personalised cards. These will contain your name (and maybe that of your wife), and sometimes your address. They should be no bigger than A5 and no smaller than A6 (postcard size).

The sentiment should be heartfelt, possibly funny (not compulsory), and brief. You want them to know you really appreciate the fact that they went out of their way to entertain you, not just to think that you're going through the motions. If they're close friends who invited you to something formal, then a simple 'Lovely!' scribbled on your card will suffice. If your letter becomes a litany of pleasures, and you mention the loveliness of the food, the wine and the guests, etc, take care, as your hosts will scan the list for the things you didn't mention ('They didn't mention the fish. Was the fish all right?'). So keep it brief. You are certainly not obliged to respond to a thank-you card (that way madness lies), although if someone sends a gift as a thank-you instead (champagne, flowers) then you should really acknowledge this, if only with a phone call.

It is traditional to address a thank-you letter for a party to the hostess only.

If you're sending a letter, it can be written or typed, but must always be signed and addressed at the top of the letter ('Dear Duncan') by you. The formal sign-off to a letter to someone you know is 'Yours sincerely'; to someone you've never met it's 'Yours faithfully'. Although a simple 'Best wishes' or even 'Best' will suffice with either.*

---

*Don't forget to write. At the back of *The Long Weekend Book* there is a 'Late thank-you letter guilt graph', which perfectly illustrates the arc of desperation resulting from neglecting to write straight away. Three days after visit: 'Just got home, had to write immediately, brilliant party, grease, grease . . .' Three weeks after visit: PS on back of envelope: 'Many apologies. Thought I'd posted this *weeks* ago.' One month: Bunch of roses. Two months: 'Grandmother fell under a train, blah blah, tragedy . . .' Six months: Never dare see host again. Nine months: 'Just spent nine months out in Zaïre and didn't want to trust local post . . .' A year +: Book dedication.

HOW TO DECIPHER MODERN MANNERS

The minefield of being 'charming'

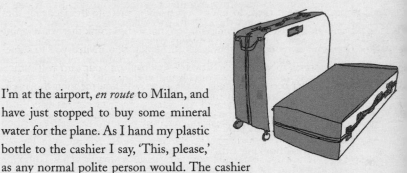

I'm at the airport, *en route* to Milan, and have just stopped to buy some mineral water for the plane. As I hand my plastic bottle to the cashier I say, 'This, please,' as any normal polite person would. The cashier rings up the price, holds out his hand and carries on talking – loudly – to one of his colleagues behind the counter.

I, of course, say nothing. There are several people behind me, but as far as I'm concerned, the cashier has so far failed to acknowledge my existence. And unless I'm very much mistaken, and have got this whole vendor/customer relationship all wrong, acknowledging my existence is principally what he's paid for.

Eventually, sensing that he might actually have to interact with his customer, the cashier stops bellowing (fact: the dumber the man, the louder he talks) and nods at the illuminated price on his till. As he fails to respond to both my raised eyebrows, I'm forced to say, 'How much?' before he begrudgingly grunts the amount.

Far be it for me to act like the man on the Clapham Omnibus, but just why are people today so rude, especially in the service industry? And when did the use of digital till displays begin to make shop assistants think that they no longer have to ask – politely, or otherwise – their customers for money?

Our parents always get misty-eyed when talking about the way our society has changed, fondly recalling the days when proud home owners used to polish their front steps, and greengrocers would help carry things to your Morris Minor. But in many respects – nationalised industries for instance – service was just as bad in the good old days. One Christmas back in the Eighties, as I was endeavouring to travel home to meet my parents, I spent about an hour trying – unsuccessfully – to get through to the ticket office at King's Cross. In those days, even though you got to speak with real people rather than suffer the Yoda-like nonsense of automated responses, the system was unnecessarily convoluted and deeply flawed. It was a system I could have easily imagined being turned down by the former Soviet Union for being too obstructive. Pretending I needed to speak with a passenger urgently, I was given the number of the telephone in the actual booking office – a number that was, apparently, not even known to the people who were supposedly manning it.

And can you guess the response when I eventually got through? 'How the bloody hell did you get this number?'

Lamenting the state of modern manners is self-defeating, a bit like complaining that old-school New Yorkers are brusque (my favourite New York T-shirt of all time: 'Before you ask, the answer is No') or that Parisian cab drivers are obstreperous – 'Les Champs Elysées? Je n'en sais rien!' ('I've never heard of it!'). And while I'm sure we'd all prefer taxi drivers who turned their radios off when we got into their cabs, people who didn't answer their mobiles half-way through lunch (So you're busy, so what? We all are. Turn it off!) and, indeed, people who didn't just start smoking without asking if you mind (and by the way, I do) . . . it's not going to happen unless we make it happen. So ask for the radio to be turned down, ask for the mobile to be turned off, and tell Fag Ash Lil that smoking actually makes you feel sick.

And as for the service industry, as it has become driven by technology, we appear to have lost any interest we once had in people skills. I don't necessarily blame the knucklehead in my local shop for being so appallingly uninterested in his job, I blame the people responsible for hiring him. Whatever happened to the staffing policy espoused by advertising legend David Ogilvy? 'If we each hire people smaller than ourselves we will become a company of dwarves. But if we each hire people bigger than ourselves, we will become a company of giants.'

Like a lot of Brits, I have always loved the attitude towards service in America, because these days the onus there is always on the server to ingratiate themselves with the customer. I don't care how insincere my waitress is when she tells me to 'Have a nice day' or asks how I am, I don't care how sycophantic and ingratiating she is when she reels off the specials like a newly minted cheerleader on Prozac. What's the problem with people smiling a little when they bring you your morning coffee? Rather that than some surly, scruffily dressed lout who thinks waiting on people is somehow beneath him (And by the way, sunshine, for the record I don't think there could be anything beneath you).

The service industry needs to wake up and smell its over-priced, over-stewed coffee, and begin subscribing to the new American mantra, 'W-cubed'. This stands for 'Whatever, Wherever and Whenever you want it', and has become the accepted catchphrase of American customer service from San Francisco to Long Island. The closest customer service gets here in Britain is to place the tips of the thumbs together with the index fingers aloft and with rapid hand movement suggest, Vicky Pollard-style, 'Whatever. Your Mum Works in McDonald's.'

The old-fashioned and frankly bizarre world of manners has gone with the wind, and the labyrinthine way in which breeding was semaphored by etiquette no longer works. Etiquette these days is different from what it meant a hundred years ago, and we no longer have such a need to know the correct way to, say, address the former wife of a duke. But common courtesy never goes out of fashion.

Let's face it, being charming or having good manners is not exactly hard work, and with a little effort, you could soon be the most charming person you know, as well as having the best manners. You should remember the following:

1   If you're walking upstairs with a woman, walk behind her (in case she falls).

2   Walk in front of her when you're walking down, for the same reason.

3   Regular door: she goes first; revolving door: you do.

4   If you're simply walking down the street with her, you should walk closer to the kerb (this used to be in case she got splashed by a horse, but it's still polite).

5   Never sit down until she has.

6   When you're flying, and you happen to have got the armrest first, give it up every now and then.

7   You can never get away with a quick glance at her chest (she'll always notice).

8   If you're drying your hands on a roller towel in a loo (never toilet), pull it down once more after you've used it.

9   Don't throw gum into the street.

10   The only time you can spit is when you're playing football or rugby, or in the privacy of your own bathroom (you should be able to do anything in your own bathroom).

11   Don't wear brown shoes after dark.

12   Always say 'Bless you' when someone sneezes, although once is always enough.

13 Never lift your glass yourself when being toasted.

14 Always tip the cloakroom attendant.

15 Always say please. And thank you.

16 If you think a woman's going to hear you peeing (and you're not at Old Trafford), run the tap.

17 Always pour her glass first.

18 You don't always have to top someone else's anecdote, even if you can.

19 Don't talk about your work (we're not that interested, as what you do for a living is not necessarily more interesting than what everyone else does).

20 Never double dip.

21 Don't take a bottle, take flowers (unless of course it's a very, very good bottle, or champagne, and even then you should perhaps take two).

22 Only text a thank-you message to someone you'd text a joke to.

23 Don't eat in the street.

24 Never eat hot food in a car.

25 Especially someone else's (car).

26 Never mention someone in an email unless you'd be happy for them to read it.

27 DON'T USE CAPITAL LETTERS WHEN YOU TEXT. It looks as if you're SHOUTING.

28 An email is not suitable for sending condolences.

29 However a letter or card will always be smarter.

30 And chicer.

31 Always signal.

32 If someone gets a bit of food stuck on their face you should scrub away at the same part of your face. Shortly your fellow diner will begin doing the same.

33 Thank people properly. Don't, like the two embarrassed ladies in Proust who agonised for days about how to thank Monsieur Swann for a case of wine, simply drop something into conversation later ('Some people have such nice neighbours' will not suffice).

34 If you don't send a wedding present or a Christmas card, we remember. And we don't forget.

35 Every woman likes a compliment, so give them. But don't do it so much that girls just think you're being creepy (or insincere).

36 Don't name-drop. Somebody said to Norman St John-Stevas, now Lord St John Fawsley, 'You are such a name-dropper.' He replied, 'Funnily enough, the Queen was saying that to me only the other day.'

37 Always RSVP.

38 If you think you've inadvertently blanked someone, go and make amends immediately. Because they'll never forget.

39 If you talk loudly on a mobile in a confined space you deserve to be mugged.

40 If you've just ordered a round of drinks, and are still at the bar when you're joined by more people, order for them too (don't think you've done enough, because you haven't).

41 If you're drinking beer in a bar and someone offers to buy you a drink, don't suddenly switch to champagne.

42 Never be first out of the cab and last to the bar.

43 Don't be a child: don't talk with your mouth full.

44 We might live in the 21st century, but still few women like hearing the 'C' word.

45 Let people finish. Even if you know what we're going to say, we want to say it anyway.

46 Don't take seconds and then leave most of them.

47 Always use an unperfumed deodorant.

48 If you're given something (a present, food, etc), don't say, 'Oh, I've got that', or 'No thanks, I don't eat spinach.'

49 If you're leaving a room full of more than four women, try not to kiss the first one, as you'll be there all day.

50 And never sleep with a woman who smokes in the street (girls should have manners too).

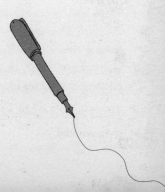

HOW TO BEHAVE AT A LAP-DANCING CLUB

Making sure you don't touch too much

First, know your lap-dancing club. Most lap-dancing, table-dancing or pole-dancing clubs have very similar and strict policies regarding what you're allowed to do, and what you're definitely not allowed to do, and these are usually discernible the moment you walk in. Probably you'll have found out already, through anecdotal evidence, or through the press. Some clubs allow much more than others, some even offering 'special services', although you should really find this out before you go. Visiting a lap-dancing club in the hope of getting a fully-fledged blow-job is a bit like going to a petrol station to buy your organic vegetables: chances are you're going to be disappointed.

Elsewhere, governmental bodies are getting tougher. In Scottsdale, Arizona, after porn star Jenna Jameson bought one of the town's leading strip clubs – Babes Cabaret – the local council declared that clubs must install four-foot-wide barriers between dancers and customers, ensuring that no touching occurs.

Like I said, know thy lap-dancing club, or else you could be severely disappointed.

I'd also be careful who you go with. I'd avoid going with large groups of men, as it looks as though you've dared each other to come, or that you didn't dare come by yourself. Go with a small group, or maybe just the two of you. Going by yourself will make you look sleazy and lonely, but going with one or two other men shows enormous confidence. The other way to show confidence is by going with a girl, and buying dances – lots of dances – for her. The best dancers will go out of their way to try and excite your companion, embarrass you and draw attention to the whole spectacle – which is all good really, especially if she gets other girls to join in.

Finally, before you go you should be prepared to tip – properly. For a £20 dance tip at least £5 if not £10. Tipping fifty per cent will guarantee that you will be able to get any girl to dance for you whenever you want, even when the club is heaving, and the men far outnumber the girls. Years ago, back in the early 1990s, when table-dancing was just taking off in the States, I asked a girl called Taylor in a dingy little club in Nashville called Show Girls if she ever 'did anything else?' In reply she said, 'The only way I'd do that was if the guy gave me so much money I'd never have to work again.' Now, I didn't take this as a No, just the opening gambit in what I imagine would have been a fairly protracted, but easily resolvable haggle.

As for drinks, choose bottles of champagne, or bottles of beer. If it's a good club then you needn't worry about being ripped off by your waitress, but if you're on the outskirts of Outskirtville (on the wrong side of the tracks, just around the corner from Nowheresville), then be cautious – it's rather easier to pour half an inch of whisky into a glass of Coke than it is to doctor a bottle of Becks.

Once inside, what do you wear that will make you feel like a confident, emancipated man-of-the-world, one who understands the latent irony and potential embarrassment of spending several hours supping overpriced flat champagne as scantily clad eastern European beauties cavort in front of you while acting as though they're actually pleased to see you? What do you wear that isn't going to make you feel like a big, fat loser?

Well, if you want to look cool then you have to put your cock on the block, so to speak.

The first thing you don't do is get yourself dressed up as though you're going to the office. I was in the Pink Paradise a few years ago, the Parisian lap-dancing club that is universally acknowledged (by the French) as being the best in Europe; and I was staggered by the number of men who came in dressed in formal suits and ties, almost as though they were going to a sales conference (or, more likely, had just come from one). This overcompensation only illustrates how uncomfortable they were with the situation.

Neither should you look too casual, however. There was one lone Japanese guy sitting opposite me wearing his polo shirt, khakis, Timberlands and imitation leather manbag. Not only did he look as if he was lost (a good excuse, I admit, although not one I've ever used) but, frankly, I think that it showed tremendous disrespect to the girls that he couldn't be bothered to smarten himself up a bit.

No, titty-bar attire is very specific, and you need to get it right in order to feel totally comfortable. The correct wardrobe is what the cognoscenti call off-duty bling (also known by its snappy acronym, ODB). This is relatively easy to achieve, as long as you follow the rules:

1 Don't wear a tie, unless it's a loud one with a fat footballers' knot (if you can't look nouveau in a lap-dancing club, where can you?).

2 Invest in a seriously OTT velvet sports jacket, in either navy or burgundy.

3 Wear your most expensive loafers without any socks, no matter what time of year.

4 Sport your most ludicrous watch and your most ridiculous cufflinks (let's face it, regardless of what kind of club you're in, if you look like a millionaire the girls are far more likely to drag their nipples over your face).

5 Accessorise the lot with a pair of jeans (Levi's), preferably bright white (jeans constrict your penis; the last thing you want to do is wear a pair of baggy flannel trousers, allowing your manhood to stand to attention for all to see).

Basically, you should look as though you've just walked off your yacht in search of a quiet drink and some harmless fun. For you this is a minor, though enjoyable, distraction, and you need to give the impression that this is your first port of call this evening, and not your last. Oh, and take a large amount of cash. You might as well enjoy yourself while the yacht is being cleaned.

HOW TO TIP

Getting to grips with the gruesome
gratuity; when ten per cent just
isn't enough

Being a good tipper* is one of those things
that, whether you like it or not, will define you
as a man in other men's eyes (and women's
too). So do it well, and don't be mean. If
you care anything for your reputation, then
stiffing staff on tips is one of the sure-fire (and quickest) ways to
sully it. You don't have to be flash, just proper.

If you analyse the philosophy of tipping, it's actually quite ridiculous, because it is totally random. If we tip waiting staff there's no reason why we shouldn't tip petrol pump attendants or the checkout staff in supermarkets. But, psychologically, we need to give tips to the people in the service industry who expect us to tip, not least because the extra money compensates for their meagre salaries. Performance-related tipping has largely gone the way of the bowler

---

*Tipping is a habit that originated in the tea gardens of seventeenth-century London, where locked wooden boxes were left on the tea tables, inscribed with the letters T.I.P.S. If customers wanted their refreshment sooner rather than later, they would drop a coin into the box as they took their seats, To Insure Prompt Service.

hat, the Routemaster bus and the local bobby. So pay up. You should also pay up when you've been given a free meal, precisely because the waiting staff rely on your tips, so if you've been given a meal for two at The Ivy, or even at your local tapas bar, leave a bigger than usual tip. It hasn't cost you anything, has it?

In restaurants in the UK you should tip between 10 and 15% of the bill, and 15–20% in America (basically double the tax and then round up). American service staff take gratuities extremely seriously – it is almost a moral duty – and I've seen waiters follow customers out of restaurants haranguing them for leaving such a measly (or British) tip – 'Was there a problem, sir?' It's no exaggeration to say that you really start haemorrhaging cash the minute your flight lands at JFK.

I always give cab drivers extra, not because I think they deserve it, but because they're more likely to turn around and give me an earful if I don't – so round the amount up by at least £1 with any journey in London, or a dollar extra in the States (if the fare is £4.30, you can make it £5, but if it's £4.80, make it £6). If it's a long journey, say from an airport, then an extra £5–20 is not unusual.

Make sure you have lots of small notes when you check into hotels, too (when you're abroad this is particularly important), as you'll need to tip the porters when they deliver your bags to your room. When they've just dumped twelve full-to-bursting Louis Vuitton cases in your suite, it's frankly not acceptable to explain, in pathetic pidgin French/Italian/Portuguese etc, that you've only got a $100 bill and that there's no way you're getting your hands on that, matey. Also, to be expedient about it, it's much better to tip when you move into a hotel than when you leave. If you're constantly asking the doormen to get you taxis, or getting valet parking to bring your rental up every hour or so, don't tip every time; just make sure you pay up properly when you check out (at least £20 for the doorman, and £10 each for the car-hops). I'd venture that the most important people to tip in a hotel are the housekeeping maids who come in to clean when you're gone. It's not going to get you any better service, but they live on scraps and free soap, so any few dollars you've got lying around are going to help enormously. Also, most guests don't do this any more, so your gesture will be more than welcome. Chalet girls, on the other hand, should get about £100 a week, while it's polite to leave some money in an envelope for the au pair or cleaner if you've been staying with friends at their holiday home or country house. (You should always check first with your hostess, as she will, for a variety of reasons – not spoiling them, not embarrassing other guests – have very definite ideas about how much she would like you to leave.)

Croupiers, meanwhile, should by rights get between 5 and 10% of your winnings, while the likes of masseuses and manicurists should get about the same. Tipping is really common sense, and whether it's the milkman, the doorman or the dustman at Christmas, or the crew on your friend's boat, an extra £20 here or there is never going to hurt (them, or you). When you're having your hair cut, for instance, it's not always necessary to tip the actual hairdresser, but imperative to tip the (young) person who washed it.

And hookers? Well, this is a difficult one as one presumes you won't be going back for repeat business. But if you are, and you're using an escort rather than a girl off the street, then it's advisable to leave a tip, not just to show your appreciation (and what appreciation!), but also to ensure that next time the service will be even better. So if you're spending say £400, you should perhaps leave £50 extra. Ten per cent is acceptable, but to leave £440 makes it look as if you've worked out the exact percentage, whereas leaving £450 makes you look generous. And if you want to tip a lap-dancer then that's completely up to you, although I'd be surprised if you had any money left to leave.

Personally, I don't often tip the washroom attendants who pass you a small towel and brush you down after you've just had a pee in fancy hotel loos. If you use the loo three or four times a night – which is quite conceivable if you're over 30 – it could cost you a small fortune just to relieve yourself, and I go out of my way to discourage the practice (the tipping, not the peeing). (Of course you might think that they deserve a tip if you've been helping yourself to the complimentary aftershave and the free mints, but then if you did either of these things I don't think you'd have picked up this book because you are so clearly, painfully beyond help.) Obviously we don't tip bar staff in Britain, but if you're drinking in America, it's always advisable to tip a barman at least 20% of the bill on the first round; then he knows that (a) you're going to be around for a while, and (b) that you're not afraid to spend money. This will also help you get served when the bar fills up.

When you should absolutely never tip is when service has already been included. Hotels are especially guilty of this, and when you're presented with your breakfast bill after your food has been laid up in your room (food that has cost the hotel less than a pound per person), you'll usually find that extra percentages have been added for Room Delivery and for Gratuity (in France this is known as *service compris*). There will also be another line, which you are encouraged to complete, for Service. I always make a point of drawing a line through it, signing the bill and looking the employee straight in the eye as I hand it back to them. I might look like a sucker, but I can assure you I am not going to start acting like one.

Restaurants are also guilty, sometimes very good restaurants. Claridge's, which remains one of the best hotels in the world, makes a policy of adding service to its bills in its bars and restaurants and then asking you to pay for it again. I've often thought that this was just a cynical way to try and get slightly drunk customers to add another 10 or 15% without properly looking at the bill (and we all leave a little more if we're drunk). Again, you should leave it blank, or, as I do, write 'ALREADY PAID' in capital letters. My childish lobbying has obviously had no effect because they still do it.

Remember that a 'suggested' service charge of 12.5% is just that, a suggestion. The added suggested gratuity on your restaurant bill is not legally binding in Britain, and there are no rules governing how much, if any, your waiter will see of it anyway. So if you're not keen on seeing your extra payment disappear down a book-keeping black hole, leave it off and leave a bigger tip, 15% maybe, in cash. More important – for you – if the food or the service have been particularly poor then leave the tip off altogether. The manager will soon get the message.

Countries where tipping is not considered essential include Japan, Australia, Thailand, China and, unusually, Italy. You should also never tip doctors, chiropodists, dentists, traffic wardens, teachers, shop assistants, tailors or priests. You must, however, always put something substantial on the collection plate in church. We are all encouraged these days to fill in one of those tax-exempt envelopes, and your envelope should never feel heavy with coins (i.e. it should always have notes in it, preferably £10+). Funeral directors should get at least £100, if you're happy with the service, that is. They have just buried someone you loved (probably), and although they do this day-in day-out, show gratitude for a difficult service handled well. A former *GQ* staffer also discovered how you should tip the RNLI. If you're a yacht skipper saved at sea you are morally – if not legally – bound to give the RNLI anything from £3,000 to £5,000 as a donation. Otherwise, according to international laws of salvage, they can keep your boat. Or, more likely, sell it.

And don't over-tip either, not anyone; or those in the service industry will just look on you as a putz, and the staff will laugh at you behind your back. Read any exposé of how a hotel really works, and you'll see that big tippers (almost always Americans, Arabs and, now, Russians) are held in as much contempt as esteem. You might get more prompt service, but you'll sort of hate yourself for it.

And if you feel figuratively short-changed, and let down by your waiter, porter, driver, or indeed lady of the night, my favourite retort is this: 'Is service included? Well, can I have some then?'

HOW TO PACK
A SUITCASE

How to arrive without all your clothes looking like linen

If you're on a business trip and travelling with suits and shirts that you'll no doubt want to wear a few hours after you arrive, then take a suit-bag, and take it as carry-on luggage. If you're travelling business class you'll be able to hang it up in the wardrobe, and if you're in coach class, just put it in an overhead locker. If the suit-bag is sturdy enough, then your clothes should be fine when you eventually arrive at your destination. Inside the suit-bag you should hang all suits and all shirts, using wire hangers as they take up less room (you should always use wood hangers at home; for travelling use the wire hangers on which your shirts come back from the dry cleaners). If you're travelling in winter, then hang your polo-neck sweaters over your shirts.

No one, obviously, relishes packing. Whether you plan ahead or throw things in at the last minute, it's difficult to be pleased with the results. And, of course, the proof of the packing is in the unpacking – when your beloved – or not so beloved – clothes invariably turn out to be appallingly creased. St Christopher can be quite mean in this respect, and although you could ask the hotel to quickly press your clothes, they'll rarely be able to do it in time. Either that, or they'll lose them. Some hotels have irons and ironing boards in the rooms, although European legislation is making this a rarity. Even so, a travel iron is never a bad idea.

So, if you're not carrying a suit-bag, open your hardback trolley suit-case and put in your washbag, spare pair of shoes (into which you have put your rolled-up socks, ties and handkerchiefs), your gym kit, and any small heavy items. Then put your trousers in the case, length-ways, with the waistband against the side and part of the garment hanging over the edge. This will be folded later to avoid sharp creases. Then turn your jacket inside out, fold it in half and carefully put it in the case. Now fold your trousers over your jacket, lay any shirts and T-shirts on the top, and put any bits and pieces around the edges and in the corners. Any sweaters should be rolled-up and placed along the edges on top of everything else (with jumpers and sweaters and the like, always try and roll rather than fold, because each fold is a potential crease).

If you get to your hotel and open your suitcase to find that what-ever you wanted to wear tonight is creased, then simply hang it up in the bathroom, over the bath, and then fill the bath with scalding hot water. Shut the door and turn off the light (in case the extractor fan is linked to the light switch). An hour later the steam should have diminished any serious creases, enough at least for you to go out in style.

You could do worse than take the advice of William Hurt's reclu-sive travel writer in Lawrence Kasdan's *The Accidental Tourist*: 'The business traveller should bring only what fits in a carry-on bag; checking your luggage is asking for trouble. Add several travel-size packets of detergent, so you won't fall into the hands of unfamiliar laundries; there are very few necessities in this world which do not come in travel-size packets. One suit is plenty, if you take along travel-size packets of spot remover. The suit should be medium grey;

grey not only hides the dirt, but is handy for sudden funerals. Always bring a book, as protection against strangers. Magazines don't last [apart from, I would suggest, *GQ*], and newspapers from elsewhere remind you, you don't belong. But don't take more than one book – it is a common mistake to overestimate one's potential free time, and consequently overpack. In travel, as in most of life, less is invariably more.'

Some tips, however: always take a shirt and tie, even if you can think of no conceivable reason for them being there. If you don't pack them, you know you'll need them. Same goes for your gym kit and your swimming trunks. If your favourite shirt is dirty, don't worry – just put it straight into the hotel laundry on arrival. And you can never have enough electricity adaptors, so buy more (just think of all the appliances that need charging at once: laptop, phone, BlackBerry, razor, etc).

Oh, and if you're rushing around in the bathroom trying to get ready in time, never put your cufflinks on while standing at the sink. Why? Oh come on . . .

HOW TO GIVE A COMPLIMENT

Be careful, be honest, be true

Remember: speaking without thinking is like shooting without aiming, so be careful when you open your mouth. When you're giving compliments – especially to women – give some thought to why you're doing it. If it's going to reflect better on you than on the person you're showering with praise, then you should really question your motives. Sometimes we pay each other compliments purely in order to make ourselves feel good. Which is not the reason to do it.

And are you going to do it in private, or in front of a whole bunch of people? If you're doing it publicly, then you need to make sure that it's appropriate, and that the object of your praise isn't going to feel embarrassed or patronised.

And don't give so many that no one takes you seriously.

If you're going to do it, then do it properly, sincerely. Don't damn with faint praise, and don't be half-hearted. And if you're being phoney, for God's sake do it so that no one notices. Women can smell phonies a mile away, and if the object of your affections thinks you're stringing her a line, she won't take too kindly to it. In fact, fall at the first hurdle, and you're toast. It can be done, though. At the end of a fashion show, it is customary for the journalists and editors in the crowd to go backstage and congratulate the designer. Now, if the show is good, and well received, then this is rarely a problem – you simply shake their hand, congratulate them and move on. But if the show is dire, and you find yourself with nothing positive to say, then what on Earth do you do? Well, one person I know, who regularly attends fashion shows, has the answer. If he finds himself unable to say anything positive about the show, he simply says one of the following: 'Sergio, you've done it again', or 'Mr Bendy Trousers, only you could have designed that collection.' Works like a dream. Every time.

You'd be surprised how many men simply don't compliment women on what they're wearing, and while I wouldn't recommend you start complimenting every woman you meet ('Hey, I *love* those shoes – where are they from?'), you should begin to notice and study what they wear. That way you'll be genuinely intrigued when you notice something you like. Women buy clothes so that their friends and acquaintances will notice them. Because if they only wore sexy clothes in order to pick up men, they'd stop buying them as soon as they got married. And if, as a married man, you think she's still buying clothes to please you, think again, pal. She remains as competitive as ever, and needs to stay ahead of the pack. So compliment her on her new shoes, her new handbag, her new lipstick shade, and especially those new jeans. 'You really like them?' she'll say (which basically translates as, 'He thinks my backside looks *great* in these jeans'). Trust me: you will always get away with it, because not only does she think you find her attractive (when you're researching a woman's outfit, you have fundamentally been given *carte blanche* to totally check her out, from her lips and her breasts all the way down to her thighs and her ankles), but by telling her you're letting her know without being vulgar or remotely pushy.

Oh, and women *always* want you to comment on their new hair – always, always, always. So start to notice. Because compliments work, and when they work, your attentiveness will be reciprocated. As George MacDonald Fraser once said of a libidinous temptress who had suddenly become 'interested', 'She didn't wink, but her voice did . . .'

The best time to receive compliments is when you least expect them. And you should try to give them accordingly. And the best way to pay a compliment is either to tell someone else – so it gets back to them quickly – or to do it in print, where everyone can see it.

Ever since I've known him, Jeremy Clarkson has gone out of his way to blame me for his sartorial shortcomings. It's hard to believe, I know, but apparently I am responsible for the anvil-like bubble perm, the billowing free-form jeans, even the mid-life crisis leather jacket. Those battered cowboy boots? My fault. The greying, frayed denim shirts? All my doing, apparently. Oblivious to the fact that I think he's the Funniest Living Englishman, Clarkson's got it in for me.

Admittedly, he has been on the *GQ* Worst Dressed Men list for five years running, but it's not as though I put him there myself (I always vote for Julian Clary and Jonathan Ross). The list is compiled from over a thousand votes from the great and the good (a.k.a. the good, the bad and the ugly), including the likes of fashion designer Paul Smith ('Clarkson is good at cars, but bad at clothes') and Clarkson's best friend, the critic A.A. Gill (Jeremy is by far the worst-dressed person . . . drop a gear . . . in the world'). He was No. 8 in 2001, No. 13 in 2002, No. 6 in 2003, No. 2 in 2004 (beaten only by Graham Norton), No. 3 in 2005 and No. 6 in 2006. As Jeremy Hackett, from men's outfitters Hackett, says, 'The worst-dressed list wouldn't be the same without him.' Indeed.

I saw Clarkson some time ago, in Cape Town, at the launch of the Jaguar XK, Jag's sporty new grand tourer. And Clarkson and I both had a great time driving it, through Stellenbosch and the wine region, down by Table Mountain, and out into the valleys. As we were about to set out in the car for the first time (he chose gun-metal grey, I chose racing green), Mr Petrolperm accosted me with his familiar finger-in-the-chest.

'So what do you think of my new outfit?' he asked me accusingly, almost forcing me to put him down.

'Jeremy, you look very . . . well, you look very Jeremy,' I said, benevolently.

'I can't bloody win!' he said, holding his hands up to the sky, as if asking for divine intervention. 'You say buy Church's shoes, so I buy them. You say Gieves & Hawkes suits are cool, so I get one. And still you say I look crap. Just what the hell do I have to do to please you?!'

This was not the first time that dear old Clarkson had lambasted me. Around four or five years previously, we were both at the same wedding in Claridge's (a fairly fancy affair, where Elton John was the best man, Richard E. Grant the MC, and Jonathan Ross the guest speaker), and I happened to bump into him on the way to the cloakroom. As I did so, I couldn't help noticing that he was wearing a pair of – how can I put this? – pixie boots. And as I was beginning to castigate him for his inappropriate footwear (it was a wedding, for chrissakes, Jeremy, not a Christmas panto), he pounced, in the way that only Clarkson can.

'OK, Mr Trendy *GQ*, look at your tie, you look like Eric Morecambe [it was large and made of burgundy velvet, so I suppose he had a point], and look at that shirt – where did you get it, Marks & Spencer!? [it was from Gucci, actually]. And as for that suit, it's ridiculous!'

'But it's by Richard James,' I said.

'I don't care, it's rubbish,' said Clarkson, his hair beginning to take on a life of its own.

'Well, tell him yourself,' I said. 'He's standing right behind you.' And he was.

But with that, the mighty Clarkson – in a perfect pot/kettle body-swerve – called me the worst-dressed man in Britain, and stormed off in a puff of unleaded, striding back to the dining-room as fast as his tiny little pixie boots would carry him.

The thing is, Clarkson enjoys being 'badly dressed', and thinks it makes him seem normal. In his defence, he says, 'I wear clothes to cover my genitalia and for no other reason.' But in reality, most of the time Jeremy looks perfectly fine, and his endearing sartorial hiccups have simply become part of his make-up. I couldn't tell him this in Cape Town, of course, as he would have rebuffed the compliment as though I were a fawning petrolhead.

So I teased him some more and set off in search of some half-decent South African chardonnay.

At dinner that night, as he worked his way diligently through two packets of Silk Cut Extra Mild, he suggested that if I had any wit about me, I would start producing a Clarkson clothing line, containing – no doubt – a redoubtable selection of billowing free-form jeans, mid-life crisis leather jackets and battered cowboy boots. Neither of us mentioned pixie boots, but then we didn't have to.

So there we are. As one of the best ways to give a compliment is in print, here goes: Jeremy, you are not the worst-dressed man in Britain.

Not while Jonathan Ross is alive, anyway.

HOW TO BE A GOOD GUEST

And what to do about peeing in the night

So what do you do when you've been invited away for the weekend at your new friends' country pile? What's the correct way to behave? The first rule is: listen. If you're asked to arrive 'around two-ish on Saturday' then do exactly that. If they want you for lunch, they'll tell you, so don't assume you can just pitch up and get fed and watered. Inviting people for the weekend is a very delicate process, and although you will be invited enthusiastically, only your hosts will know the complete details of the weekend. They will have an exact idea of how they want the weekend to unfold, and will have a fairly good idea of when they want you to arrive and leave. Consequently they will try to direct you carefully, tentatively, without being rude, and you should be sensitive to this. (If you get the impression that they'd like you to leave sharply after lunch on Sunday, then that's exactly what they want you to do.)

You should make the effort to arrive looking calm and feeling upbeat. Nobody wants to open the door and hear about your awful day/headache/terrible journey, etc (I don't).

The rule for a guest is: you pay. For everything. Your hosts' fridge will be full, as will the cellar, and they may even have prepaid for some events (cinema, theme park, kids' adventure playground, etc), but if you venture anywhere where payment is needed (restaurant, pub, pub, restaurant), *you do it*. Don't argue, and don't let yourself be persuaded otherwise: just do it. As not doing it is rude. Doesn't matter if it happens three or four times over a weekend, just put your hand in your pocket. If there are other guests there, then you will no doubt be fighting to pay each bill – the sensible thing is to have a quiet word with the other guests before the first excursion: 'We'll do tonight and then you do tomorrow, OK?'

You should also bring a gift when you arrive, what the Americans call a bread and butter gift – a case of wine, vintage champagne, chocolates, flowers (already in a vase – no hostess wants to disappear to the kitchen to tend to bouquets), a hamper, a candle, a box set of CDs or DVDs. Or if both you and your hosts are that way inclined, drugs.

And be careful of your pets, as your hosts might not love your dog quite as much as you do.

When dinner comes around, you'd better sing for your supper. I don't care if you're feeling under the weather, or a bit miserable, just pull your finger out and act like you're having the best time in the world. Because if you don't it's unfair. Be amusing, tell jokes and anecdotes, and tailor your behaviour and conversation to the mood of your hosts. Don't grandstand, just try to be excellent company. After all, if they're good friends of yours, you owe it to them. And you want to be invited back, don't you? If your hosts want to stay up till four, then stay up with them (and if they start yawning, have the good sense to go to bed).

You should mingle and smile when introduced to new people. Mix it up, and introduce strangers to each other. Don't get plastered (immediately), and flirt with older people to make them feel special. Delight in the food and ask where the wine is from. Admire the host and hostess's outfits, and express relish in the environment (comment on the garden, children's photos, etc). Don't be insincere (they're your friends, remember?), but remember to do as much as you can to make your hosts feel they made the right decision inviting you. Don't treat your break like a holiday – give as good as you expect to get.

Be mindful of what Quentin Crisp once said: 'The well-mannered person ardently wants social relations to run smoothly.' If you're a vegetarian and you're presented with a dish containing meat, don't complain; it's not your host's problem, it's yours. If you've been coming to your hosts' home for years, then by all means get up and make a pot of coffee in the morning, but try not to wake them. If you're visiting new friends, don't overstep the mark. Wait until they get up themselves. You can use the time waiting for them to surface by going to the local village and buying the Sunday papers (all of them). And if you're too late for that, then do the croissant run.

Strangely, the one thing that everyone worries about when they're staying with friends is what to do when you have to get up and go for a pee in the middle of the night. Do you flush, or not? If you have an *en suite* bathroom then it doesn't matter, although it's probably just as well not to flush in case you wake someone up. But if you're being asked to use a loo half-way down a corridor, maybe between your bedroom and that of your hosts, then do you flush, or not? If you don't flush, for fear of waking your hosts, then how are they going to feel when they nip into the loo before you wake up, only to find a pan full of pee? Personally I think the only thing you can do is flush, and just hope no one wakes up. And I'd also sit down to pee, so as to make as little noise as possible. Then close the lid and quickly pull the chain.

While parlour games have obviously gone out of fashion, people still like to play things like Charades and The Name Game. Also known – quite pretentiously – as Forehead Detective, this involves everyone sitting round in an approximate circle. Each member of the group is given the name of someone famous (or someone you all know) by the person sitting on their left, who writes it on a piece of paper and then sticks it to their forehead (cigarette papers used to be popular, now it's Post-it notes). This creates an immediate team spirit, mixed with a slight sense of unease, because while you can see who everyone else has stuck to their face, you can't see who's on yours. Each person then takes it in turn to ask yes/no questions about their character until they guess who they are. Perennial favourites are Graham Norton, Boutros Boutros-Ghali, Joan Collins, Jenna Jameson, the Archbishop of Canterbury, Norman Tebbit, Jordan, Simon Cowell and the one person everyone in the room knows you hate.

And always, always send a thank-you letter. You don't have to go overboard like Mr Collins in *Pride and Prejudice*, but a simple acknowledgement is always necessary (and another gift wouldn't go amiss).

HOW TO COMPLAIN

Sometimes the only option is to be rude

Bizarrely, not only has the Internet become a place where you can indulge those corners of your personality you perhaps don't always want to share with everyone else – a sort of concierge service of the arcane, the prosaic and the decidedly odd – it has also become a facility for doing your dirty work for you.

If you're sick of spending forty minutes trying to get through to some dodgy call centre, waiting to complain that your microwave/fridge/iPod dock/mail-order Thai bride has so far failed to arrive, then you can, if you so desire, call complaindomain.com, give them twenty pounds, and they will do the complaining for you. They'll take up your case, keep you updated and get you any due compensation. BT, MFI, PC World, Dell, Comet, British Airways – no one is safe from their perpetual nagging.

But why on Earth would anyone want to use it? After all, that would take away the fun of calling someone up in a heated bate and screaming at them down the phone for ten minutes. Which, frankly, is not something I think I'd ever want to deny myself.

Complaining is something of an art, one I like to think I have mastered completely. I don't actually like complaining, but I have become extremely good at it. And while I would never advocate being rude simply for the sake of it, where any semi-nationalised service supplier is concerned, or any insurance company, any airline, indeed any organisation that feels it necessary to employ a small army of people whose sole occupation appears to be waiting for you to call up and complain, intransigence works.

The terrible truth about complaining is the fact that if you're insistent, and borderline rude, then you will get results. Call up BT and refuse to get off the phone until you're happy and you'll get things done. While it would be lovely to think that everyone on the end of a call centre help-line is there to actually help you, we all know that this is rarely the case. And rudeness works.

You would have thought that deregulation and an increasingly ferocious marketplace would have made British Telecom improve their services to the extent that they are no longer used as an example of poor service. But no, not in my house. Now that you can choose network providers, handsets and software packages like you can choose breakfast cereals at your local supermarket, wouldn't you have thought that BT would have streamlined themselves into a slick, fully-functioning 21st-century telecommunications company? Me too.

If I ever want to remind myself of what Britain used to be like, when nationalised industries seemed to take great pride in treating the consumer like a member of the Soviet underclass (and here I'm basically talking about British Rail), then all I have to do is ask BT to try and help me. Quickly. Efficiently. And with a modicum of charm. But seeing that this never happens, I think I'm well within my rights to be as rude and intransigent as they are. Which I am. And, as I say, I'm very good at it.

Complaining is not a science but a skill and an art. As with most skills, the more people practise, the better they become. As with most arts, the trick is to recognise natural abilities and when it's best to use them. *Watchdog* advocate converting your fury into determination and controlled indignation. Complaining involves a little psychology, a worked-out strategy, an awareness of tactics and an appreciation of the resistances you are likely to meet. And if all that makes it sound as if it is a battle, you may need to be warned: sometimes it is.

The thing is, it doesn't have to be this way. Hotel groups, travel companies, banks, energy suppliers, telecom companies and airlines have now made it so difficult for any of their customers to actually speak with a human, that by the time you actually get through to someone on the phone, you are usually so frustrated and angry, having had to press a monotonous sequence of numbers for the previous twenty minutes, that when you hear a real person ask, 'Can I help you?', the answer is usually, 'Yes, actually, you bloody well can. And I hope you've got the answers I'm looking for because if you don't you're going to be talking to me for a very, very long time.'

The trick with these people is to refuse to be intimidated, to be prepared for the long haul, and to refuse to take no for an answer. Always ask for the person's name, so that if you get cut off (or, more likely, if they cut you off), then at least you have a name to ask for when you call back in approximately twenty seconds' time.

Usually, you're simply trying to get the idiot at the end of the phone to understand that something his company are responsible for, has, somehow, gone wrong. The trick here is (a) to get them to acknowledge this, and (b) to get them to do something about it. And the way you do this is by being belligerent. It's a sad truth, and one that my wife refused to believe for years until, like me, she realised that the only way to get anything out of anyone on the phone is to be as forthright as possible.

However, you should only ever call up to complain if you actually want to achieve something. If you're just annoyed about a particular aspect of the company's service, or you want to let them know how angry you are at the attitude of their deliverymen/hours of business/lack of customer service, etc, then don't bother. You won't achieve anything and will only make yourself more wound-up. Only get the angry stick out when you actually want to make something happen – when you are making a complaint about the non-arrival of a sofa, receiving the wrong airline tickets, or (more likely) the fact that the idiot from BT installed your phone incorrectly.

To circumnavigate the infuriating automated phone-answering systems, various websites now offer 'cheat sheets', that list the sequence of numbers you have to punch in order to get through to a human (holidaymakers urgently needing to contact Thomas Cook, for example, can bypass the automated phone system by pressing 1, then 2, then 5).

But as for British Telecom, if I were you I wouldn't bother learning the cheat sheets. I'd simply change your service provider.

HOW TO BE PHOTOGRAPHED

What do you mean, you are standing up?

It is remarkable just how many sophisticated, worldly-wise and successful
men instantly freeze when someone puts
a camera in front of them. Men who have stood
in front of five hundred constituents, five thousand shareholders,
or presented to a room full of bored clients with low blood sugar
levels rarely seem to know what to do when someone asks to take
their picture. Do they smile, frown, cross their arms or head for the
hills? Look through any trade magazine, company brochure, sales
catalogue, national newspaper or family album and it would appear
that many men can do all of these at once.

I've seen hundreds of celebrities being photographed, and the ones
that get the most out of it are those who use the camera as though
they were taking the picture, rather than the photographer. You need
to treat the lens as though you own it, and don't let it intimidate
you.

Being photographed is not that different from being filmed. 'In a
close-up, the camera lens magnifies your actions, so you have to know
how to scale down the action of your performance without losing
the intensity as the shot gets tighter,' says Michael Caine. 'In fact,

oddly enough, your mind should work even harder in a close-up than it does during the other shots because in the close-up, the performance is all in your eyes; you can't use the rest of your body to express yourself.'

I've seen Caine being photographed several times, and the cliché about celebrities 'turning it on' for the camera is certainly true with him. He is a master at it, and treats the camera as he would a journalist. 'OK boys,' he'll say, 'Here we fucking go, what do you want?'

Caine's friend, the celebrity photographer Terry O'Neill, has photographed him over 150 times, cataloguing the myriad personalities and celluloid guises of a Very British Institution. 'Over the years I've shot him so often that it became something of a holy grail for me to photograph him without his glasses. A lot of critics think that Michael's power lies in his specs, but they couldn't be further from the truth. With Michael, it was always his eyes that made people notice him.' It's the same with most people in front of the camera.

Firstly, when having your picture taken, you should never try to be someone you're not. Don't pose, or try to look cool, because you'll just end up looking like Gary Numan (or, worse, David Brent). Don't frown either. Smile, look contented and pleased to be there. Never cross your arms, as you will look defensive, awkward and unnecessarily aggressive. Similarly, don't slouch or put your hands in your pockets as it will seem as though you're not really bothered how you look in the picture. And for God's sake try not to look smug, as people will hate you.

Celebrity fashion photographer Mario Testino likes to say that he gets his subjects to relax their mouths during shoots by asking them to say 'Wogan', which rounds their lips. While it's rather strange that one of the world's most fashionable photographers gets some of the world's most beautiful girls to mouth the name of Britain's most ardently middle-of-the-road DJ, I wouldn't advise any men doing the same: it will make you look like a monkfish (and not in a good way).

If you're photographed a lot, or are about to be, it's easy to work out which side is your best – we all have one, and five minutes spent in front of the mirror while you're shaving will work it out for you. Tilt your head downwards a little (never lift your chin up), and look up a little with your eyes. If you are being shot full-length, it is advisable that the photographer has the camera just above your waist; this is so the top and bottom halves of your body are in proportion. How many times have you seen a huge head and pin feet because the photographer was taller than the subject, or the reverse when the photographer was way smaller or, even worse, sitting down?

It's a good idea to try and chat to your photographer so you can get a variety of facial expressions. Many shots will be awful, but you will stand a good chance of getting a few really great ones, and after all with digital cameras you can just delete what you hate instantly. Make sure you see the Polaroids or the chosen digital pictures and simply choose the ones you want. Photographers learn how to get the best out of people, but every one of them has a particular style, and that style might not be best suited to you – so ask to see the pictures before they're edited (you need to remember that this exercise is about you, not the photographer).

Never let yourself be intimidated. I was once being shot by David Bailey – who's notorious for trying to intimidate his subjects – and I'd only been in front of the lens for a few minutes before he called me 'a long streak of piss'. He softened immediately when I told him the actual phrase was 'a long streak of *paralysed* piss' (an old RAF term). He made up for it by telling me the filthiest joke I've ever heard (told to *him* by Walter Matthau, and unfortunately not workable in print).

Checking the light source should be the job of a good photographer (or, increasingly, their assistants), but there are several things you should remember. A side light will present deep shadows on the opposite side of the face; and a low light can make sinister scary movie shadows above the nose and on the forehead. A front-facing light can be best. Polaroid is the kindest medium as it bleaches out all blemishes, but black and white is often far more flattering and 'classic' than colour. In fact a black and white photograph is nearly always more flattering than a colour pic. If you're really nervous about being photographed, then it's wise to be shot in your own environment, and to have your wife or girlfriend around to make sure you don't look ridiculous.

Some people just shine in front of a camera, regardless of whether they're trying to or not, whereas the rest of us have to learn how to act as though we're enjoying it. Being photographed is a trick like any other, and if it's going to become an issue in your life, you should learn how to cope with it.

Some specific tips. If you're bald, a judicial crop across the forehead will obviously be flattering. If you're slightly portly, a head shot might be better than a full-length photo. And beware the wide-angle lens, especially if you're carrying weight. And if you're being photographed for a consumer or fashion magazine, don't assume the make-up artist has your best interests at heart; she probably has, but give your opinion if you have one.

Finally, don't 'do' something for the camera; you will look like a prat. Be confident – always be confident – but don't show off.*

---

* And it's true: if you wear glasses you will look more intelligent, and a suit will always give you a stronger silhouette.

HOW TO TURN THIRTY (AND THEN FORTY) WITH DIGNITY

Welcome to your mid-life crisis

I admit, I'm a cliché, OK? Six weeks before my thirtieth birthday I went barmy: demented, berserk, moonstruck-mad, good old-fashioned ape-shit crazy. Old age was approaching like a jail on wheels and I just couldn't cope. Didn't anyone understand? Obviously, no one had ever turned thirty before, at least no one I knew.

I had all the symptoms: fretting over wasted youth, worrying about my future. Was I an underachiever? Had I hit all the right goals? I was so depressed, I got anxiety attacks every twenty minutes. For those of you who have never experienced such a thing, let me tell you it isn't just a figure of speech. I first got one when I was attempting to buy a flat a few years before, and couldn't understand why I was curled up on the floor of my room in the Watergate Hotel in Washington (where I had come to review the Rolling Stones), unable to breathe, and panicking about whether or not I was about to make the right decision. I was scared for my sanity, and the only thing that made me feel any better was calling up the estate agent in Maida Vale and telling him I didn't want the flat (I didn't so much conquer my demon as decide not to buy it).

This time was different, as my approaching marker concerned all aspects of my life. Was I in the right job? Was I developing as a person? Should I be married by now? Did I have the right friends? Why was my waist expanding? I was in trouble, and I knew it.

Then there was the celebration. It had to be the party to end them all. When you're thirty, I surmised, everything had to be special. But what should I do? Where should I go? Who should I invite? And would it be special enough? I was worrying so much, I felt as if I was planning a multinational's millennium party . . . worried that I was turning into Mad Jack McMad.

With twelve hours to go and nothing planned, it was all decided for me – I was struck down with gastric flu. Psychosomatic, my girl-friend said – decision displacement, faking it – but then she hadn't spent the night clutching her stomach, trying to get through to God on the big white telephone (thankfully he was always engaged). Anyway, if it had been psychosomatic I would have probably been clutching my balls: the most common psychosomatic symptom is a dull ache in the testicles, usually, I am assured, when you've been unfaithful and are worried that you may have caught something.

So I made my thirtieth birthday toast with water. The next day I felt the same – anxious, pensive and all the other words that mean anxious and pensive – only now I had hit the age of thirty.

In reality though, I'd actually hit thirty about three years previously – at 27. That was when I, like most men, first took stock of myself, started taking myself more seriously; when I disembarked from club-land, stopped punishing my liver and threw out an awful lot of clothes (and I do mean awful). Twenty-seven also brought warnings of a small paunch, while clumps of hair had begun to disassociate them-selves from my scalp.

Of course, there are parts of me that will forever remain sixteen, and parts of me that have always been middle-aged (the more I think about this, most of me actually), but it's a shock to be confronted with your thirtieth birthday; you have to learn to act your age. This can be a problem, because there's bound to be a part of you that feels forever young. 'You're in your early thirties?' said Martin Amis at the time. 'You're probably intellectually persuaded that you're going to die, but I bet there's ten per cent of you that thinks that everyone else is going to die, and as you look in the mirror you think: there is this interesting exception in my own person. There's this illusion that life is always going to be there. Around your late thirties, that goes.'

To accept mortality inevitably leads to a close examination of your own life. You start contrasting your life with those of your peers; you compare partners, jobs, salaries, houses, cars, clothes, temperaments, looks, physiques, ambitions, and the likelihood of you fulfilling them.

And, if the pieces don't fit, it feels as if you're on a time bomb, frantic at the thought that there are only so many years left to put said pieces in place. It can make you mercenary and callous, force you into a gym, or help you change jobs (please don't do this just for the cash; I've taken two jobs in my life simply for the money and both times it was a mistake). And it can do all of these things at once. Turn thirty and the way you look at the future changes fundamentally, because there isn't so much of it left. Your ambitions change, too: some diminish, others start to look plausible. When you hit thirty you set your sights higher, but you'll probably want to move the goalposts, too.

There are those, predictably, who treat thirty with indifference; those who think it is no different from turning 29, and carry on regardless ('all it means is less frequent erections and the advent of nasal hair'). Some ignore it ('I was oblivious, and it wasn't until I was about 36 that I realised I'd been acting like a 25-year-old for the last ten years'), while others just slow down ('You realise you have to act more seriously. Past 28, going into 30, you realise you can't drink, smoke, or abuse your body as much as you used to or as much as you'd like to. You have to learn to be more frugal. Also, you get great satisfaction seeing people who are 22 or 23 screwing up. You cloak yourself in smugness and think, shall I tell them or not?') Some simply use it as a reason for clearing out their wardrobes. 'No matter what fond memories they evoke of the first time he wore them,' I read recently, 'there are certain garments from a man's past that he should never seek to wear again: a thin leather tie, rainbow-coloured braces, those little underwear briefs with cartoon superheroes printed on.'

The biggest problem with turning thirty is knowing that forty (or 39 and 12-twelfths) is only ten short years, or 120 very short months, away. The horizon changes and you find yourself looking down a road with middle age at the end of it. Forty is serious, a legendary figure bathed in an unearthly glow. By the time you reach the Big One, you had better know exactly what you're doing; so if you're in any way uncertain, turning thirty gives you a good excuse to worry about it.

'Turning forty is a big event,' says Amis. 'But it didn't come on the stroke of midnight. No, there's just a biological delay before you begin to understand that you're going to die. A coarsening of the features happens with this realisation. Because it's such a blow – as if a loss of individuality occurs. This individuality you had and that you thought was eternal. When you discover that you're not an exception to the ageing process, when it emotionally hits home, it's as if that writes a few years on your face immediately. A sort of sadness sets in . . .'

For many men, turning thirty seems like the first nail in the coffin. But then, a decade later, they realise how young they were, and how much was ahead of them. This always happens when you look back, whether you're eight or eighty. When I was 22 or so, I realised with irritation that I was too old to be a pop star – something which these days is not the case (Morrissey didn't become a star until he was 26, and I dread to think how old the Pet Shop Boys are). I think I always knew that turning thirty was a phoney benchmark. In fact I remember thinking that I'd probably look back on 'thirty' as a breeze, an event so unimportant as to hardly warrant recollection. I was sure of it.

I thought that in ten years' time I'd be busy faking a mid-life crisis to remember what it was like to reach the mere stripling age of thirty. I know I'll be the same when I eventually reach fifty.

The thing you have to understand as you approach any serious benchmark is the fact that you will always, always be apprehensive about it. And the other thing you need to understand, is that you always feel better once you've passed it. It is a copper-bottomed fact that as we get older, men get better at everything, including, saliently, sex.

And that, really, is all you really need to know.

Mr Jones

Things you should have done by the age of thirty/Things you shouldn't do until you're over forty

Made a million/Spend a million

Got fired/Fire somebody

Dated a lap dancer/Pay for sex

Bought a first edition of a Martin Amis novel/Own a first edition of a Kingsley Amis novel

Quit smoking (cigarettes)/Start smoking (crack)

Developed a taste for classical music/Develop a taste for jazz

Spent a night in jail/Bail a friend out of jail

Made a killing on the market/Lose it all on the 4.15 at Sandown

Caught a 35lb marlin/Catch a trout on a dry fly

Run the NYC Marathon for charity/Pay someone you sponsored

Had an AIDS test/Have a prostate cancer check-up

Had meaningless sex with a minor celeb/Make love
to a living legend

Stopped going Dutch with women/Start paying
the full 12.5 per cent

Gone off-menu/Order for the table

Stopped arguing with your parents/Start arguing with your kids

Fucked 'up the payroll'/Fuck 'down the payroll'

Slept with a woman twenty years your senior/Sleep
with a woman twenty years your junior

Abandoned your first novel/Turn it into a screenplay

Started reading the business pages/Start making
the business headlines

Taken a girl to a football match/Vow never to take
a girl to football again

Swum in three oceans/Ski on three continents

Joined the mile-high club/Get your pilot's licence

Cleared a pool table at one visit/Compile
a snooker break of over fifty

Learned to snowboard/Go back to skiing

Saved a life/Make a life

Recognised that guitar rock will never die/Celebrate the fact that guitar rock will never die

Understood that *The Godfather* is the greatest film ever made/Understand why *The Godfather Part II* is better

Received a compliment with equanimity/Find it in your heart to give a compliment

Set your mobile to vibrate/Have someone to answer it

Convincingly faked an orgasm/Accept that she's done the same

Stopped parroting catchphrases/Get a motto

Had anal sex/Have an anal examination

Changed your political opinions/Lose your political opinions

Moaned about things/Complain about things

Learned a foreign language/Learn to speak the Queen's English

Started on Proust/Give up on Proust

SEX
&
SENSIBILITY

HOW TO SEDUCE A WOMAN

If I said you had a beautiful body would you hold it against me?

First, choose the right place. Although you can never choose who you fall in love with, you can always choose where you look. As Philip Roth's father says to him in *The Plot Against America*, 'That's what I always tell my boys. Marry like President Washington. It's as easy to love 'em rich as poor.'

Secondly, choose your women carefully. Check out the way she looks at men as they pass her, check out the way she looks at you. Are you going to be wasting your time? Is she a prowling SINBAD (Single Income No Boyfriend And Desperate)? What's she wearing? After all, to paraphrase Michael Caine's mum, 'If it's not for sale, what's it doing in the window?' Or, as Vince Vaughn says in *Wedding Crashers*, 'A tattoo in the middle of the lower back – might as well be a bullseye.'

A Capricorn's advice? Never express interest in a woman until she's expressed an interest in you. That way you'll be a *lot* less disappointed.

1   Don't forget that you're trying to be immediately remarkable rather than permanently satisfying. You are not perfect, so hide your faults.

2   A public kiss is not foreplay.

3   In her eyes, sexy beats cute, smart beats sexy, and funny beats everything.

4   But never use humour when things are going badly, because they'll only get worse. Just look at David Brent.

5   On a first date, never ask for a *ménage à trois* (it's French for 'in your dreams').

6   A kiss is an expression of affection, not passion. Trust me.

7   If she laughs at your jokes, smiles most of the time, touches your arm every now and again, and teases you (very important, this), then the signs are good.

8   Be generous. 'Women are an investment, and the more you spend on us, the more seriously you take us.'

9   If, however, on date three, she takes you to an unbelievably expensive place, and treats you – let her. She'll find it sexy and empowering.

10   She thinks metrosexuals are, well, a bit gay.

11   Read her body language: if her lips are pouting or she tilts her head, she likes you; if she turns her head towards you but the rest of herself away . . . or if she puts her hand behind her head, she doesn't like you at all.

12   You can never, ever compliment a woman too much. The best advice I've ever heard on the subject? 'You can never, ever, under any circumstances, no matter how florid or excessive you might think you sound, exaggerate the splendour of a woman's recently unclothed body.'

13   For women, shopping is foreplay, just like beer is for you. As is talking, *lots* of talking. Sorry, but it's true.

14 Don't muck around in the office. Remember: don't shit where you eat.

15 If you're flirting on the phone and want to move to the next stage, always challenge her in some way – tell her she ought to ask for a rise, or encourage her to say something to a friend, or execute something at work in a particular way; anything, basically, that creates a bond between you as well as making it easier for her to call you back to let you know how it all went.

16 When you meet her, try to be just ever so slightly less drunk than she is.

17 As Billy Crystal said, women need a reason to have sex. Men just need a place.

18 Sexual euphemisms to be avoided: 'put Barney in the VCR', 'lead the llama to the lift shaft', 'get up in the hat rack', and 'climb back on the horse' (although this is perfectly acceptable when used to describe your first alcoholic drink the day after an especially heavy night).

19 Texting has obviously made flirting and seduction easier. But use it sparingly. Effectively, but sparingly.

20 Let her catch you looking at her. She put a lot of effort into how she looked before she came out, and she will enjoy being appreciated. Just don't ogle her breasts. Ever.

21 Never say, 'Can I buy you a drink?' Say, 'What are you drinking?'

22 *The Game* by Neil Strauss is an exhaustive account of how the author turned himself into an extraordinarily successful pick-up artist. The book's glossary includes (1) The three-second rule: *noun*: a guideline stating that a woman should be approached within three seconds of first seeing her. (2) Group therapy: *noun*: the idea that women of beauty are usually accompanied by friends, and to meet her, a man must win the approval of her friends while actively demonstrating a lack of interest in her. (3) Similarly . . . Neg: 1. *noun*: an ambiguous statement or accidental insult delivered to a beautiful woman a pick-up artist has just met, with the intent of actively demonstrating to her (or her friends) a lack of interest in her. For example: 'Those are nice nails, are they real?' 2. *verb*: to actively demonstrate a lack of interest in a beautiful woman by making an ambiguous statement, insulting her in a way that appears accidental, or offering constructive criticism.

23 Cologne is good (Stella is not cologne, nor is Budweiser or Beck's).

24 Commit the colour of her eyes to memory. She will test you on this, a lot sooner than you think.

25 Women want to know that you're capable of taking care of them, but not that you think they need taking care of.

26 'It doesn't matter how good he is in bed. If he can't get me a taxi in the rain, he can forget it.'

27 When you finally get to kiss her, gently suck her tongue.

28 Sexy girls want you to want them for their minds . . . and smart girls want you to want them for their bodies.

29 You undo a bra thus: grasp either side of the clasp and push the sides together – this will cause the hook to disengage from the eye. By now you should really have learned to do this with one hand.

30 Every man knows that sex should never be the most important part of a relationship, although you should make sure you're sexually compatible. After all, if the sex is good, it's twenty per cent of a relationship. If it's bad, it's ninety per cent.

31 There is also the option of 'going ugly early', but I'm not sure we need to get into that right now.

32 One final tip, from Chazz Palminteri, as Sonny in *A Bronx Tale* (1993): 'All right, listen to me. You pull up right where she lives, right? Before you get outta the car, you lock both doors. Then get outta the car, you walk over to her. You bring her back to the car. Dig out the key, put it in the lock, and open the door for her. Then you let her get in. Then you close the door. Then you walk around the back of the car and look through the rear window. If she doesn't reach over and lift up that button so that you can get in, dump her.'

HOW TO BUY FLOWERS FOR A WOMAN

Don't make the wrong floral stance

You might not know this, but every man needs a florist. He doesn't just need the telephone number of one (don't ever book flowers via email), he needs a name and a relationship, needs to be able to call up at the last minute and say to Igor (or Randolph or Pumpkin or Lydia Folkestone-Hovercraft), 'Look, can you get a bouquet to Gerrards Cross by seven o'clock?' You need the name and the relationship because you're calling at ten past six and if your mother-in-law doesn't get her flowers by the time she goes out to dinner (you've forgotten her birthday again, you oaf), then your domestic relations could experience something of a little cold spell.

So choose a florist, and use them regularly. Learn to trust their judgement, once they've fully understood your needs. They will see you through romances, break-ups, births, deaths and ill-advised flings. Women tend to like lilies and orchids, but good florists will always suggest something innovative. Don't forget that much of their business is taken up with corporate entertaining, and they no doubt work for a hotel group and various restaurants too. It's their job to know what's 'in', so to speak. As flowers are expensive (the minimum you should spend is fifty pounds including delivery), the foliage you 'pad' the bouquet out with is crucial, and your florist will have a good steer on this too. Sometimes it's best to go with one single colour, rather than an arrangement, as this can look stunning.

Make sure you send them to her office. She loves this. She will know everyone is staring as she walks back to her desk from reception clutching a bunch of flowers the size of a small tree. And she'll feel like a princess on the bus home.

Think about the message carefully. Who else will see it? What stage is your relationship at? 'Meet me in the Westbury, 7.30, Room 213' will be a lot more effective than 'I'm surprised you can walk after last night' (especially if the flowers are delivered by someone from the mail room). If you're sending flowers to a client to apologise for something, don't compound the crime by referring to it in too much detail on the card, just in case someone from his company sees it.

Vary the size of the bouquet: sometimes a small bunch of freesias is divine, and sometimes some long gladioli with willow branches up to three feet long will work. Or pussy willow mixed with laburnum. These are all easy ways to make an impression. Currently the vogue is for orchids or the like in vases or pots, because they require no maintenance at all.

'These days flowers go in and out of vogue like lapel sizes,' says a friend of mine who sends flowers for one reason or another at least twice a week. 'Just as you're getting used to Casa Blanca lilies somebody comes along and makes phalaenopsis orchids the flower *du jour*. Chrysanthemums, like shell suits, are terminally naff; while carnations, once the pariahs of the flower community, are – like cowboy boots, their sartorial equivalent – enjoying a bit of a renaissance. But be careful. Try too hard, go over-exotic or too stark and white, and you'll just end up looking like a flower victim.'

There are a million reasons to send a woman flowers (OK, maybe not a million, but a lot). To say I Love You, to say Sorry, for birthdays, anniversaries, babies, promotions, or, when you're still dating, just to say, It's Thursday, and I still love you (or better still, when you're not dating). Basically there isn't a woman alive who will not appreciate flowers. They are the result gift. Frank Sinatra wooed Ava Gardner by filling her hotel room so full of roses that she was almost asphyxiated by the aroma. But in a good way.

Flowers have also become a default business gift, and are the easiest, swiftest, most pleasing thank-you present. They work best when they're unexpected, and trust me, if you've had a row with a client, or want to thank someone for a favour, few things work as well as a surprise bouquet. Try not to buy red roses, as they're really old-fashioned. If you have to – you know she likes them – then mix them with berries, twigs and trailing ivy (and make sure you order an odd number – even numbers are common). Finally, don't buy flowers from a petrol station or a supermarket, or from the bloke standing by the traffic lights as you drive home. But if you do, unwrap, cut and arrange them yourself before she gets home.

HOW TO BUY LINGERIE FOR A WOMAN

Making her feel special without making her feel cheap

The first rule here is, Be Careful. After all, you don't want your significant other looking like an extra from a cheap metal video, do you? *Do you?* Lingerie usually tells a woman what sort of woman you'd like her to be, rather than what sort of lingerie you'd like her to wear. And as she knows what type of woman she is already, she's not going to appreciate you buying her tacky sex-shop skimpies. Synthetic scarlet underwear, crotchless panties, bra tassles, peep-holes, fluffy trimmings and leopard-skin suspender belts are all woefully naff. You should also avoid seamed stockings (tacky) as well as basques and fishnets (if she wants these, which is unlikely, she can buy them herself).

The second rule is, Know Her Size (check the labels in her clothes, stupid). She will probably respond well to the fact that you know her sizes, regardless of what you've bought her and regardless of whether she likes it or not. In Britain bra sizes are still measured in inches across the back and underneath the breasts, and range from 30, 32, etc up through 40 and beyond. Cup measurements are universal, ranging from AA (boy breasts) through to HH (probably not natural). Panties or briefs (the industry doesn't recognise 'knickers' any more) come in even dress sizes, from 6 and 8 right up to 16; or occasionally from XS to XL. And if you're buying (tasteful) suspender belts, they should be in the same size as the briefs.

When you enter the store, make sure you turn up alone, and sober, as lingerie assistants get sick of men coming in together after some Dutch courage, making crass gags and asking them to try things on.

Choose carefully. It's always a good idea to know what sort of underwear your girl likes, as there's a huge difference between sports bras in plain cottons and more showy things in satin, silk and lace. Also, bear in mind her skin tones and hair colour, because if she's pale, say, then ivory or white lingerie could make her look wan and washed out; if she's black, champagne is more fetching than white, and if she's a redhead, avoid oranges and pinks. Sports bras are better for small-chested girls, while Wonderbras are fun but not the type of thing your love interest will want to wear all day (they're very stiff, like old corsets).

And spend as much as you can afford. Buying cheap lingerie is almost as bad as buying cheap jewellery. And for God's sake pronounce it properly – something along the lines of lansheree, and not lawnju*ray*.

Buying lingerie works; not necessarily in a 'result' way (she was likely to sleep with you anyway), but it will flag up the fact that you still find her desirable. And if you have to buy lingerie for your woman to spice up your sex life, then there was probably something wrong with it in the first place. So congratulate yourself for taking the initiative.

HOW TO FIND THE G-SPOT

Honestly, it's in there somewhere

For eons, women were inclined to complain that their man could never find their clitoris. A more recent bugbear has been the G-spot, which women still complain we can't find, and which for years we thought was simply a myth. Sorry, guys, it isn't. It is your girl's equivalent of the prostate and, if handled correctly, can send her into orgasmic spasms. So you'd better learn where it is.

Ready: Get your lover to lie on her stomach.

Aim: From behind, gently stimulate her clitoris until she is fully aroused. Then slide your finger gently inside her and, on the front wall of her vagina, press carefully until you feel a small area that is slightly different in texture.

Fire: Imagine your finger is rubbing a dirty mark on very fine material. Keep on until the area becomes more enlarged. She'll soon yell. You'll smile. You've hit the spot.

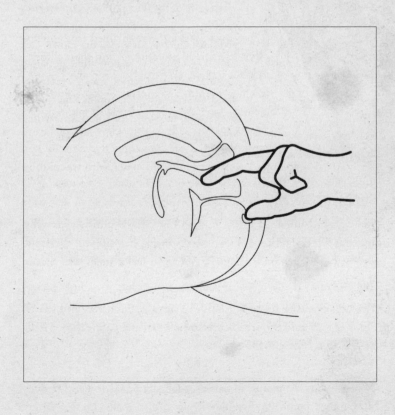

HOW TO GET FIT

Because it's actually quite easy

Ever aware of the fluctuations in the world's waistline, cognisant of the fact that Ronald McDonald has swapped his clown suit for a tracksuit (he is now the company's 'global ambassador of fun, fitness and children's well-being'), and having turned a certain age, for some time now I have had my very own personal trainer. Alasdair. Or, as I have rechristened him, The Fitness Perv.

Like all trainers, Big Al (as he likes to call himself) is something of a zealot. Always early for our appointments, always full of new ways to make me suffer ('I've come up with some new circuits: you're going to die'), always ready with freshly honed abuse (a keen advocate of political correctness, his favourite retort is 'Stop being a girl').

Big Al (which I still refuse to call him) never lets you forget he was once in the army, and even on bitterly cold days will turn up for work in a vest and a pair of jogging shorts that he says were standard issue but to my eyes look suspiciously like a thong wearing a valance.

When I started training in earnest (actually in Hyde Park), I dutifully turned up on my first day in my baggy khaki shorts, a bright orange logo T-shirt and a pair of secondhand Nikes given to me by a friend. Alasdair – who if he ever leaves personal training would have a frankly subsistence-level career as a stand-up – asked if I was about to go on holiday, which I found funny once, but not every time I turned up to train. And so after a while – having briefly toyed with those grey sleep suits they give you when you fly long-haul with Virgin – I did what any self-respecting consumer would: I invested in some proper gear.

Now, I've never been the biggest fan of training shoes, have never seen the point of wearing them as an alternative to loafers, Oxfords and the like (they make grown men look like children, make children look like infants, make infants look like aliens). Neither have I understood the cultish veneration that surrounds them, nor the relentless obsession with 'box fresh' variety: these days there are trainers which light up, trainers which tie their laces together, trainers which masquerade as proper shoes, even trainers – I believe – which will play the banjo and do your tax returns (often at the same time). So the idea of buying a pair was anathema to me, until I convinced myself that they would be used solely for practical purposes.

Then came the T-shirts. Too mean to run in my designer Ts, I'd started off wearing old rock'n'roll T-shirts, the ones proclaiming allegiance to a zeitgeisty pop group (in my case the Ramones and Kraftwerk, and in Alasdair's probably Atomic Kitten or Gary Barlow), but felt I'd sort of outgrown them. I once saw three portly men in a restaurant in Marylebone wearing commemorative tour T-shirts: Bob Marley (predictably always a favourite), Rage Against the Machine (a touch idiosyncratic, I admit, like System of a Down or Queens of the Stone Age), and, of course, a ubiquitous U2 number (apparently celebrating some long-forgotten eastern European jaunt of the late Eighties). And they all looked like Very Sad Men, men whose arc of achievement hadn't quite got off the ground, whose benchmark of success was being in seat 36, Row K of the Hammersmith Odeon twenty years ago. It was less the unreconstructed childishness of this that intrigued me, rather the banality.

If men are prepared to do this, I thought, then why don't we apply this chest-beating to other events in our lives – T-shirts that announce to the world that we ate in Granita in 1992, or moved to Notting Hill in 1995? How about 'Soho House (rooftop bar) 1999'; 'Gascony 1993'; 'BMW 320SE 1991–1994'; or, an idea I think would definitely catch on, 'Jean-Paul Gaultier, the Lurex years, 1984–1987'? For the record, the only T-shirt slogan I've ever really liked was 'Dip me in honey and throw me to the lesbians'.

And so I became a fitness perv and invested in The Kit. I bought two pairs of Asics trainers complete with Adidas lace-locks (one pair for gym work, another for outside), a couple of Nike drifit tops of varying thicknesses, drifit shorts, Nimbus cushioned socks, a North Face Gore-Tex jacket (for when it's really parky), a Polar heart rate monitor watch, some Peak Performance vests, a North Face rucksack, some Ron Hill jogging pants, cotton and Lycra Ron Hill running gloves, and some Oakley Blades with interchangeable hi-definition lenses, for running into the sun. Oh, and, just to spite Alasdair, a Superman outfit.

Believe it or not, losing weight, getting fit and staying healthy is not rocket science as some personal trainers may lead you to believe.

The so-called 'celebrity' trainers seem to effortlessly get their celebrity clients into great shape in the shortest time possible with amazing results. What they fail to tell you is just how many sessions their client does each week, how long for, and what nutritional guidelines they are following. If you had the same amount of free time, not to mention the money to spend on personal training, you too would be in the best shape of your life.

What these trainers fail to tell you is that fitness is based on three simple rules:

1   If you want to lose weight – eat less and train harder.

2   If you want to gain weight – eat more and train harder.

3   Lastly, if you don't use it you lose it.

It's as simple as that.

Eat Less and Train Harder

OK, so for rule one what do you really need to do? 'Eat less and train harder' – is it really that simple? Er, yes, actually. All these amazing workout routines and fad diets are not going to work unless you stick with them long enough for you to see a change.

If you reduce your calorie intake by eating a well-balanced diet and reducing the quantity you eat, then combine that with increasing your calorie expenditure through exercising more, you will get fitter, and the by-product of getting fitter is usually losing weight.

If it really is that simple, then why don't more people achieve their health and fitness goals? The answer is that we are becoming more and more sedentary and with it we are becoming more and more lazy. Everything nowadays is produced for our convenience, everything from the food we eat to the transport we take to get us from A to B. The answer lies in our motivation and determination to succeed. It's the same with careers and business: some achieve and lead while others simply follow. It takes hard work and guts to succeed, a trait not many people possess.

However, all you need to achieve your goals are three things:

1   Belief in yourself that you can do it.

2   Goals.

3   Determination.

OK, what about the science to it? Very simply, there are two types of exercise you need to do to become fitter. The first is aerobic exercise in such forms as running, swimming, cycling, rowing and walking. The second is resistance training, which is any type of exercise where you have to move a weight for a number of repetitions.

Both will get the heart rate up, both will burn calories and both will help you to burn more body fat. However, one without the other is very ineffective and results will not be seen nearly as quickly.

To get fitter, you have to increase what you are doing exercise-wise each week by five to ten per cent. The variables that can be changed to achieve this increase are:

1   Frequency – how often you train.

2   Intensity – how hard you push yourself.

3   Time – the length of your training sessions.

4   Type – which exercises you undertake – i.e. running, swimming, circuits, etc.

Manipulating these variables will ensure that you stay on course and you achieve your goals. Easy? If it is, then why don't more people succeed? Goals are the answer.

Goal Setting

To really achieve you have to have goals. So before you start training set yourself two types.

The first is your personal goal, the reason for exercising – for example, getting down from a 36-inch waist to a 32. The second is an achievement goal where you have to get fitter in order to complete it. It could be a 5km run, a charity bike ride or a walking holiday in the Lake District. The key is that it *has* to be something that you would not be able to achieve if you had a go right now but something you *would* be able to do if you were fitter.

The goals should be set over three stages and they should have the SMART principle applied to them all (Specific to your needs, Measurable, Attainable, Realistic and Time lined). The first set of goals are to be reached within a year and this means that you have an end point from which you can work back. The second set of goals should be targeted from the six-month point. You should aim to be slightly more than half-way towards your goals, because as you get closer to the end of the year it will become more difficult for you to achieve results as your window of opportunity diminishes (the 25 Christmas lunches you won't want to miss out on). The third set of goals should be set at the six-week stage. This is just long enough for a change to be noticed but short enough to keep your focus.

These goals will allow you to monitor your progress and see that you are really achieving through your training.

Nutrition (Getting It Right)

Counting your calories nowadays is quite a simple thing to do, as nearly all packaged foods have their nutritional values marked on the packaging, making it easy for you to understand their content. To help the body with losing or putting weight on and getting healthier, follow these simple guidelines:

1   Drink two litres of water per day.

2 Eat three to five vegetables per day. These should be your main source of carbohydrate.

3 Reduce your starchy carbohydrate intake (pasta, rice, potatoes, bread and alcohol) and try to get most of your carbs from fresh vegetables and fruit.

4 If you do eat starchy carbs, eat them before 6 p.m. at night.

5 Leave two hours between eating and sleeping.

6 Supplement your diet with Omega 3 and 6 essential fatty acids.

7 Take a regular pro-biotic supplement or eat plenty of organic yoghurt.

8 Avoid sugary food (e.g. chocolate) and soft drinks.

9 Avoid fatty foods such as fish and chips.

10 Only drink three nights of the week and, when you do, drink a small amount. Red wine is good for health benefits but vodka is the best for losing weight.

People tend to over-eat and therefore have an excess of calories in their diet. Some kid themselves by thinking that if they eat out and go for the healthy option it will be good for them. However, food in restaurants tends to have plenty of hidden calories, so you don't know just how many calories you've really eaten. Eating out three or four nights of the week will increase the number of calories you consume over the week significantly and in return the body fat piles on.

After reading the above you will probably realise that if you want to put weight on (lean tissue as opposed to body fat) then the reverse is applied. Train harder but eat more, so the body can rebuild the muscles to cope with the workload. As I said, it's not rocket science.

The third and final rule is: if you don't use it you lose it. The body needs a constant stimulus for it to develop and change. If you don't exercise, your body doesn't adapt and it stays in a state where the only stimulus is your usual routine . . . sitting behind a computer all day and then fighting to get a seat on the train to sit down – when you have just spent the past nine hours doing just that. Nothing will happen unless you become more active and adopt exercise as part of your lifestyle.

HOW TO GET THE BEST ROOM IN A HOTEL

Don't take no for an answer

Fact: the first price is never the best price.

If it's the height of the season, or there is a convention or a trade fair in town, or the hotel is full, then you'll probably not have much luck haggling. But in all other circumstances, hustle like crazy.

How do you find out if the hotel is full? Simple. Ask what they have available. Hotels are either full or partially full, and if they're not full you'll be offered a variety of differently tiered rooms. This means you can start to haggle over the rate.

So do not accept the first rack rate you are offered. Always ask if they can do a little better; ask if they have something else; ask if they have any promotional rates. Ask if they have a corporate rate, and when they ask what company you're from, you've won the first battle. Say you're going to be staying in town a lot and need to have a hotel of choice, and that you'd like them to be that hotel. Can they do a deal on that? Tell them the place over the road is cheaper. They'll ask if you've stayed with them before, and if you have, then make a big show of the fact that it cost you a lot less last time. Keep on going until they offer you a better price. Because there is always a better price. Always remember:

most of the time, hotel rooms sit empty, so anything they can charge for them is gravy. The rack rates are arbitrary anyway (and there's always a ten per cent surcharge added to every room rate to cover theft – ashtrays, robes, teaspoons, etc).

You should take nearly as much care with your hotel room as you would with a flat rental. Maybe not for just one night, but if you're going to be staying there for a while, make sure it's the right one for you. Here are some questions to ask about the room they're offering you:

1 Which floor is it on? In older hotels, the first floor will have the rooms with high ceilings, although some people are obsessed with being near to the top. These days, the higher you go up in a hotel, the better the rooms. But in any grand hotel that was built before 1890 (when the lift was invented), the best rooms were always placed on the first floor, so the gentry didn't have to walk up so many stairs.

2 What's the square footage, the volume and the floor plan?

3 Does it have a bath as well as a shower? This isn't as silly a question as it sounds. I was once given a penthouse suite in The Excelsior, one of the better hotels in Florence. It has a double balcony, looking over the city as well as the Arno, and is one of the most beautiful European hotel suites I've ever stayed in. Yet, for some perverse reason, it doesn't have a bath. It sounds churlish to moan about it now, but as I had had to leave the house at 5.30 in the morning in order to catch my flight, without having a shower, and as I had a long night ahead of me, when I checked in a bath was all I really wanted. But with only 45 minutes to spare it wasn't worth trying to move to another room. So I had a shower and then felt guilty for being spoilt.

4 Is the room near the lift?

5 Is it above the bar?

6 Does it face the street?

7 What's the view like?

8 How big is the TV? (What do you mean there isn't a TV?)

9 Does it have a king-sized bed or two singles?

10 What else do you have in case I don't like it?

When you check in, remember the concierge's name. Forge a relationship. If there's a problem, or you want something done, you can then ask for them by name. Don't be intimidated by them, or treat them as the sort of person whose sole purpose in life is to screw money out of you. Concierges are there for a purpose, so use them.

Also, never use the phone in your room. Ever. This is one of the ways in which hotels make money, and the mark-ups are astonishing. In 1998 I went to New York to interview Sharleen Spiteri, the lead singer with Texas, for the *Sunday Times*, and the publicity company put me up in the Mercer Hotel in SoHo, at that time one of the most fashionable places to stay in Manhattan (meaning the door staff were too cool to open them for you, let alone talk to you, room service was practically non-existent, you could never get a drink at the bar and it was prohibitively expensive). I stayed in the room for two nights, had nothing from the mini-bar, ordered no food from room service, had no clothes dry-cleaned and didn't watch any porn on the TV. Didn't even order a newspaper. My bill? $250 thank you very much. For phone calls, most of them local. Please, please, use your mobile.

The fact that a hotel is big doesn't necessarily mean its service is going to be exemplary. Often the reverse is true, even in some of the better ones. Some of the hotels in Las Vegas, for instance, are so gargantuan, that it can take over an hour for your luggage to reach your room. In places like this it is sometimes advisable to carry your bags yourself. Similarly, as the hotel wants you to spend as much time in the casinos, restaurants and shops as possible, room service is notoriously slow. (Note: The Four Seasons is the only hotel in Vegas without a casino, and consequently the service is a lot better.)

In some of the newer boutique (small) hotels, when you check in an assistant manager will often show you to your room. Don't tip her; only tip the bell boy who delivers your bags.

Some tips:

1 Never go back to a hotel where the hangers are attached to the wardrobe rail (don't you trust us?).

2 While the breakfast hangers always say that you need to hang them outside your door by 1.30 a.m., usually they aren't collected until around 4.30, so as long as you do it before then, you'll be OK.

3 If you're going to be receiving a lot of faxes (another way the hotel makes a ton of money) or packages, instruct the concierge, the operator and the person who mans the 'business centre' that you want all of this stuff delivered immediately, otherwise it will sit downstairs until you decide to ask someone about it. Be very careful here. Each time you send or receive a fax – indeed, every time you say the word or conjure up a mental image of a fax – your hotel adds another arbitrary £50 to your bill.

4 If you're going to be lounging around your room all day, put the Do Not Disturb sign outside your door, otherwise you will be accosted every ten minutes by maids trying to clean your room. And sometimes they'll barge in, just as you're about to start flicking through the new issue of *Trouser Snake*.

5 Buy bottled water from a convenience store on your way back to the hotel. You will no doubt be dehydrated and want to drink a lot of water, and if you drink the bottles in the mini-bar they will cost you a small fortune.

6   If you're looking for same late-night 'company', don't bother with the concierge, because although they're all meant to possess a mental Rolodex of suitable names and numbers, many will take umbrage at you for asking. Much better to use the local equivalent of the Yellow Pages (or so I'm told).

7   Figure out how the air-conditioning works before you go out for the evening, because when you come back you'll be too tired/drunk/lazy to try and turn it up/down/off.

8   Ditto the centralised lighting system (I once spent twenty unsuccessful minutes in my room in the Hyatt in Shanghai trying what I thought was every permutation in an attempt to turn off a halogen spotlight in the wardrobe).

9   Always look at the bottom of the sink when you're in the bath; then you'll really see how much effort the hotel has put into its interior design.

10   Check-out time is usually 11.30, but most hotels will let you stay until 2 p.m. before threatening to charge you.

HOW TO GET AN UPGRADE

Securing that elusive seat in Business, Club or First

After a certain stage in life, when you get on to an airplane you really want to be turning left, rather than right. Not only is it the only way to fly, but if you travel a lot for business – when you are presumably flown Business Class – then flying Economy or Coach for pleasure can actually counteract the enjoyment of going on holiday.

So unless you're so flush that you can always afford to fly yourself, and your girlfriend or wife, and your family Business Class, then getting an upgrade becomes extremely important indeed.

The best way of achieving this is by developing a relationship with someone of importance at the airline, someone who can be called upon every now and then to press the right buttons and make the right calls. This becomes a lot easier if you are a member of an airline's frequent flyer programme. British Airways has a great scheme, and if you belong to their Executive Club, Silver Card holders can use their lounges when they're flying BA but only in Economy, while Gold Card holders can use the lounges whenever they want, regardless of what carrier they're on. If you aren't flying Club or Business, the use of a lounge before and after a flight can help a lot, let me tell you.

1   If you're a frequent flyer and become known to the airline, then you stand more chance of getting SFU (Suitable For Upgrade) typed next to your name on their computer.

2   Airlines often overbook Economy seats because they have so many no-shows, so although it sometimes helps to book seats on unpopular routes at inhospitable times, the opposite is often true. If the check-in staff try to bump you to a later flight, or offer you a financial inducement to do the same, suggest that everything could be solved if they move you into Club.

3   You could also do worse than buy an Economy ticket and then ask if it might be possible to get an upgrade when you check in. Ideally you can ask to use some of your frequent flyer miles, but if you don't have enough (and let's face it, when do you ever have enough?), then charm helps enormously; if you can manage to make the check-in staff laugh, and you're smiley and well-dressed, there's no reason why you won't get bumped into a fairly empty Club section.

4   Call ahead by all means, although you will usually be told that any upgrades are made at the discretion of the check-in crew. This is sometimes true and sometimes not, so try calling.

5   Also, let them know what you do, and suggest that you might be able to put a lot of business their way (if you genuinely can, that is). If you're the head of a department that regularly sends employees abroad, or the manager of a rock group or hotel chain, it will not be that difficult to generate a relationship with someone at the airline.

6   Pity can often work, and if you're ill or have a disability, or have an especially convincing sob story to tell, then you might be chosen to move towards the front of the plane.

7   If the check-in queue is long, you can always try to check in at the Business Class desk, and then begin your story there. Once they've taken your details, and they have your passport in their hands, and they can see that you only have carry-on luggage and that you're obviously not a psychopath, they might find it just as easy to bump you up.

8   Never try to bribe anyone, and never shout and scream if charm doesn't work. The only time that being belligerent and intransigent works is if the airline is at fault and you have a long line of people behind you waiting to check in. Occasionally I have turned up late for a flight and been told that there is no room onboard. If this happens it is perfectly acceptable for you to behave like an absolute arsehole and start raising your voice. The airline won't want to cause a scene, nor will they want to hold up the flight, so your predica-ment will soon be solved.

9   Fundamentally, however, the best way to get an upgrade is to travel alone, only have carry-on luggage, be bright and charming without being pushy, and look the part. If you look like you should be travelling economy, you will be staying in economy, no matter how good you are at blagging.

10   There is a caveat to all this, of course, and it concerns the dirty weekend or the romantic mini-break. If you're whizzing your loved one away for a while, and have planned everything in intricate detail, right down to the type of taxi picking her up from her office, and the type of flowers and champagne waiting for you when you check-in to your swanky hotel room, you really don't want to break the spell or the momentum by haggling for an upgrade for you both at the airport. In this instance, pay the extra, will you?

HOW TO PROPOSE

Because there's always a right time

I proposed to my wife on a Sunday, at Ascot, back in September 1996. I'd spent the previous evening at a work dinner in Bond Street, and had spent most of the night sitting next to one of her closest friends. While I'm still fairly sure she hadn't been briefed by my future wife, her friend's conversational gambits were rather suspicious: 'She's such a lovely girl, you know . . .' . . . 'How long have you two been living together now?' . . . 'Do you ever want children?' . . . 'You were engaged once before, weren't you?' . . . 'How old are you again?'

Normally, this sort of conversation would have had me heading for the nearest vat of industrial-strength Rioja, but that night the words coalesced into a cartoon lightbulb above my head, shimmering and shaking in the candlelight as though drawn by ancient and unsteady hands. Pop! Of course! She was the one! How could I have been so blind as to drag my heels?!

I needed to act immediately. Making totally unbelievable excuses, I rushed out of the dinner and grabbed a taxi home. Only to find my future bride asleep and totally uninterested in being shaken awake.

So it had to wait until the following day.

As we were walking around the paddock, inspecting the horses, I turned to her and did it – asked her to marry me. Even though I didn't kneel (it was raining), she totally knew what I was going to do, as she smiled, said 'Of course' and then kissed me on the mouth. For some innate reason, women always know when you're about to propose, so I would advise any of you who might consider changing your mind at the last minute to think again; she'll already think you're going to do it, and is going to be seriously miffed if you suddenly decide not to. In fact, she won't just be seriously miffed – she'll probably throw a drink in your face, punch you in the throat, kick you in the shins (really hard) and then sleep with all your friends. Immediately. So don't do it.

Our euphoria was somewhat tempered when we finally found all our friends back in the enclosure.

'You look rather pleased with yourself,' said Simon, absent-mindedly playing with his (by now useless) betting slips. 'What have you been up to?'

'Well,' I said, trying not to look too smug, 'we've just got engaged.'

And after a man-hug, hearty congratulations and two hastily poured glasses of decidedly non-vintage champagne, he said, without a hint of irony, 'Why?'

Perhaps he had a point. Every one of the three couples we went to Ascot with are now divorced. Heigh-ho.

I've often thought that men only get married when they're walking along the path of least resistance – i.e. when they're experiencing a weak moment. There he is, quite happily bouncing along as a bachelor, eating when he likes, sleeping with whoever he likes, drinking too much, watching rubbish television, wearing his boxer shorts two days running and, all in all, having a high old time of it . . . when all of a sudden, CRASH! – he runs into a woman who knocks him off his feet. Six weeks later he's planning marriage, and isn't quite sure what hit him.

There is another theory, that men simply settle down when they get tired of running around. This means that, having reached the age of 34, say, they suddenly think they ought to be married, and so marry the woman they happen to be with at the time. This might sound callous, but there is often more than an element of truth in this.

Also, there is another notion that a man will marry the first woman he dates who isn't as high-maintenance as all the bunny boilers he dated in his teens and twenties. Low-maintenance girls are best, after all.

This much we know: relationships are difficult. And courtship, though exhaustively codified and comprehensively analysed, is still a minefield of frustration, confusion and unexploded emotions. I reckon Spike Milligan had the best idea: he thought our sex lives would be immeasurably improved if our genitalia were actually in different places. He once suggested that life would be a lot easier if men's genitalia were attached to an index finger, and women's were attached to their shoulders. This would obviously mean that in order to initiate an interest in a woman, all a man would have to do is to go up to her on the train and tap her on the arm. Job done. Instead we have to move around each other like repelling magnets in ever-decreasing circles.

But if you've finally decided to pop the question, then try to do it with as much style as possible, because your wife will remember it for the rest of her life – every detail.

So here we are: I didn't buy a ring before asking, as I wasn't sure what to buy and anyway was worried it wouldn't fit. I would advise doing the same, as that way you can go shopping for the ring together. Trust me: she'll like this – not only will she get to choose exactly what she wants, but she'll know you paid a proper amount of money for it too (diamond marketeers like to try and get you to part with around a month's salary for a ring). It's also not necessary to propose in an especially salubrious location. The mere fact that you're doing it is enough. Yes, you can book the best table at an amazing cliff-top restaurant in a beautiful resort; and yes, you can fly there for a long weekend; and yes, you can have a hideously expensive dress sitting in a box, gift-wrapped, waiting on the bed. And yes, you can have a bucket filled with chilled champagne, and the hotel room floor strewn with rose petals. But you can save all that for later. Just ask her. Surprise her at work. Wake up and bring her your news with her tea. Or champagne. Drive her out into the country. You could even send her a handwritten note by courier. Or ask her to meet you in a particular hotel bar (or suite) in the middle of the afternoon. You could write the question in marker pen on a piece of ribbon and slip it into her glass, or have the waiter deliver a message. Alternatively, record yourself asking her to marry you ('The last three years have been the best years of my life. Lucy, will you marry me?'), and then either courier over the CD or trick her into watching it together. Or rent a billboard for your message, or get the captain to ask on your behalf over the intercom as you're taking off from Heathrow.*

You can do all of this and more. But what she really wants is for you to ask her in the first place. Everything else is just gravy.

If you're a traditionalist, then you should really ask her father before you ask her. Don't worry about this, as he's going to say yes. If you don't ask him beforehand, then call her parents as soon as she's said yes, along with all the other people that matter. Be especially careful with her mother, as she's been thinking about this day ever since her daughter was born (so don't bugger it up).**

---

* Ways not to propose: just before or after you've come (she won't believe you), or done for you by a DJ on the radio (unspeakably naff).

** Never tell anyone you're planning to propose. It will leak. And then you'll ruin the whole damn thing.

HOW TO REBUFF AN ADVANCE

Because sometimes you have to

You've been pinned against the wall now for what feels like an hour and a half. She's discovered that you tangentially know a friend of hers and she's taking you through the fascinating story of how they met. She keeps asking you if she's boring you, which only makes you go out of your way to convince her otherwise. Your smile is so thin as to be imperceptible, but the SINBAD (Single Income No Boyfriend And Desperate) in front of you is oblivious, so intent is she on finishing her excruciatingly boring story. Not only that, but whenever her eyes catch yours, you feel like you have a For Sale sign on your lapel, and you don't like it.

She is talking too quickly and flicking her hair too much and you've seen her sort before. She's a long way from being a psycho or a bunny boiler, but she has 'high maintenance' embossed on her forehead in capital letters. You know the type: she's the girl who pushes her food around her plate while bombarding you with questions she doesn't give you time to answer (women who take ages picking at their food are always trouble); she's the girl who flirts with the waiter; who asks if you like her top, when said top barely covers her chest. The girl who thinks nothing of calling you at work and expecting you to listen to her for 45 minutes.

SEX & SENSIBILITY 169

She's attractive in that French way, the *jolie laide* way, and is probably great in bed. But you've been down that road, and it always ends in a car crash. These girls are great initially, but as soon as you've been with a few of them, you realise the protracted nightmare of the aftermath far outweighs any fleeting sexual nirvana. So she fucked your brains out, now she's going to make the rest of your life hell.

You'd move on, but you've already circled the room twice, and there's *absolutely* no one here you know. And you can't leave because you're waiting for someone, so you're stuck – listening to a tedious, and potentially dangerous woman. The only thing worse, you think to yourself, would be if she were to make a pass at you. And – Oh my God! – it's just about to happen.

As you manage to get a word in edgeways and start telling her an equally boring story – in the hope that she'll get the message and push off – she interrupts you. 'Look, I shouldn't really say this, but . . . well, would you . . . would you like to come back to my place for a drink? Or something . . . You know, now?'

Well, the easiest thing to do would be to tell her you're actually gay, but seeing that you've already mentioned several of your ex-girlfriends, and it's painfully obvious that you're not, that's not going to wash. Plus, she'd think you were joking, because no one would ever dare say that (and if you hadn't mentioned the ex-girlfriends, you wouldn't have dared say it either). Also, there's the possibility that she might think she could be the one to turn your head, so to speak.

Your other default excuse would be the fact that you're seeing someone else, but you've already foolishly told her you're single. Plus she looks like the sort that might make a scene.

So what do you do?

Easy. You look interested, look longingly into her eyes, say you can't right now, but that you really, really want to see her, take her number (carefully, repeating it as you go), and promise, p-r-o-m-i-s-e to call tomorrow. Never call.

If you're dealing with someone who's actually quite rational, and who isn't going to be fobbed off with that, then be honest(-ish), and say you're not sure. Say you like her but need some time. Act old-fashioned if you like, and say you're not about to jump into the sack with anyone right now.

Or, if you already have a platonic relationship with the woman, and actually really like her, say you don't want to ruin the relationship. Say you value her friendship too much. She's going to be slightly embarrassed, but at least she gets to keep you as a friend.

Of course in other situations you can simply act dumb, and pretend you have no idea what's going on.

Once, a long time ago, I was at a party on a Saturday evening in Covent Garden. It was the opening of a fashion mall, and the crowd was full of models, photographers, publicists, agents, journalists, fashion designers and the usual people who turn up for these things. I was single at the time and, uncharacteristically, was actually looking forward to going out on a Saturday night.

I was driving, so hardly drank, and by about eleven I'd had enough (talking, that is, not drinking – I hadn't had nearly enough of that). Just as I reached the top of the stairs by the exit, I was approached by the PR of a (female) fashion designer, who – having had rather more than me to drink – told me her boss had taken something of a shine to me. I laughed it off and changed the subject, pronto. You see, while *** may have been interested in me, it was in no way reciprocated. (I don't tell this story out of conceit – I don't think I've ever told anyone before – and it's pretty much an isolated case. I'm just using it as an example.)

Anyway, we were soon joined by her boss, who, having previously never acknowledged my existence, proceeded to try and charm the pants off me. She made it clear that she knew I was single, and started flattering me no end. At this point I wandered off towards the door, only to bump into a couple of friends. And as I left them – I really was going home now – *** came up to me and said, 'What do I have to do, get down and beg?' I was shocked, although obviously didn't let on, and I made the kind of face you make when you didn't quite catch what someone said, and then said something anodyne and dull about how boring the party was. I think I just sort of stood there, swaying backwards and forwards. Luckily the music was so loud I could hardly hear what she was saying anyway. I wasn't about to walk off, as that might have compounded her embarrassment (if she had any, of course). I certainly wasn't clever enough to know that by acting stupid I'd let her down in as gracious a way as I could, but I sort of knew that doing nothing was probably the best policy. At least I knew that if I continued to act uninteresting rather than uninterested, then she might lose interest.

Which, very quickly, and I've no doubt much to her relief as well as mine, she did.

In the end, there is no satisfactory solution to this problem. Men are dogs, and would, to quote an old girlfriend of mine, 'fuck sand if that were the only option'. So when a woman approaches a man, and he turns her down, he's *really* turning her down.

HOW TO END A RELATIONSHIP

'Darling, I think I need some space . . .'*

Rule One: be kind. Hopefully, you're only ever going to leave this particular person once, so try to do it with some dignity. Or, to be callous about it, imagine she's a job and you might want to one-day work there again (sometimes it's OK to think like a woman). Seriously, why be a bastard about it? You could begin being unreasonably sexually demanding (even more so than usual), or you could start humiliating her in bed, or embarrassing her in public. If your ego can take it, you could begin having sex with the sort of agricultural gracelessness that will have her running for the nearest hills (or taxi rank). But all you're doing then is forcing her to make the decision herself, which is cruel and adolescent.

Think again. Have a plan. Tell a white lie, a kind lie . . . According to lore, the three great lies are:

---

* Alternatively . . . Slip out the back, Jack . . . Tell her you're gay, Ray . . . Say she looks like the Queen, Gene . . . Go on about your ex, Tex . . . And all the great sex, Rex . . . And how it was the best, Becks . . . Tell her the thrill has gone, Ron . . . And then play her the Eagles song, Don . . .

(1) 'I love you.' (2) 'The cheque's in the post.' (3) 'I promise not to come in your mouth.' It is the lesser-known fourth one, the Get Out Of Jail Free card to end them all, that you have to play now: 'I just don't love you enough.' How can she argue with this? You're admitting you love her, admitting that you're honest enough to know that you don't love her as much as you need to in order to pursue a serious relationship, and she will also infer that you're not sleeping with anyone else. It implies that you have wrestled with the decision for ages (who knows, maybe you have), and that having considered the possibilities, you think the best option would be to bow out now: 'It's not fair on either of us.' She will be distraught, and may even hate you for a while, but at least she can rationalise it by knowing that you didn't just spitefully dump her, and that you actually considered her feelings, and the implications of staying together when things weren't perfect.

And you know what? It's true.

Never say, 'It's not you, it's me.' She will hate you for being such a wuss. Ditto, 'I need some space.' We all know this means, 'I am a louse, and have actually started seeing someone else but am much too much of a baby to admit it.' There are those out there who will never end a relationship until they have another one waiting in the wings (or a few, spinning like plates, outside the theatre), and you must go out of your way to make sure that you are not seen to be doing this (even when you so obviously are).

Be a man about it. Do it in person. Never by phone, letter or – God forbid – email. In the early 1990s there was a spate of stories in the press about various celebrities dumping their partners by fax, and let's face it, it's just not on. You need to be more of a mensch about it. But if you do decide to do it in person, you don't necessarily need to do it in private. She's less likely to cry/crack your head open/call you a See You Next Tuesday if you're in a public place. Try a museum café; it's what she would do. This happened to me once when I was dumped, and my soon-to-be-ex-girlfriend compounded the crime by arranging to go to the cinema with a friend twenty minutes after telling me my services were no longer required.

If you are dumping someone by phone – and let's be honest, we've all done it at some point in our lives, no matter how much we pretend to ourselves we haven't – don't, having done the dirty deed, suddenly say 'I've got to go,' as this will only encourage her to carry on talking (and talking). Just say, 'I'm going now, goodbye,' and ring off. She really will hate you, but if she only warranted a phone call in the first place then you probably don't care too much about that.

Never dial drunk, as you will always, always regret it. We all get a little maudlin after one or twelve drinks, and what you should never do is call your ex in this condition (in fact you shouldn't really call anyone in this condition). Because you're not being true to yourself. All you will probably be is, (a) lonely, and feeling sorry for yourself, (b) looking back on the relationship through rose-tinted beer goggles, (c) horny, or (d) all four. But do yourself a favour and delete her numbers from your mobile. That means you also need to stop answering 'unknown' phone calls, as it could so easily be her. Chances are she will be dialling drunk herself, and the last thing you need is for her to start crying down the phone for two hours. Or, even worse, to lure you back in with the promise of a night of uncomplicated sex ('No strings, just friends'). Sex with an ex is never uncomplicated.

And never write her an explanatory letter. You'll regret it, as it's the sort of thing she'll bring up when she calls you at three o'clock in the morning to harangue you for dumping her six months earlier ('You said you fell in love with me when we were in Venice. Was that before or after you slept with me? Also, what did you mean about Jackie? Did you ask her out first?' etc etc).

Allow yourself to feel genuinely sorry for yourself. Sure, it's not easy being on the receiving end of bad news, but it's no trip to Hawaii for the bearer of the tidings either. You are a shit, but don't beat yourself up about it. You had a dirty job to do, and now you've done it. So wallow a little, but don't do it for too long. Don't dwell on the ramifications of your decision; just get out there as soon as you can. Climb back on the horse. You are obviously allowed a decent mourning period (if only to convince other women that you're not a complete and utter sleaze-bag), but you need to get back on the train as soon as poss. Sleep with any woman who appears remotely interested, even the ones you definitely won't be taking home to mother (come to think of it, you should probably put these ones at the top of your list). If a woman wants to sleep with you, in your current situation and state of mind there is really no obvious reason for you to say no. And if, after sleeping around for a while, you realise what a terrible mistake you've made, let's hope she still thinks you didn't love her enough. Because you obviously do.

It goes without saying that all of the above applies only to the semi-serious relationship, and that anything deeper requires a library of thought. Splitting up becomes more difficult the more entrenched you are in a relationship, and if you own property together, are married, or have children, then the implications of separating have a weight to them that hopefully you will have evaluated ad nauseam. Be true to yourself at all times. But remember this: if you're a married man and it's you who wants the break, financially you are on a hiding to nothing, as the courts always favour your wife. And if you have kids, well, I think you know what that means . . .

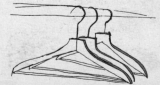

STYLE
&
FASHION

HOW TO GET THE PERFECT WARDROBE

Every suit, jacket and shirt you'll ever need. And everything else besides

This much we know: women's handbags, like the glove compartments in their cars, can be very dangerous things to open. Forgotten sanitary towels, bank statements, loose change, nail scissors, an Eagle Eye Cherry CD (you'd forgotten about him, hadn't you?) . . . they're all in there, along with five-year-old lipsticks, Q-tips, sticking plasters, phone numbers scribbled on the backs of bus tickets, the occasional half-eaten fruit bar and even an old boyfriend or two.

I know, I've been there, as I'm sure you have.

Perversely, their wardrobes tend to be just as cluttered – Tardis-like havens full of scarcely worn ballgowns, scarves (lots of scarves), boot-cut jeans and summer dresses all piled on top of each other, sullenly waiting to be taken to the charity shop. Oh, and about two dozen handbags, and forty pairs of shoes. Nearly every woman I've ever known seems to treat her wardrobe like that cupboard under the stairs, where things are pushed in, but rarely retrieved.

And we men, for our sins, seem perfectly happy to follow suit. Why, I don't know. Just because we now spend nearly as much on clothes as our loved ones, let's not adopt their habits. There are rules, you know, and we should adhere to them.

Practically speaking, the easiest and most efficient thing you can do with your wardrobe is divide it into two sides – winter and summer. Essentially, that's shirts, suits, jackets and shoes, because everything else will be folded away in drawers.

Casual jackets, overcoats and evening suits should be pushed to the side of your wardrobe (you'll wear them less than most things), while the middle should be full of formal stiff-collar shirts and suits. Some of the shirts should be designed to be worn with a tie, while others – by the likes of Interno 8 – should have high collars that can be worn without. As for suits you'll need them in pinstripe, grey, navy, black and Prince of Wales check.

Ideally you should try to keep your suits evenly spaced so they don't rub against each other, and take them out of their suit-bags and dry-cleaning polythene so they can breathe. You'll probably have to do this every couple of months as you're not going to remember to organise your wardrobe every morning. A few of your hangers should have a circular wooden moth repellent slipped over the hook.

You should get your suits pressed or dry-cleaned at least twice a year, and if you stain or spoil the fabric get it cleaned immediately; if you shove it back on the hanger you'll ruin your investment. There are those who say you should never dry-clean a good suit because the chemicals ruin the fabric, but honestly the only worry you should have is the possibility that a suit might be fused instead of stitched (it's cheaper), in which case it will wrinkle under heat.

Every year you should spend an evening going through your wardrobe, and do the following:

1   Throw away anything you haven't worn for a year.

2   Throw away anything of which you have two.

3   Throw away things you've kept for purely sentimental reasons (in my case a black velvet bomber jacket with a fur collar, fake tiger's talons and the word 'Gigolo' appliquéd on the back in silver plastic; if you also happen to have one of these, dump it now, although I appreciate the fact that you almost certainly don't).

4   Bin anything soiled or torn (apart from your foxed shirts).

These days the world is full of so-called style gurus, and everyone's an expert on some aspect of modern consumer lifestyle, whether it's fashion, food, sex, interior design, whatever. But where fashion is concerned, salient information seems hard to come by; these experts either expect you to look like a Regency dandy, or the star of a reality TV show. Being well-dressed doesn't mean you need to look like a dandy, doesn't mean you have to walk into your local branch of All Bar One sporting a fez, silk pyjamas and a brocade dressing-gown. Neither does it mean you have to wear a tracksuit and a load of bling.

Apparently there are two rule books: one that reads as if it was written in the eighteenth century, and one that was apparently scribbled on the back of a drug dealer's business card about five minutes ago.

For men, dressing well is essentially about good taste and common sense. To wit:

Accessories: Most Japanese households have an eighteen-inch shoehorn by the door, as they tend not to wear shoes indoors and are forever taking them off and on. A lot of European hotels are now doing the same, and I suggest you get one (a big shoehorn that is, not a European hotel).* Signet rings can be worn on the pinky finger of either hand, unless you're married, when they should go on the hand not sporting your wedding ring. The design should be worn so that the viewer, rather than the wearer, can see it.

Blousons: When buying a blouson or leather jacket, always buy the one with the snuggest fit. That way, you'll look cool. If you buy it too big, you run the risk of looking like an eastern European cab driver (not cool).

Boots: Only wear them for practical reasons.

Coats: Buy a Covert coat, a cashmere over-coat, a raincoat and a Husky (see below).

Cufflinks: Never wear cufflinks that you can't put on imme-diately. Say you own a beautiful pair of gold monogrammed cufflinks, two oval-shaped discs joined by a chain; and say it takes you about thirty seconds every day to struggle to put them on; and say you wear them every day to work. If you work for 45 years fairly consis-tently, taking into account holidays, a sabbatical and illness, you will have spent eighty hours of your life putting cufflinks on. That's about eighty hours too long.

The Default Jacket: You can never go wrong with a navy-blue single-breasted jacket, and – like your penis – you should never really be caught without one. You can wear it as part of a suit with a shirt and tie; with jeans and a white T-shirt; even, if the mood takes you (weirdo), with a pair of khaki threequarter-length trousers and a string vest. In fact you can walk into a smart hotel looking like a hobo – in your dirty white jeans, your crumpled blue shirt and your unshaven mug – but throw on a navy jacket and you suddenly look like George Clooney. I once saw a man walk into the dining-room of Mount Nelson Hotel in Cape Town wearing a white lace shirt and what looked like a pair of pyjama bottoms. He was unshaven, was wearing a pair of decidedly dodgy shoes and was communing with his mobile phone with an almost adolescent glee (film producer, obviously); but because he was wearing a blue jacket he looked perfectly at ease. Trust me, it works (which is why Clooney wears one himself).

Gloves: Remove them before shaking someone's hand (even if it's really cold!). If it is too cold, wave.

Hairstyles: If you're thinking of getting one with a name (mullet, Mohawk, quiff, Hoxton fin, etc), don't.

Handkerchiefs: Now that we're not wearing ties so much any more, take more care with your pocket square, the handkerchief you put in your breast pocket. Like your shirt, it will become the focus of the top part of your body.

The Husky: What do you wear when it's too warm for overcoats, and too chilly just for suits? When it's not really winter and not really summer? What do you wear when, as my mother used to say (on a daily basis) when I was small, 'The weather can't make its mind up'?

You get up, have a peek out of the window and notice that it's bright and sunny outside. So you ditch the thermal vest and the rollneck and opt instead for a shirt and tie (you figure it'll be too brisk to wear it open-necked), a lightweight central-heating suit (i.e. one that can be worn indoors), some casual hybrid shoes (half loafer, half trainer) and no coat. But five hours later, as you're darting out of the office for lunch, you're hit by torrential hail, arriving at Le Petit Gros Cochon sodden, irritated and looking like an amateur human being (didn't you know it was raining, you klutz?).

Alternatively, as you work your way through your ablutions, you notice that it's pouring outside, so you wrap yourself up in a sturdy, heavily-lined suit, a freshly polished pair of Lobb brogues and a thick Aquascutum raincoat. Later in the day, as you rush back to work from a meeting, you stumble into a sauna: the sun is blazing, the park is full of secretaries in slingbacks and miniskirts, and taxi drivers are staring at the only man in the square wearing a raincoat and an embarrassed smile.

Sounds like you? Sounds like me. Back then, anyway. There is an easy way round the weather problem: buy a Husky. Honestly. I know you probably don't want to walk around town looking like you've just come from the Pony Club, but a Husky is what you need to complete your wardrobe. It's light, possibly the lightest coat you can buy; it's a sensible length, just below the waist, just covering the suit jacket; it's boxy, making it perfect for wearing in the city; you can turn the collar up, making it possible for you to feel, albeit fleetingly, like Eric Cantona; and – and! – it's relatively cheap. The best Huskys are made by Barbour, ironically enough, and they come in essential colours: black, navy, a deep bronze and the classic racing green.

There is a caveat to all this, though. While a short quilted jacket can be the personification of British sartorial elegance, especially abroad – walk around Milan and Tokyo and you will see an abundance of them – you absolutely cannot wear one after dark. You won't, like Cinderella, turn into a pumpkin, but wear a Husky to a dinner or a hotel bar in the evening and you'll look like a Japanese salaryman who got drunk and forgot to go home.

Hybrid Shoes: The 21st-century business uniform is another one entirely, and largely consists of camouflage pants (or similar), expensive, imported Japanese T-shirts covered in ironic logos, and training shoes or hybrids. Many companies that shot up in the wake of the Internet boom of the late 1990s have no dress codes at all, such things being anathema to their company ethos. When asked if his own company had a dress code, Google bigwig Eric Schmidt said, 'You have to wear something.' First popularised by Prada in the mid 1990s, a hybrid shoe is a cross between a formal and a casual shoe (a loafer, say, crossed with a bowling shoe), and is now acceptable even in old-fashioned formal situations.

Jeans: You'll always need a pair of jeans, preferably Levi's, and preferably 501s. They should be dark, should fit like well-cut trousers, and have no holes or loose bits of thread (those days are over). Most men who wear jeans seem to assume that they can just fling them on with impunity, perhaps thinking that their very shapelessness (the jeans, not them) will disguise a multitude of sins. In reality the opposite is true, and it's actually far more important to get a pair that fits you perfectly.

They shouldn't be too baggy, nor too tight, and they should be exactly the right length: not too short, not too long, and not rolled back to show four inches of stitching. Jeans should break on your shoes like old-fashioned trousers, bunching up by just half an inch.

- According to a poll among American women in 2005, the sexiest thing a man can wear is . . . 'Rugged jeans and a plain white T-shirt'.

Long-Sleeved T-shirts: Get some.

Patent Leather Shoes: Yes, but only with evening dress.

Scarves: These days you can wear one even when you don't really need one: make it cashmere, make it grey, and wear it with grey or navy suits. You can even wear them in the office – if they're tied properly (see: How to Properly Tie a Scarf).

Shirts:

- Invest in double-cuff shirts.

- Fly-fronted shirts, which hide the buttons, elongate the body.

- Foxed shirts (i.e. those that have begun to look a little threadbare on the collars and cuffs) are probably the only shirts you need to wear at the weekend.

- Don't wear a tie with a soft-collared shirt.

- Always tuck your shirt in while your trousers are still undone.

Shoes & Socks:

- Don't wear over-shoes.

- Use cedar shoe-trees at home and plastic ones when you travel.

- You might think shoe-bags are poncy, but they come in handy when you're throwing a pair of shoes into an overnight bag.

- There should never be a gap of lily-white flesh between the top of your socks and the bottom of your trousers when you cross your legs.

- Wearing trainers with a suit will not make you look younger and hipper, only like a stand-up comedian.

- Unless you're wearing a boot, the only socks you need are thin socks.

- Try matching the colour of your socks to your trousers or your suit. If not, wear black. All the time.

- Don't wear brown shoes to work, unless you're sporting a grey or blue suit.

- Never wear brown shoes with a black belt, or vice versa.

- Buy Oxfords, brogues, loafers and Derbies. Only medievalists wear sock garters.

Shoe Polish: Just buy black and use it on your brown shoes too.

Shoe-Trees: You only need one pair. Put them in the last pair you wore, and swap them around when necessary.

Suits: For work you'll need a dark blue suit, a white shirt and some dark ties – this is still the classic business garb of corporate America, symbols of a lifetime of allegiance to IBM, the FBI or 'the city'.

- Always buy single-breasted.

- The better the jacket, the more casually it can be worn.

- Never do up the bottom button on your suit (and never only the top one if you're wearing a three-button jacket).

- A one-button, single-breasted suit with side vents is timeless and modern. It's also exceptionally well balanced, elongating the body and giving an elegance to your silhouette. A two-button suit also looks good, while being slightly less dandified. A three-button suit can make the body look slightly square.

• If you're wearing a patterned suit, don't wear a patterned shirt.

• The wool your suit is made from should be a Super 150.

• 'When a man puts on a suit, he changes his behaviour,' says Tommy Hilfiger. 'It's the businessman's uniform. The style, the cut, the fabric and the fit are signifiers of his individuality and rank.'

• 'When you sit down, sit on your jacket a little. That gives you a good line.' – William Hurt as Tom Grunick in *Broadcast News* (1987).

Sunglasses: Take them off if you're talking to someone not wearing them.

Sweaters: It's fine to wear a thin, V-neck cashmere sweater under your jacket, with or without a tie.

• You can never own too many Smedley rollnecks.

Ties:

• Get some knitted ties – maybe not for now, but for later.

• Necktie acquisition: any time you see a tie you like, buy it. If you decide to wait and come back later, it will be gone.

• Don't wear tone-on-tone shirts and ties. If you do, you'll look like a pundit on Sky Sports. I always choose the shirt first, although some men pick a tie and then choose a highlight colour from the tie to match the shirt.

• Don't tuck them into your trousers.

• British regimental stripes slant from top left to bottom right; American stripes tend to slant top right to bottom left.

- Never wear a tie that is lighter than your shirt.

- If the narrow bit is longer than the fat bit, try again.

- Never leave a tie knotted at the end of the day.

- To keep them in the best condition, hang them or roll them.

Tips: Choose your clothes carefully, but don't talk about them, please, as one mention of a bespoke suit has been known to suck all breathable oxygen from a room and render everyone unconscious.

- Everyone needs nice things they can eventually get sick of.

- Colour is over-rated: stick to a classic palette of ink navy, charcoal grey, white, pale pink, black, chocolate brown and camel. Try to avoid yellow and green. And never use the word palette.

T-shirts: Don't tuck them in, except where local etiquette demands, e.g. on the golf course.

Trousers:

- Never have more than two pleats either side of your fly-front.

- Your trousers should always break on your shoes, unless you're wearing skinny, tapered, mod-type pants.

- If you don't want to wear jeans, wear moleskins, chinos or Bedford cords.

Underwear:

- Boxer shorts or jersey Calvin Kleins.

- Never wear anything other than white underwear with white trousers (and if you're tucking it in, make sure you can't see your shirt, either).

Watches: You'll need a good chunky sports watch (Tag Heuer*), a classic Rolex (mine dates from 1948), and maybe a modern classic, like Cartier's Roadster. Don't buy cheap watches: you can be walking along a deserted Caribbean beach, wearing only a pair of shorts, but if you're sporting a big, expensive watch then you're still well dressed. Fact, as David Brent might say.

• Your watch-strap should match your jewellery.

Wellington Boots: Green or brown by Aigle, Le Chameau or Hunter. Try to make sure they have a neoprene lining.

Look at it this way. A classic principle of drama going back to Aristotle states that if you take all the characters of a play and roll them together into one person, you end up with a profile of the author. Well, think the same about your wardrobe.

---

* My Tag Heuer came courtesy of *Private Eye*. A few years ago they wrote some tedious and inaccurate piece suggesting that because I was plugging the watch brand so much in *GQ*, I was obviously receiving free watches (forgetting the fact that, as an upmarket consumer magazine, it is part of the magazine's mandate to suggest luxury brands to its readers). I wrote to the letters page explaining that in my career I had never been given a Tag Heuer watch, only to have the CEO call me a few days later offering to give me one (I chose a classic black-face Monaco). I actually composed a thank-you letter to *Private Eye*, but I was overcome by a rare attack of good judgement and didn't send it.

HOW TO DRESS YOUR AGE

What do you mean, you're still wearing trainers?

How old are you feeling right now? Are
you feeling like a born-again teenager, loping
around the house in baggy, voluminous jeans, an
oversized hoodie and a pair of training shoes the size of
King Kong's Ugg Boots? Or are you dressed like your dad, sitting in
front of the fire wearing a pair of battered old yellow cords, a V-
neck cardi under your jacket, and a pair of brogues that were last
polished when the old king was still alive?

Or are you just dressed like yourself? Frankly, I doubt it. I don't
think we ever dress our age, and we tend to spend all our lives
pretending to be older or younger than we actually are. Cast your
mind back to when you were thirteen or fourteen; all you cared
about was looking seventeen or eighteen. It was certainly all I cared
about. I remember I had a pair of cream-collared Oxford bags that
Ellen MacArthur could have used to get her across the Atlantic; a
fantastically ugly, tight-fitting French shirt with a ridiculous
butterfly collar; and a pair of gargantuan, two-tone platform boots
that even Geri Halliwell in her prime wouldn't have worn. Did I
look older than I was? Of course not, I just looked like every other
suburban thirteen-year-old boy who was desperate to look five years
older than he was.

These days I wear clean-cut three-piece pinstripe suits, expensive bespoke shirts and ties, and bench-made chisel-toed shoes that are so highly polished I once saw my wife use one as a mirror in the back of a taxi when she wanted to reapply her make-up. Do I look older than I am? Probably. But then I'd rather look like a generic City gent than do what most 'creatives' do in their thirties and forties, which is try to look like they're still in their teens.

Don't you hate them? They're the 'guys' who turn up at your office for a meeting wearing pink camouflage trousers, old-skool sneakers and a T-shirt with some sort of cartoon drawing of a Japanese gorilla on it. They'll give you a funny handshake and flick their fingers just like rappers do (and boy do they like rappers). And to listen to them talk you'd think they were all brought up in the projects in the South Bronx, and then shipped to a school in Jamaica where they were taught to speak only with a mid-Atlantic accent (and t'ing). 'Wiggas', they used to be known as, although I've always called them prats. Nearly everyone in the advertising industry acts like this, as does anyone who has anything to do with computer graphics or the dotcom world. In fact in a lot of modern Internet companies (hitherto known as dotcom.uk), you are contractually obliged to look like this, no matter how old you are. You can skip the goatee beard and the baseball cap if you speak with an Oliver Twist vernacular, but you'll never be allowed to ditch the box-fresh trainers.

There are those who say that these days men can wear anything they like, and that because fashion has become so much more democratic, and so much more mass market (even at the luxury end) – not to mention the fact that in many respects the generation gap seems to have vanished – we have *carte blanche* to wear something from American Apparel one day, and something from Hermès the next (And On The Third Day We Wore Them Together!). You know the sort of thing: at 8 a.m. you're a street-styled teenager, mucking about on your iPod. By 11 a.m. you've become a forty-year-old businessman, sitting behind your desk at work. At 7 p.m., you're a relaxed thirtysomething about the house, before turning into a mid-twenties success story, dressed up to the nines in time for a night out. And let's face it, if you can afford a Tag Heuer Monaco, does it matter if you're 18, 45, or indeed 60?

This is all very well, I think, as long as you don't reinvent yourself to the extent that you no longer wear the clothes that everyone else your age wears. Because if you do that, you'll just look silly. And small children will laugh at you in the street.

My advice to anyone who has any aspirations to look younger than they do is simple: don't. Or rather, DON'T. It's forgivable, I think, even endearing, to try and look older than you are. And while it might seem gauche when a spotty, whey-faced eighteen-year-old turns up for work on his first day in the type of suit that was last fashionable when really awful, cheap-looking suits were last fashionable, at least they're attempting to interact with the grown-up world. Trying to dress like someone ten, twenty, even thirty years younger than you only makes you seem sad, desperate, and out of touch (and I'm not even mentioning Cliff Richard, Noel Edmunds or Des O'Connor).

If you're in your twenties then you should be wearing vintage Converse All Stars, some skinny jeans you found in a secondhand store on the fringes of LA and weird-looking T-shirts with funny logos that can only be bought over the Internet; if you're in your thirties you should be sporting a dark, top-of-the-line Hugo Boss suit, stripy Paul Smith shirts and a pair of heavily worn-in Tricker's brogues; and in your forties you'll probably be needing a Savile Row bespoke suit (Richard James, Kilgour, Spencer Hart or Gieves & Hawkes), Interno 8 shirts (big collars worn without ties are still massive 'up west'), and a brand-new pair of Lobb Oxfords.

But there we are. I have to go now, as every now and then I like to spend an hour or so dressed up as the funny-looking one in Franz Ferdinand. No, really.

HOW TO DRESS FOR A WEDDING

And the groom wore . . .
a silver lamé shell suit?

For a woman, the rules are simple: look stunning without upstaging the bride. For men, things are slightly less prescriptive, and unless the groom has decided to wear morning dress, then the safest option is to look as spic and span as possible.

When I got married I was Savile Row head-to-toe – royal-blue Richard James two-piece, three-button summer suit with lilac lining, pale blue gingham Richard James shirt, and a silk lilac Richard James tie. Shoes were black bench-made Oliver Sweeney Oxfords, with black dress socks. I had a white buttonhole, as did the best man and the ushers. From what I remember, and from examining the wedding photos, most of the male guests were wearing the same – two-piece summer suits in fairly upbeat colours, white or plain colour shirts, vivid ties and polished black shoes. As they all wore buttonholes, each and every one of them looked incredibly smart. They looked, in fact, as if they were all off to a wedding.

These days, people tend to treat weddings a lot more informally than previous generations, and in the same way that few of us wear our Sunday Best to church (see below), dress codes at weddings appear to have relaxed. In some ways this is a direct result of the modern celebrity matrix, and as gossip and paparazzi magazines continually feature the glitzy and unconventional weddings of the rich and the famous (or at least the sort of people who fill the pages of gossip and paparazzi magazines, who aren't necessarily rich or famous, just pushy), so everybody wants to try and out-do them. But please don't treat the aisle as a catwalk – that's the divine right of the bride. And the marquee is not a nightclub, so don't be showing off your new zebra-print duster coat or your seriously bling leather jacket. Be discreet, restrained, proper.

If the invitation says Morning Dress Optional, then you should really wear morning dress, because the soon-to-be-happy couple are subtly letting you know that they'd be awfully chuffed if you made an effort (as they've known many of their friends for a very long time, and while they can almost guarantee that their parents' friends will dress up, they can't be so sure about you lot).

The full formal version of the wedding outfit is often limited to the ushers, and includes the following: a black herringbone morning coat (potatoes have jackets; this is a coat), a buff linen single-breasted black waistcoat, morning suit striped trousers, white formal shirt, regimental tie, black lace-up shoes, black felt top hat and white gloves.

And don't worry if you turn up and you're the only man in morning dress/lounge suit/black tie etc. As I say, these days weddings are less about ceremony and more about emotion. And if you carry it off with style, all the other men will wish they had gone off-piste too.

What you can't wear are chinos, brown shoes, chambray or denim shirts, cords or trainers. Always wear a jacket, no matter how awful it is. And if you truly are dreadfully dressed, the rest of the guests will no doubt think you're the eccentric country cousin, a dishevelled toff, a sort of Craig Brown type who wouldn't dress up for a wedding even if it were his own.

Essentially, you should look as if you respect the institution of marriage. I'm an enormously big fan of the *Spectator*, but as any regular reader knows, you get used to the more than occasional madcap

– or silly bonkers, as my youngest daughter might say – piece explaining why, say, French farming subsidies can be blamed fairly and squarely on the Labour government's aggressive declassification of the red telephone box. One such piece appeared a while ago, when one of the magazine's regular – and particularly erudite – loons suggested that the moral fragmentation of the country could be put down to the fact that men don't wear hats any more. Silly bonkers? Maybe, although I think the old duffer may have a point.

I go to church approximately two Sundays a month, and have become rather troubled by some of the clothes the congregation deem suitable for an hour and a half spent in the presence of The Man Upstairs. Don't get me wrong, every civilian who decides willingly to enter the portals of a house of God should be embraced with loving, open arms – though 1.7 million people in Britain attend church every month (actually up one per cent on the previous year), Sunday attendances are down two per cent to just over 900,000, and as you can imagine, this figure is dominated by people over the age of fifty – but couldn't they all dress as though visiting God has slightly more resonance than visiting their local branch of Somerfield?

Frankly, I think you should put as much effort into what you wear to church as you do when you're going to a nightclub, and I don't mean by wearing those gold lamé boxer shorts, either (not two days in a row, anyway). Do I think you should wear training shoes when you're taking communion? No. Do I want to stare at the back of an Arsenal away strip or a fifteen-year-old button-down lumberjack shirt when I'm singing *Agnus Dei*? Take a wild stab in the dark. Yes, I admit to once wearing a pair of white Birkenstocks on Palm Sunday, but it was an extraordinarily hot day and they were nestling underneath an unbelievably expensive Paul Smith lilac silk suit at the time.

When you're next in church, just imagine you're going to court instead. That should do the trick – because, let's face it, in a way you are.

HOW TO WEAR MORNING DRESS

What a grey day!

It's only in the spring that men's minds turn to morning dress. The wedding season will be upon us any minute (a season that seems to start earlier every year), while Royal Ascot starts in June – and if you're going, and you don't want to have to hire one again, then it's best to get a morning coat made (every man should really wear morning dress to the races, and if you want to enter the Royal Enclosure or any hospitality box, it's obligatory – if you're improperly dressed you won't get past security).

If you're going to Ascot then you should wear a grey morning coat – it's smarter – but if you're going to a wedding then you should really only wear black (only the groom and the bride's father should wear grey), preferably with a subtle herringbone pattern. You will also need the following: a pair of traditional black-and-grey-striped trousers; a white, pale blue or pale pink shirt; a grey or polka-dot tie; a grey waistcoat (single- or double-breasted, it doesn't matter); black (polished) Oxford shoes (loafers and monkstrap shoes are also all right); a pair of grey buckskin gloves; a matching handkerchief square; and a grey top hat. It's perfectly OK to wear a grey top hat with a black morning coat, although if you're in the unusual position of being asked to wear morning dress to a funeral, the hat should be black.

Take extra care if you're hiring the outfit – which, I would imagine, is what you'll probably do – and make sure you get fitted way in advance of the event. Sartorially, few things look worse than rented morning dress, especially the hat. Rented hats not only get battered, bruised and stained, but it's highly unlikely that you're going to find one that fits perfectly. Why not get a bespoke morning dress outfit made, including the hat (especially the hat)? Then you'll never have to worry again. You might only wear it a few times a year, but who wants to get caught in a rental shop?

True to its name, morning dress should only be worn during the day. If you're caught wearing a morning coat after dark, legend has it that the ghost of David Niven will accost you from behind, quietly tap you on the shoulder and, in perfect Received English, politely ask you to go home and change. Old boy.

HOW TO WEAR BLACK TIE

Understanding the ever-changing world of the human penguin

It doesn't matter what industry you work in, at some point during the year you will be required to squeeze yourself into your penguin suit, wipe the unsavoury-looking stains off your dress shirt, find your straggly little elasticated bow-tie and present yourself at the nearest grand hotel for an excruciating night of cheap wine, slow food and the inevitable pass at the boss's wife.

And where evening dress is concerned, we have it rough. While women can get away with murder – wearing cheap push-up bras, a couple of yards of hastily arranged crimplene and some old stilettos – we have to turn up to black-tie events looking like every other pleb in the room, dressed only in an old tux, a frilly yellowing shirt and a pair of shoes you haven't seen, let alone worn since this time last year. In 2005 Britain's dry cleaners removed the unpleasantness from an estimated eight million suits, while we spent some £60 million on cleaning, steaming and pressing. And most of this was spent on evening dress.

Now, I've had some great times at black-tie do's, but then I don't look forward to them as though they're my 21st birthday party, stag party and wedding all rolled into one. In this I appear to be alone, as most men who put on a DJ seem to take it as a licence to behave as though they've just come ashore after twelve months at sea.

My worst experience in black tie happened a few years ago at a sales conference held at the Lygon Arms near Stratford-upon-Avon, one of those state-of-the-art, top-of-the-line, generic ye-olde-worlde hotels that specialise in wood-panelled snugs, multi-course menus and eastern European chambermaids. As I excused myself from a seemingly interminable dinner and made my way to the loo, I passed the bar by the lobby, only to be accosted by a large, drunk and obviously partially-sighted German. Blocking my path he asked me if 'there might be any service' as the bar was looking decidedly unattended. With hindsight I like to think I gave him an arched eyebrow, a knowing wink and a witty riposte, although in reality I simply stammered, '. . . er, I don't know, I'm not a waiter.'

The whole point of black tie, the whole reason all us men look like we do (identical) is in order to allow women to shine. But in this age of male emancipation, where we are almost taken as seriously as women in department stores, isn't it time we started getting our own back?

Even though it's very difficult for any man to go off-piste without appearing to be trying too hard – think about those fools from the accounts department who sport the revolving bow-tie, the paisley cummerbund, the robin-red waistcoat or the T-shirt with a bow-tie printed on it – I haven't worn a bow-tie to these events for years. A couple of winters ago I lost my tie after an awards ceremony in London (I can only assume it's still tucked away behind some night-club banquette with a crumpled packet of Silk Cut, an unsmoked cigar, an extravagant credit-card receipt and the phone number of a waitress interested in 'work experience'). And while I realise it's tanta-mount to wearing training shoes to a wedding, or coming out of the men's room with a small map of Alaska on your chinos, since then I've simply worn a crisp white shirt with a big strong collar . . . and no tie. I may look like an out-of-work gigolo, but at least I don't look like the tool from Accounts.

Rock stars, meanwhile, can not only wear what they like, we expect them to. In 2005 I went to Swarovski Fashion Rocks, the glitzy Prince's Trust event in Monaco. For my sins I was the Chairman of the event, and so the night before had been invited, along with all the performers (Jon Bon Jovi, Mariah Carey, Jamie Cullum, etc) and the fashion designers (Giorgio Armani, Tommy Hilfiger, Roberto Cavalli, etc), to a cocktail reception at the Grimaldi Palace to meet Prince Albert. And, true to form, most of the male guests dressed in a modern-day approximation of traditional black tie, namely black suits, embroidered black shirts, patent leather shoes and lots and lots of jewellery. Ozzy Osbourne – who, as well as being The World's Most Extraordinary Living Rock Star (copyright all newspapers), is also something of an under-appreciated natty dresser – turned up in quintessential alternative black tie: bespoke black frock coat, black dress trousers, a simple black T-shirt, snakeskin boots, a huge belt buckle, John Lennon sunglasses, and a bloody big cross on the end of his necklace.

And, push-up bras, crimplene and stilettos notwithstanding, he wasn't going to let the girls get away with anything. Having just paid his respects to Prince Albert, Ozzy caught sight of Isabella Blow, the lovely, but rather eccentric Fashion Director of society bible *Tatler*. Isabella has a penchant for somewhat gargantuan hats, and on this occasion had decided to wear a headdress that had what appeared to be a birch tree sticking out of it (it stuck out from her head so far that she had to come through the door sideways). Proving that The World's Most Extraordinary Living Rock Star has lost none of his faculties, he turned to me and whispered, 'Bloody hell, that looks like the first symptoms of bird flu.'

However, here are the rules. In the first place, as Frank Sinatra said, a tuxedo is a way of life. 'When an invitation says black tie optional, it is always safer to wear black tie,' he once said. 'My basic rules are to have shirt cuffs extended half an inch from the jacket sleeve.

Trousers should break just above the shoe. Try not to sit down because it wrinkles the pants. If you have to sit down, don't cross your legs.'

1   Only three colours are acceptable: black, midnight blue and burgundy (the latter only in velvet; most evening suits are made from barathea wool with silk crossgrain lapels).

2   Jackets (single-breasted, please) should really only have one button or two, although three is just about acceptable.

3   Jacket lapels can be shawl, peak or notch: all are OK.

4   Only wear white dress shirts – with a ruffled or pleated front, and wing or turn-down collar.

5   Shirt studs look great, otherwise your shirt buttons should be covered or hidden by the flap on your shirt.

6   Learn to tie your own bow-tie (see How to Tie a Bow-Tie). Acceptable colours are black, midnight blue, burgundy or white.

7   Wear a white silk handkerchief peeking out of your breast pocket.

8   Never wear a belt on your trousers; by rights they will have side-straps.

9   Wear black or navy silk socks, long ones (there are few things worse than showing some pebbledash shin between where your trousers end and your socks begin).

10   Cufflinks should be carefully considered; if in doubt, err on the side of caution.

11   All your jewellery should be the same metal (i.e. if your watch has a silver strap, then your rings and cufflinks should match).

12   Men don't really wear cummerbunds any more.

13 Ditto the evening waistcoat.

14 If you're travelling, and your dinner suit arrives creased, just hang it up in the bathroom and run a bath or a shower for half an hour, and the steam should see to them.

15 Shoes can be as feminine as you like (with bows if you like), as long as they're patent leather or highly polished (even loafers could be acceptable – e.g. Gucci classics).

16 Shoes should be as plain as possible; for instance, you should never wear brogues after dark.

17 A 'white tie' invitation not only means you have to wear a white tie, you have to wear tails, too.

18 And always remember to polish the bottom of your shoes; if it was good enough for Sinatra I think it ought to be good enough for you.

19 Oh, and carry mints; an evening of over-indulgence is never going to be kind to your breath.

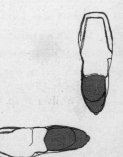

HOW TO WEAR WHITE TIE

The one outfit guaranteed to turn any man into a movie star

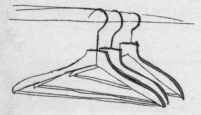

While black tie essentially means a tuxedo (or, in German, a smoking jacket), white tie always means tails ('white tie and tails'), and is one of the most formal outfits you can wear, an outfit that will very much make you look and feel like an old-fashioned idea of a 'gentleman' (if, indeed, the thought appeals to you).

If an invitation says 'white tie', 'cravate blanche' or 'full evening dress', then tails are expected to be worn. Few of us are bombarded by white-tie invitations these days, but we should all know what to do, just in case (and all of us should do it at least once).

This is a uniform like no other, and there is little point going off-piste. There is an old proverb that defines genius as 'an infinite capacity for taking pains', and the same could be said of white tie. Wearing it won't turn you into a genius, but wearing it properly will definitely teach you to put clothes together perfectly. Because if you don't, it won't work (and rather than ending up looking like David Niven, you'll look like a conductor).

So what do you need? Well, the kit is as follows: Your tailcoat will be black and single-breasted, with black silk lapels – and should never be buttoned up. Your black trousers will have two parallel silk stripes down the seams. This distinguishes them from evening dress trousers, which only have one. (Note: your trousers should never, ever have turn-ups.) Your stiff white cotton piqué waistcoat can be double- or single-breasted, and will have lapels. Your cotton piqué or pleated shirt will also be white, with a wing collar. (If you wear shirt studs, make them white, although your cufflinks can be as bling as you like.)

Your white (real) bow-tie will be made from cotton piqué, and your shoes will be pointy black patent leather (worn with thin silk evening socks). The bottom of the waistcoat should never extend lower than the bottom of the front of the tailcoat, while the back of the tail-coat should line up with the back of the knee. And considering how often you're going to use it, you're almost certainly going to rent it.*

---

* If you're wearing white tie during the winter, then wear a black overcoat and a white silk scarf. You could also wear a black top hat and some white gloves, but seeing that you'll have to take them both off when you arrive at your party, this seems like an indulgence (if not a total waste of time).

HOW TO INTERPRET DRESS CODES

Lounge suit, smart casual, and Hollywood Black Tie

Your mail falls through the letterbox with a reassuring thud. People still like you. People are still paying you. People who couldn't care less about you are still sending you bills (they're not dumb; they know that other people are still paying you). One envelope is suitably intriguing, being larger than most of the others, and considerably heavier. So you open it first, and find what's known as a 'hard card', a gold-embossed invitation to something suitably swanky. And then you put it on the mantelpiece, next to the one you received yesterday for the opening of a wallet in an area of London you've never heard of (you're not going to it, wouldn't be seen dead at it, but you don't want to throw it away because it looks so ridiculous).

And then you look a little closer, and you notice, where it usually says Black Tie, White Tie, Morning Suit or Lounge Suit, or even, in some cases (where irony obviously has never been an issue, or indeed a topic of conversation), Smart Casual, it says, bold as brass, Hollywood Black Tie.

So what the hell do you do now? Black tie you obviously know, while lounge suit is not just what you wore to the office, only maybe with a different tie, the sort my mother probably once called 'snazzy'. A lounge suit is a smart two-piece 'event' suit in a deep midnight blue, or two-tone charcoal or black, freshly pressed or dry-cleaned. That suit you saw in the magazine at the weekend, or maybe the one you saw in *GQ*? Now's the time to buy it. In the spirit of old-school elegance you could also wear a small cravat or a 'twilly' (an extremely thin cravat that you tie around your neck like a small scarf), which will at least make your look seem *intended*. Lounge suit is almost an anti-dress code, as it underscores the fact that the hosts aren't asking you to e-s-p-e-c-i-a-l-l-y dress up; you can if you like (they'd like you to, if they were honest), but they're not going to bust your balls if you don't. It is a great leveller, a democratic dress code, and all you really need to know about it is the fact that the Blairs used to put 'Lounge Suit' on their social invitations to Downing Street.

And if an invitation says Smart Casual you simply don't go to it (Alan Partridge has killed that one off for good).

But Hollywood Black Tie?

Believe it or not, this is the dress code *du jour*, and can be found nestling at the bottom of invitations to everything from award ceremonies and cocktail parties to office functions and weddings. It's like telling people you're in the know while making them feel slightly nervous at the same time. 'Ooh, Chantelle, it's Hollywood Black Tie, what shall I wear?'

Well, Hollywood Black Tie started off meaning some sort of suit not worn with a bow-tie but maybe with an ordinary black tie. But actually it has become a catch-all term and in reality means anything you like. So if you want to wear an open-necked shirt, do so. If you want to wear a white dinner jacket, a silver lamé ruffled shirt and a pair of *diamanté* jeans, go ahead (although I would advise you don't leave the house). If truth be known, HBT was invented so that lazy rich film actors and multi-millionaire rock stars wouldn't look so ridiculous turning up at black-tie events wearing their gym kit or their girlfriend's pyjamas. To wit: 'Oh my Lord, it's Ozzy/Marilyn/Robbie/Brad . . . and they're wearing, er, . . . pink satin shorts . . .'

Which means if you're nabbed by the corporate affairs director as you're hovering over the buffet, trying not to spill two glasses of Pommery over your fluorescent orange jumpsuit, pick up your lamb, couscous and potato salad, smile and whisper, 'Hollywood Black Tie. You like?'

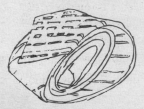

HOW TO PROPERLY TIE A SCARF

You don't want children laughing at you in the street, now do you?

Those of you who read the *Sunday Times* will know 'A Life in the Day', the back-page column in the *Sunday Times Magazine* where the famous and the fabulous (and occasionally both) talk us through a typical day in their lives. The column has been going since God was a boy, and has been repeatedly and merci-lessly copied ('A Room of My Own', 'Me and My Mantelpiece', 'My Wastepaper Bin and Me', etc), although I'm sure most people don't know why it was started.

Contrary to what I believe to be popular opinion, it was not invented so that the erudite and the wealthy could tell us all the simply marvel-lous things they get up to, but rather the opposite. It was meant to itemise the minutiae of their lives, like what type of tea they drink, what they think about before they go to sleep, how long it takes them to drive to work. Prosaic stuff, not the weird and the wonderful.

This obviously bypassed one particular subject, a former pop star who had fallen on, well, let us say less than eiderdown times (this was in the early 1990s, I think). Worried, perhaps, that his poten-tial record-buying public might not be impressed with the reality of his day-to-day existence, he turned in a quite ridiculous, and literally extraordinary diary: 'Woke at six and wrote a novel; at half eight I took the dog for a walk, bumped into Salman Rushdie and Bono and decided there and then to record a tribute album to the Zimbabwean farm people; drank a bottle of whisky; wrote a book of poetry; had lunch with Nelson Mandela and Kylie Minogue (I paid); recorded a fourteen-part TV series on early Etruscan architecture; had a lie down; drank another bottle of whisky; flew to Marrakesh for the launch of a global hotel empire, and jetted back to Blighty in time to have wild and furious sex with **** ****.'

Well, years ago I started a column in the *Independent* founded on the same principles as 'A Life in the Day': rarely going in for sweeping statements on the Zeitgeist, pontificating on the state of the nation, or the moral implications of wearing a safari suit in a built-up area, or sporting moleskins after Easter. Instead, the column focused on the minutiae of the stuff in your wardrobe, the stuff you wear every day. Such as: should the bottom of your tie hit your waistband, or fall just below (the former); what's the best, short, lightweight coat (the green Barbour Husky); what to do about the small, scuffed spot on the heels of the shoes you drive to work in (polish them every day or wear Tod's driving slippers).

And, pertinently, how to wear a scarf. Surely we don't need to be told how to wear a scarf? I mean, we're all grown men, aren't we? Tying a scarf is just like tying your shoelaces, isn't it? (parallel horizontal, in case you were wondering). And we were taught that by our mothers, weren't we? There has never been anything remotely stylish about tying a scarf, no matter what colour it was, and no matter who designed it. A scarf was a scarf was a scarf.

These have always been a couple of accepted ways of throwing a scarf around your neck: you either simply tied the ends together like a piece of string, leaving a big, fat knot beneath your chin as it jutted out of a duffel coat or a puffa jacket; or you pretty much did the same thing, only pulling the scarf back under itself, as you would a tie, folding it over and giving it a flat front (underneath a thin over-coat or a Crombie).

My friends, those days are gone for ever. Today, there is only one accepted way to tie your scarf, so you'd better get used to it. And what you do is this: you take your scarf and fold it in two; you then wrap the scarf around your neck and then push the two ends through the loop created by the fold. You finally tighten the scarf by pulling the two ends away from you until the knot has reached your neck. Got it, Tonto?

Everyone I know seems to be tying their scarves like this (even those friends who pretend not to care how they look), with many of them leaving the things on as they walk around the office. However, I'm not quite sure whether this is some sort of style statement (scarves indoors!) or just a way of letting me know that the central heating isn't what it used to be.

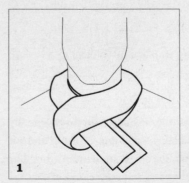
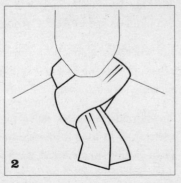

HOW TO TIE YOUR DECK SHOES

All that you know is wrong

I never did make a good Cary Grant. I could do the voice (if Tony Curtis could do it, then surely anyone can), but I always had a problem with the clothes, especially the sailing clothes.

When I tried to approximate his style – the scrambled egg-free blazer, the white open-necked shirt, the cravat and the khaki Oxford bags – I'd either end up looking like the actor Leslie Phillips ('I say, would you like any help with that, my dear?') or, more alarmingly, and a lot more frequently, a frighteningly accurate homage to Alan Partridge.

But when you're on a boat, you have to reinvent yourself to a certain extent, or else you look not so much like a fish out of water as a city slicker with no sea legs.

Now, I've done Cowes, sailed across the Solent, cruised towards the green flash in the Caribbean, and bailed water out of a twelve-foot yacht during an electrical storm off the coast of Brittany, but I've never been particularly *au fait* with the whys and wherefores of nautical dress. For years it's been an ongoing process of trial and error (mainly error, to be frank). However, I think I may have arrived at some sort of solution, or a compromise at the very least.

The first thing you need to do is throw away the blazer. Wear a blue jacket in a summer-weight fabric if you like (Richard James, Kilgour, French Connection, Jasper Conran), but nothing with metal buttons. You will end up looking like an extra from *Carry On, Faux Admiral*, believe me. Much better to change the buttons to white. Then choose a cotton piqué polo top (dark colours are best, although white and yellow also work), a pair of chinos (Gant, Nautica, Land's End, Gap), or maybe a smart pair of knee-length shorts (Paul Smith, Hackett). You're also allowed to have a pair of sunglasses swinging around your neck, a money pouch on your hip and a large and expensive water-proof watch, and you can sometimes get away with a hat, either a Panama hat or a baseball cap (although never worn the wrong way round). On no account ever wear a pair of socks on a boat; if you do you will be forever identified as a fool (not only that, but a fool on a boat).

It's always the little things that say the most about a man: the knot in his tie, the turn of his cuff and the cut of his jib. For those without a jib, who still favour a nod in the nautical direction, there is the deck shoe. You *have* to wear them onboard. A style classic, this moccasin-inspired item of footwear has for years been as stylish onshore as off. Most lawyers and solicitors tend to wear these at the weekend (every weekend), but this is what they're really designed for. However, all men on dry land, and most of those who sport them on boats, wear them the wrong way. No idle styling detail, the lace that runs around the shoe is actually an integral part of its design. When tying your deck shoe, pass the lace under and over the side lace, before tying both ends in the traditional way in the middle. The point of doing it this way is to help keep your foot in the shoe and yourself on the boat. You have been warned.

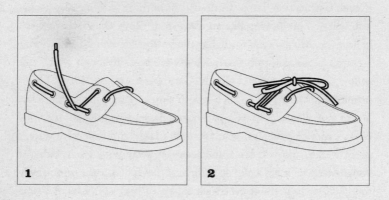

HOW TO WEAR A TIE

Because it ain't as easy as you think

As most of you should know by now, the minutiae of fashion are fairly prosaic. And God, as always, is in the details. This especially applies to those of us who, through no fault of our own, tend to wear a suit to work. Every day. Yeah, for sure, if you're going to leave the house each morning dressed like a nineteenth-century dandy or an Afghani rebel, then the rules are fast and loose, just as they are in fancy dress. But if you're trying to look 'proper' (as well as 'cool' and 'dignified' and all the other things associated with dressing properly), then the rules are what you are going to have to learn.

Take ties, for instance, and in particular the often uneasy tie-shirt-belt relationship. This is the sartorial threesome from hell, although if you get your tie right, it should be a lot less bothersome. Ignore for a minute which sort of tie is fashionable right now – recently the large, extravagant tie was superseded by the thin tie, which was then knocked into touch by the knitted tie, which was then taken over by the flat-bottomed tie – because fashions come and go. The trick is to know what to do with it when it's hanging around your neck.

In the early 1980s I used to work with a rather portly accountant who would come into the office every morning with his tie covering his enormous belly like some miniature suspension bridge. The tie would hang over his belt so that it nestled on his fly, while the other end protruded from underneath his knot like a little four-inch mistake. He did this – hello! – to try and disguise the fact that he was a bit overweight; but obviously it didn't work.

Other men I know always try to make sure that both ends of the tie line up, regardless of where they fall on the shirt. This means that both tips could end up a couple of inches above the belt, which looks just as ridiculous as one end hanging over your, er, privates.

The third mistake that men make when tying their ties is probably the worst of the lot: tying it so that the thin end hangs down below the bigger one. It doesn't matter if it only hangs down by a fraction of an inch, it is wrong, wrong, wrong, and you will look ridiculous because of it. The hard-and-fast rules are these:

1　The shirt placket (the strip of material running down the centre of your shirt with the buttons on it) should always be vertical, never twisted, and should always be aligned with the belt buckle.

2　The tip of your tie must never fall below the belt.

3　The thin end of the tie should never fall below the fat, front end.

4　The tie should never be tucked into your trousers.

5　Always slip the thin end of the tie through the strip of horizontal fabric on the back of the tie, which will stop it swinging about when you bend over to flirt with the new girl from Promotions as she's struggling to get to grips with the photocopier.

HOW TO TIE A BOW-TIE

Look like Cary Grant or Hugh Grant in a flash

Far too many men are scared of learning how to do this, but it really is quite simple. Here goes:

1   Place your bow-tie around your neck and leave the right end dangling one and a half inches longer than the left. Simple enough.

2   Now slowly cross the longer end over the shorter end and pass the longer end up through the loop.

3   Now grab the shorter end and – here's the tricky part – carefully form the front loop of your bow-tie with it.

4   When you feel the loop is right, hold it with your thumb and forefinger and drop the longer end over it as we've drawn here. It's not so tough, is it?

5   Next, form another loop with the longer end and pass this loop behind the front loop and between the crossed ends you formed in step two.

6   You can easily adjust your bow-tie by simply pulling on the loops and ends.

7   You are now officially ready for a night on the town.

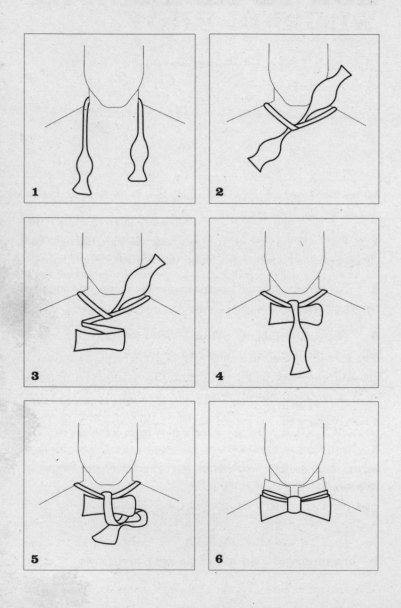

HOW TO TIE A WINDSOR KNOT

Because frankly you ought to be able to by now

This is one of those hoary old things you find in arcane gentleman's guides, and is still considered to be one of those things a man of breeding should be able to do with his eyes closed. Every man ought to, and it is actually incredibly easy to master (almost as easy as the four-in-hand, the one you use every day). All you need is a little bit of practice. I know, what say you try it every morning before you go to work, say in front of the mirror, then you can wear it all day!

The knot is so-called because it was meant to be the brainchild of the Prince of Wales, later King Edward VIII, and later still the Duke of Windsor (the exportable dandy) when he abdicated. There is now evidence that his father, George V, actually wore what became known as the Windsor, although his son certainly appeared to popularise it (preferring to wear his ties with a spread collar, which is still the best way to show one off). You can actually achieve the same effect as a Windsor by using the four-in-hand on a very thick tie, and there is now proof that this is actually what the Duke did himself. Lord Lichfield, the current Queen's cousin, photographed the Duke tying his tie in a four-in-hand in the 1960s in an effort to dispel the myth, but to no avail.

Whatever. Men wear a Windsor because it makes the knot look fat, and this is how you tie one:

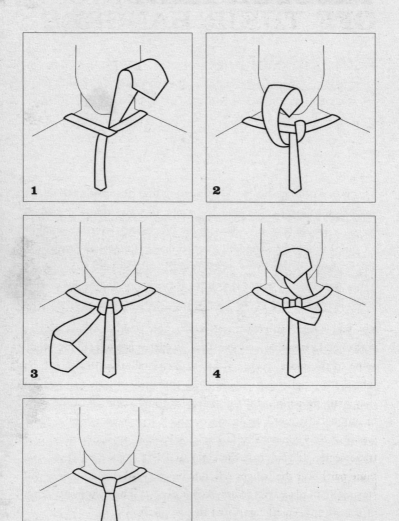

HOW TO STOP YOUR TROUSERS SLIDING OFF THEIR HANGERS

Better on a hanger than on the bottom of your wardrobe, eh?

How many times have you opened your wardrobe door to find trousers that have fallen off their hanger and are lying in a shapeless pool on a pair of shoes, looking like some sort of half-hearted Claus Oldenberg soft sculpture? Well, there are simple ways to avoid this. You could buy hangers with some sort of rubber clasp (good), or those old-fashioned hangers that have a closing 'gripper' bar (bad – they can crease your keks). You could also buy hangers with metal grips that you can affix to the waistband (if you study some of the more arcane guides to men's tailoring then you'll be told that by rights you should hang your trousers upside down so they hang properly). But the failsafe method is an old Savile Row technique that, until being discovered a few years ago by *GQ* (it was leaked by someone at Gieves & Hawkes), was something of a trade secret. If you cross the right and left trouser leg (from the same pair) over the hanger rail, one on top of the other – they will stay safely in place. According to our expert, 'The cohesive friction of the cloth keeps the garment in one place.'

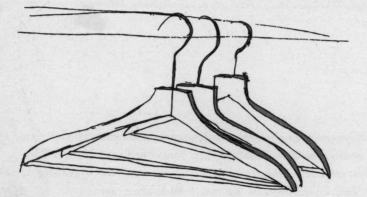

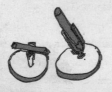

HOW AND WHERE TO STICK YOUR MONOGRAM

Should it show at all with your jacket on?

For some men, the idea of monogramming their shirts is still as ridiculous as having their portrait painted. It is, they think, an act of hubris, of potential folly. I must admit I felt a bit like that, until someone gave me a monogrammed shirt as a gift, and then I very quickly got hooked. If you think it's naff then just ask yourself this: is it any more ridiculous walking around with someone else's name on your shirt rather than your own? According to *The Official Preppy Handbook* (1980), 'Preppies have known it for years: who needs LV or YSL when you can lay claim to a discreet EBW III?'

'The monogram, like its tribal antecedent, the tattoo, is a clear social marker,' we said once in *GQ*, and this has never been so true. Wear a tattoo and you'll look like a footballer or the member of a boy band (or, worse, someone who'd like to be a member of a boy band); sport a monogram and you'll look intriguing. You'll also look like someone who doesn't mind sticking their head above the parapet, which in business is a very good thing indeed. Now that stealth wealth has become a socially accepted prefix (-suit, -car, -woman, etc), the tell-tale signs hidden in your luxury consumer purchases have become even more important. Who wants to walk around in logo-intensive clothing when you could simply have a little monogram in a suitably discreet place, semaphoring your innate superiority?

There is nothing that can't be monogrammed, although I would draw the line at scarves, belt buckles, door knockers, shower curtains, lampshades and ashtrays (and frankly I don't think you should ever really monogram your car, not unless you're the sort of man who owns a customised Bentley, in which case you're obviously rich enough not to care what anyone thinks). It is perfectly acceptable to monogram wallets, rings, golf club covers, luggage, sweaters, hip flasks, napkin rings, handkerchiefs, pyjamas, playing cards, bed blankets, pillowcases, soap and cufflinks, and recently it has also become chic to do the same to briefcases, BlackBerrys, iPods and laptops.

Obviously the prime targets are still shirts, and it is increasingly important how your initials look and where they go. You should really only use your initials, as it somewhat spoils the effect to have 'Duke', 'Babemeister' or 'Lurch' carefully stitched on to your collar. The initials should be in small block capitals, with or without points (full stops). It's fashionable to have the stitching in a contrasting colour to the shirt, though I prefer the same colour, especially white-on-white. Old fogeys will tell you that the monogram should not show at all when you have your jacket on, and should be hard to find when you have it off. But that is an extreme view that doesn't really wash today. The important trick is to make sure the monogram is on the left, regardless of which part of the shirt it ends up. Monograms can be stitched into the (left) collar, on the breast pocket (or where the breast pocket would be), on the left hand body of the shirt (just below the rib cage), or – increasingly these days – on the (left) cuff. And a favourite for American Ivy Leaguers who fancy themselves as dandies is the monogram on the left sleeve at the elbow.

This is totally stealth, as no one ever sees it there.

HOW TO COMMISSION A SUIT

Please, no belt loops!

There is so much rubbish talked about bespoke suits, especially these days, when every so-called style magazine has a bi-monthly column about how to do it properly. The only thing you really need to know is that it's incredibly easy to do, and that there is no mystery about it whatsoever. Neither is it prohibitively expensive, and if you shop around it shouldn't be that much more expensive than buying an off-the-peg suit from a top-name luxury designer. Basically you should please yourself. Today, Savile Row is a far friendlier place than it was fifty years ago, catering to a far more modern man – you.

There are many things to recommend a bespoke suit. There are the fittings, where you are made to feel like the most important man on Earth (which is a change, perhaps, from how you might be treated at home or at the office). There's the knowledge that no one is walking around wearing anything quite like it, and there is the slight decadence of paying rather a lot of money for something that many men find unnecessary. There's also the childish, but still quite satisfying feeling when, having been asked where you bought it, you say your suit is bespoke. Actually.

These days you shouldn't really have more than two fittings for a suit, sometimes three. The process will begin with a discussion of what is wanted and the taking of the measurements, after which the tailor will cut the suit – using an arcane collection of rulers, chalks and scissors – before sending it off to an outworker, who will work up the suit into a rough shape for the first proper fitting, putting in the canvassing and the pockets. At this first fitting the tailor will make various alterations before ripping apart and then recutting the suit. Here he could realign a collar or a shoulder, pull in the waist, recut the armholes (which should always be tight) and slightly lengthen the vents. The suit will then go for finishing, where the linings, the edges and the buttonholes are sewn into place. Rarely will a suit be touched by more than four pairs of hands. Then there is the final fitting, where the only sounds coming from the customer – you – should be coos of delight. The whole process shouldn't take longer than six weeks from soup to nuts.

'The worst thing you can do is try and disguise someone's body shape,' says master tailor Doug Hayward. 'You should play to your client's strengths. Essentially people are buying my taste, not my clothes. I don't try and force my personality on people. You shouldn't make a suit that's going to overpower the person; they have to be able to look and feel comfortable in it.' This is sound advice. I started having suits made because I was an odd body shape, so thin that it was difficult to find suits to fit (and this was back in the 1980s, when suits tended to be boxy and more suited to the stockier, squat body shape). So get your suit cut to fit you, not to disguise you – you will never be that taller, shorter, fatter or thinner person, so find a tailor who can flatter your body (without surgery).

One of the best things, I think, about owning a made-to-measure or bespoke suit is the label. In an off-the-peg suit the label is usually just a big logo, seemingly stencilled on to your jacket as though it, and you, were a piece of numbered and catalogued merchandise.

Where's the individuality in that, do you think? But with a bespoke suit you get a whole different take.

If, say, you were having a suit made by Angelo Galasso at Interno 8, on the inside of the jacket you would find a largish and quite splendid label with your name woven into it in a beautiful script. If you were to pop round to Richard James and do the same thing, the label would be nestling inside the inside pocket of your jacket; on it would be printed your name, and the month and the year it was made.

And if you came out of Richard James, and headed south down Savile Row you'd hit Spencer Hart, the shop opened by Nick Hart when he left Chester Barrie. Hart's labels are something else again. Look inside the wallet pocket in your jacket and you'll read the following: 'Hand made for [your name here] in the year of 200[*]. Spencer Hart sincerely hopes you get laid in this product.'

I mean, really, what more could you want from a suit?

1 Bespoke means 'spoken for' (just so you know).

2 A so-called made-to-measure suit is basically just a basic, pre-existing template pattern that has been roughly altered to fit you, and isn't bespoke at all.

3 How you look tells the world how you feel, and there is no earthly reason why you shouldn't own a bespoke suit (or twenty). You need to look smarter than your average lumpen officetarian.

4 According to Doug Hayward, 'The basics of a suit you don't mess about with: single-breasted with two or three buttons, side vents, straight jacket pockets with flaps, two inside pockets, straight-leg trousers (no one has waistcoats any more, thank God). You make it simple and you make it well. There's no great secret to it, you bring your taste to it and, of course, the way you actually cut the suit.

Tailoring is the same everywhere, it's just how you interpret the rules.'

5   Having said that, never be intimidated by the tailor. You are the client, after all. A tailor is there to give you advice, and if, for some bizarre reason, he doesn't seem interested in doing what you ask, then go somewhere else.

6   I would agree about the side vents, as they're very English, but these days would opt for a one-button suit, and would ask for slanted pockets.

7   As for fabric, choose a good quality sober colour. Don't get carried away – you don't want your friends to think you're moonlighting as a pimp.

8   Choose your lining carefully. Your first inclination might be to go for something outlandish, but I'd either go for a contrasting colour, or something classic – white, black, grey, pale blue or mauve. Not red (never red).

9   You'll be offered functioning cuff buttons, and you should ask for four – although only the bottom two really need work.

10 Do you need a ticket pocket? Maybe – it looks quite cute.

11 Do you need turned-back cuffs on the sleeves? Probably not, not if you intend getting a lot of day-wear out of it.

12 Always try to have as few pleats as possible on your trousers, as they are terribly old-fashioned.

13 Always wear a favourite shirt when you go for a fitting, as you should never show more than half an inch of cuff, and you should wear a shirt you wear a lot.

14 The more colourful your suit, the less often you will wear it.

15 Make sure that the buttons are horn buttons, that the lapels are hand-stitched lapels, that there is felt under the collar, and that there is a canvas interlining (if there isn't, and your jacket is 'fused', it will crinkle the first time it is dry-cleaned).

16 Your suit should have rope shoulders, where the tops of the sleeves stand proud of the shoulders.

17 Velvet lapels? Why not.

18 Nipped-in waist? Definitely.

19 It is sensible to have two pairs of trousers made, as they will wear quicker than the jacket, and as two batches of fabric are never the same, will be difficult to replace.

20 Zips or buttons? Zips are a lot more practical.

21 Don't ask for belt loops – no bespoke suit has them.

SPORT
&
LEISURE

HOW TO BEHAVE IN A CASINO

Because it ain't like the movies

Does the thought of going to a casino make you want to don a dinner jacket and come over all James Bond? Well, casinos are very different these days, with five-star restaurants and luxurious bars serving premium liquor. Many of them feel like glorified top-end nightclubs, and encourage the same sort of deportment. So while you're not allowed to tip the gaming staff in Britain, you can still tip barmen and waitresses. Big time. You should be dressed appropriately, and I suggest you wear a tie, just in case. You have to be a member to gamble on any licensed premises, although this can usually be arranged on the night, as long as you bring a passport (your own, dummy) and another serious item of identification, like a driving licence.

There is a huge difference between casinos in American and Britain, which is why Americans like gambling here so much. Class rears its head over here, and if you're gambling in one of the chi-chi casinos, like Aspinall's or 50 St James, both in Mayfair, then you really do feel as though you're stepping back in time. Going to a casino in Vegas or Atlantic City is not much different from going to a McDonald's or a Burger King (the service is pretty much the same), which is why a lot of Brits like going there: it's classless, unceremonial, and requires almost no effort or skills other than an ability to lose money. Going to a casino in London is much more fun and rather more grand. And when you lose money here, it really hurts.

When you arrive at a casino, it's best to spend at least half an hour acclimatising yourself, making a tour of the tables to see what the stakes are. Then you should find a table that suits your prowess, pace and wallet. Playing in a casino is very different from playing at someone's house, and the sort of practice you get here will stand you in excellent stead. As a newcomer it will be difficult for you to grandstand, while it will be almost impossible for you to get the measure of the croupier or indeed the other players. It will, however, make you better at shielding your cards, and playing to a certain level without having any undue influence on the game.

And keep a cool profile, be confident and act like a success, especially in the way you are dressed. The croupiers will notice if you behave accordingly or not, so just play your part. When you're gambling in a casino your only objective is winning, and psychological subtleties will be wasted on people you're never going to see again.

All players must be at least 21 years of age with no exceptions. If you're playing a slot machine with your young nephew by your side, a security guard will quickly appear (dispatched by casino surveillance) and ask you to leave. But you can walk through the casino with your youngster in tow; as long as you're on the move, you're OK.

Almost all casinos offer craps, blackjack, slots, video poker and roulette. The major casinos will, in addition, have live poker, sports betting, baccarat, keno and an ever-growing list of table games.

'Table' games, especially blackjack and craps, offer the novice the greatest challenges. However, these games remain two of the most popular in Vegas. Free daily lessons at most Strip casinos will let you slide up to the tables with confidence. Don't hesitate to ask any question you like at the table. If a dealer doesn't answer, or is rude, walk away to another table – or indeed another casino. At some of the smaller and less crowded gambling houses, dealers will take the time to orient players to new games. If you're a newcomer to the tables, avoid the larger houses, especially at peak hours, because the personnel may be too busy to help you.

Before you sit down at a table, look at the notice that announces the minimum and maximum bets. Most casinos offer a range of betting minimums, but the low minimum tables tend to be packed. For example, blackjack tables have minimums of $5 to $500 and maximums up to $10,000. Predictably, minimums in casinos on the Strip are generally higher than those of downtown casinos. Timing is also important, and Vegas casinos tend to be busy between noon and midnight, especially at weekends.

The seats in a casino are for players only. Most dealers are instructed to ask non-players to move. And don't try to engage the dealer in conversation, don't put money or chips into the dealer's hand, don't throw chips or money at the betting layout, and never move another player's bet. Although dealers are trained to be friendly, they must also pay attention to the game and be alert for cheats. If you try to gossip with a dealer he'll ignore you, as distracting dealers is a trick frequently used by sharks. If you want assistance, the best person to approach is one of the floor managers, as their duties include social-ising with players. If you have a query about a game, ask the dealer to call an inspector.

Security requirements prevent dealers from shaking hands with players, to stop them from covertly passing across chips. Don't leave your chips unattended at the tables, as they're quite likely to be stolen. The exception is poker, where the dealer will watch the player's chips during a leave of absence from the table.

Never straighten up or move another player's bet. If you need to place your chips on someone else's chips and their bet is ambiguously placed, query the bet with the dealer before making any moves. Players should not touch any gaming equipment or cards unless instructed to do so by the dealer. In some casinos, blackjack players are not allowed to touch the cards at all, while in poker, where players hold their own cards, the cards must be kept in view at all times. Players should wait until all the winning bets have been paid out before placing bets on the next game. The dealer will give the cue by announcing, 'Place your bets' when it's time for the next game to begin.

Dealers have set procedures that they must follow, such as paying out all winning bets in a specific order, so even though you may be in a hurry to leave the casino it is useless to request that your bet is paid out before your turn.

Your personal electronic items are also frowned upon in the casino. No electronics, including cell phones, can be used while seated at a casino game. In the sports book of the casino, pagers and cell phones cannot be used at all. Casinos are traditionally camera-shy, but the no-photography rules that for years protected players are no longer as stringent. If you decide to listen to music, make sure you do not delay the game. Many poker players think they are cool if they sit at the tables with their iPods. However, some of these players can be extremely annoying, since they are often unaware that it is their turn to act. If you listen to music at the table, make sure you keep focused on the action around you (which means not listening to Radiohead or anything else unnecessarily distracting).

Obviously games tend to be looser late at night, so if you're trying to break yourself in, maybe this time is the right time. This is partly because more casual players play then. But regardless of when you play, just remember to pay attention to your opponents' stacks in no-limit games. Sometimes, they will have very high-value chips buried in their stacks. Make sure you know how much your opponents have before making bets that may put you or them all-in.

And be a good winner. As J.P. Donleavy says in *The Unexpurgated Code*, 'Gather up your winnings without smiling. Nor does it do to leave a casino laughing your head off after breaking the bank as it can give the impression to all the crowd watching that you are a rank amateur who has never won anything before.'

Hunter S. Thompson was responsible for my first trip to a casino. It was 1992 and I was working on the *Observer*, specifically helping relaunch its colour supplement. For the inaugural issue it had been decreed that we should fly Thompson, the king of gonzo journalism, to London from his formidable bolt-hole in Aspen, Colorado, to attend the Braemar games in Scotland. There, so we thought, Hunter would be able to write about both the Royal Family and the British royal press pack with his usual, er . . . colourful irreverence. Hunter S. Thompson, the author of *Fear and Loathing in Las Vegas, Fear and Loathing on the Campaign Trail '72, The Great Shark Hunt* and hundreds of equally rabid journalistic exploits, here, on British soil, with his customary cigarette-holder, hip-flask and jaundiced view of the world, with *Observer* journalist Robert Chalmers along to ride shotgun. The crumbling House of Windsor! The dreaded paparazzi! And the savage Hunter S! All in the same place at the same time? With their reputation! It seemed too good to be true. And that's exactly what it turned out to be.

Hunter had only been to England twice before – once in 1974, on his way back from a drug-fuelled trip to the Ali-Foreman 'Rumble in the Jungle' fight in Zaïre, when there was some serious unpleasantness at Brown's Hotel and the Chelsea Arts Club in London. The second was in 1980, when he came to stay with his legendary partner in crime, the illustrator Ralph Steadman (he was, by all accounts, a more than troublesome house guest). On another occasion, when Hunter was due to fly to Scotland to make an address at a biker's convention, he only made it as far as Denver, having had something of an altercation with an irascible taxi driver and several unforgiving bottles of vodka.

'I was at the Roxburghe Hotel in Edinburgh and all these Hell's Angels had arrived, desperate to meet him,' says Steadman. 'I was given the task of telling them that he hadn't arrived. It would have been like telling a mutinous crew there was no food left. I was prepared for him not coming. I was surprised that they weren't.'

Unfazed by this litany of disaster, we were confident of controlling America's most unwieldy and drug-addled reporter. After all, there were reports from the US that he'd calmed down somewhat recently, and his preparatory faxes to London seemed quite demure, almost lucid: 'I am profoundly excited by the challenge of dealing with these people,' he wrote in one, 'who may or may not be utterly strange to me.'

Of course Hunter never delivered. In fact, he never even made it to the Highlands. But in the few days he was in London he managed to cause his customary havoc and to leave a trail of wanton destruction in his wake. In the week he was here he managed to run up an extraordinary bill at his hotel, while his recreational pursuits seemed to largely consist of smoking grass, hoovering up cocaine and drinking whisky, beer and gin in vast quantities. On one sojourn to an East End pub he had the following on the table in front of him: two large Bloody Marys, a pint of bitter, a coffee, two pints of orange juice, a triple Scotch and a hefty vodka and tonic.

On the Sunday night we had arranged a party in Hunter's honour at the London Metropole, the Edgware Road hotel where he was staying (in a £300-a-night suite). But the guest of honour failed to show. Having already missed several flights to Scotland, he had decided, at the height of his amphetamine psychosis, to hop on a plane back to Colorado, leaving P.J. O'Rourke, a motley crew of *Observer* bigwigs and myself all standing around – to use one of Hunter's favourite expressions – with our dicks in our hands.

'Some people will tell you that London is a nice town,' Hunter wrote to us on his return. 'But not me. I will tell you that London is the worst town in the world. For a lot of reasons, but fuck them. Just take my word for it. London is the worst town in the world. You're welcome.'

As the party didn't manage to stagger out of first gear, after a while we reconvened to the Victoria Casino across the road. It being a Sunday night, I had hardly any cash on me, but within forty minutes I had made £350 playing roulette. Probably the least-demanding form of casino gambling, roulette offers a remarkably theatrical way to work a table. Even though you are totally at the mercy of the croupier and his spinning wheel, the fact that you're placing chips on to the green felt gives you a sense of grandeur that you'll never really have playing blackjack or poker. You might even feel like James Bond.

For me, my after-dark experience was exactly the right sort of baptism, although the next time I visited a casino, in Las Vegas a year later, I lost $200 in ten minutes. Sweet.

Blackjack

The pit boss is probably more important at this table than at any other, principally because he is so involved in the game.

• Once you've placed your bet, don't touch it until you get paid.

• If the cards are running against you, don't keep asking for a new deck. If you don't like your cards, move to another table.

• In most casinos when a man sits down at the blackjack table to play, he will immediately be assessed by the pit personnel: 'How much is he good for?'

- Don't walk up to a dealer and tell him he looks bored, or make him shuffle an eight-deck shoe just to make one £5 bet, lose, then walk away.

- Once the hand has been completed, don't turn your cards over to help the dealer. They have a routine on the pickup and you're just slowing them down. Besides, dealers need to lay the cards a certain way so the cameras can see them.

- If you're playing a game in which your cards are dealt face up, don't touch them. In the past, casino bosses told dealers to slap the hands of players who touched cards. Things are more player-friendly nowadays, but the rule remains. In games dealt face down, the situation is different. In those games, you pick up your own cards.

- When you join a game, especially at higher-denomination tables, ask if the other players want you to wait until the shuffle to start playing. Sometimes players who have been on a roll will want to finish out the shoe before changing anything. Don't expect the same courtesy at low-denomination tables. Space is at such a premium that it's a bit much to expect someone to wait at a $10/£5 table.

- Please, resist the urge to give unsolicited advice. Blackjack players are especially bad about this.

Slot Machines/Video Poker

If the casino is crowded, limit your play to just one machine, as it's rude to do anything else. And if you don't, you'll look like one of those sad, fat, white-trash ladies that the casinos bus in to Atlantic City from Pennsylvania.

• When taking a break or looking for change, a player will put a cup on his seat or on the handle indicating he is still playing that machine. Heed these signs. Separating a player from his favourite slot is like messing with the cubs of a mother bear.

• Why are you playing slot machines, you loser?

Craps

Don't try to hand cash to the dealer to make change. The dealer is not allowed to take any cash or chips directly from the customer. You need to place your money on the felt, before the shooter gets the dice, and ask the dealer for 'change only'.

• In craps, when you are the shooter, roll so that the dice hit the back wall of the table.

• Keep your hands off the table and out of the way of the dice being thrown.

• Tables have rails all around the game to store your gaming chips. Use them. Also, underneath there is shelving for your drinks.

• If you're the shooter, give the dice a good toss across the table. Never try to slide dice across the layout thinking you can control the outcome. The first time the boxman will call out, 'No roll.' The second time, possibly a slap on the wrist. The third, you're out.

Roulette

Roulette is a game where you exchange money for chips. The colour-coded chips are not allowed to be bet or intermingled by your friends or family. If both you and your spouse are playing together, you'll need to get separate-coloured chips.

• Dealers will leave the winning bet on the layout. Your winnings will be slid to you. It's your responsibility to remove the winning bet if you don't want to play it the following spin. Outside wagers (red/black, odd/even, columns, etc) will be left alongside your original winning wager.

• Wait until the dealer lifts the marker off the previous winning number before starting to make bets on the next spin. Until that marker comes off the layout, the dealer is paying off bets from the previous spin and wants no confusion over what is an unpaid bet and what is a fresh wager.

• The first player to bet with cash chips takes precedence, and no one else may bet with the same value cash chips. Other players will be warned that someone is betting with cash chips as the dealer will announce, for example, 'red on' or 'pinks on' (depending on the colour of the cash chips).

• When betting chips of mixed denomination, stack them with the highest denomination on the bottom and the lowest on top. It makes it easier for the dealer to read your bet size, and also is a casino safeguard against cheats who attempt to cap a bet with a large-denomination chip after they know the result.

Online Etiquette

There are a few points of virtual casino etiquette that one should adhere to when gambling online. Just like being at a real-life social event, it's good etiquette to be polite and courteous to everyone else in the gaming room. This goes a long way to show you have respect for the other online gamblers in the room.

Another very important point of etiquette is knowing how to play the game before you decide to play for real money.

Most important, should you choose to fold while playing, don't discuss what you had in your hand. This can ruin the game for the others at the table. Please remember that most virtual casino websites have time limits that you need to adhere to when it's your turn to play. It is best to make quick but smart decisions to keep the flow of the game. Lastly, try not to go overboard with the online chat feature. Unless everyone else is talking, keep it to a minimum. Tonto.

HOW TO WIN AT TEXAS HOLD'EM

Because any day now you might need to

'Whether he likes it or not, a man's character is stripped at the poker table; if the other players read him better than he does, he has only himself to blame. Unless he is both able and prepared to see himself as others do, flaws and all, he will be a loser in cards, as in life' – Anthony Holden, *Big Deal*

The rules of poker are simple, it's the playing that's tricky. Boosted by the popularity of playing online and televised tournaments, poker is once again the card game that everyone wants to play. Although instead of Five Card Stud or Five Card Draw, the game everyone's playing these days is Texas Hold'em, whether it's online, at home, at live tournaments or in casinos.

To play, each player is dealt two private cards face down. These are the 'hold' cards, and the first round of betting starts now. The two players to the left of the dealer (or the 'button') each make a blind bet to get the action started, one small and one big. In turn, each player must either call (meet the existing bets), raise (by an amount equal to the existing bets or more, depending on the agreed limits) or fold (chucking in your hand). If no one has bet anything yet, you can also check (or pass) – bet nothing but stay in the hand with the right to call.

Once betting is done on the hold cards, the dealer lays five 'community' or communal cards face up in the middle of the table, and if you are still in the hand you make the best five-card hand you can from the seven available. The first three community cards are the 'flop', and another round of betting takes place once they are dealt. The sixth card is the 'turn', and the last, deciding card, is the 'river'. The great thing about Texas Hold'em is that anyone can play it – even you.

Texas Hold'em strategist Bill Burton says that Position, Patience and Power are the keys to winning. 'The most important decision you will make is choosing to play a starting hand. The biggest mistake a player makes is playing too many hands. Being aware of your Position in relationship to the dealer is important in Texas Hold'em. You need a stronger hand to act from early position because you have more players acting after you who may raise or re-raise the pot. It is important that you are Patient and wait for Powerful starting hands to play from the correct position.

'Deciding whether to continue playing after seeing the flop will be your second biggest decision. It can also be one of the most costly decisions if you continue after the flop with an inferior hand. It is said that the flop defines your hand. That is because after the flop your hand will be 71 per cent complete. Where does this figure come from? Assuming you play your hand out to the end, it will consist of seven cards. After the flop you have seen five cards or 5/7 of the final hand, which is equal to 71 per cent. With this much of your hand completed you should have enough information to determine whether to continue. Poker author Shane Smith coined the phrase Fit or Fold. If the flop does not fit your hand by giving you the top pair, or better or, a straight or flush draw, then you should fold if there is a bet in front of you. If you played a small pair from late position and you do not flop a third one to make a set you should throw the pair away if there is a bet.'

Philip Perkins, another poker expert, agrees. 'Most people that are unsuccessful are the ones that like to play every hand and chase cards,' he says. 'Be selective on the hands you play and you will increase your odds greatly. Get an understanding of how the other players at the table are playing – loose, or tight? This is important to know because the person playing loose is very hard to bet out of a hand and the players that are tight usually only play when they have a monster hand.

'A loose player likes to bluff a lot, and one way to feel a loose player out is to raise his bet or check raise him and watch how they react. Remember mentally how they reacted in each betting round, so if it does come to the showdown and you see their cards, you have just been given a great read on their style of play. A tight player generally only plays the "nuts" early on, but then they know you have a read on them and their style of play, so in the later rounds they try stealing the pot with a big bet. If you have a feeling they might be trying to steal the pot, again raise their bet. If a tight player is quick to call, more than likely they have a hand, so fold. Otherwise with your raise, a tight player will put you on a higher hand, fold and wait until their hand comes along.'

Because more people are playing poker than ever before, and because there is now a vibrant online community, as well as a fairly serious TV fraternity, there are now many more accepted ways to play. Poker players have become celebrities, and instead of simply monetising their skills, have turned into performers too. Recent books such as *Aces and Kings: Why They Win – the Secrets of Poker's Greatest Players* pay as much attention to the personalities as they do to tactics.

Before you start playing, learn the lingo – learn as much Pokerese as you can. It's a fun game, for sure, but when you play you have no friends – you must play with a ruthlessness reserved for . . . poker. Don't take anything personally. Don't lose your cool. In fact don't show any emotion at all. As Lee Robert Schreiber says in *Poker as*

Life: 101 Lessons From the World's Greatest Game, 'Anger will ultimately hurt you more than anyone to whom you may express it.'
Learn to take your losses, and mistakes, on the chin, and never
complain. And you have to understand that there is no such thing
as bad luck, even if you don't really believe it. Be resilient. Don't be
superstitious. Be positive and have complete faith in yourself.

One of the most traditional ways to play is the 'tight-aggressive'
style, described above, where you wait for a big hand and then play
it forcefully. This way you ignore less good hands, and bow out
quickly. One player who ignores this style is Daniel Negreanu, the
high-flying thirtysomething high-school dropout who's best friends
with Leonardo DiCaprio and Tobey Maguire. He believes it's
becoming increasingly difficult to win playing this way because
everyone's at it, and favours a more scatter-gun approach. 'In the
old days, there was this myth that you have to play tight and only
play certain hands,' he says. 'Poker has evolved. The mathematics
behind what everybody thought was correct – the "book play" – is
absolutely not correct any more [because there are so many less
experienced and often reckless players coming to poker]. It's way
too conservative.'

You can observe a lot just by watching – so watch. For example: if
someone who usually talks a lot shuts up, he's got a *good* hand; also,
when a player begins staring at his cards, it probably means he's going
to bet. Also, when a man is anticipating confrontation, or feels he
has a hand worth pursuing, he will invariably start flexing his muscles,
sit up straight, lean forward or deepen his voice.

This works the other way too, so try to make sure you don't have
any involuntary gestures to signify getting a particular card (i.e. don't
start rubbing your leg if you've got a lot of picture cards). Don't play
poker with women, as it's far more difficult to get inside their heads
(usually because you will, at some point in the evening, imagine what
it's like to be between their legs). Play for proper money, because if

the stakes aren't high enough, then you've nothing to lose. Don't throw good money after bad, and cut your losses as soon as you think it's appropriate (i.e. when you know you're not going to win the hand).

Be prepared for the long haul, because if you start at 7 p.m. then you're not going to be finished before midnight, and if you're with serious players then you could be there all night. If you have to go at a certain point, tell people when you sit down, not five minutes beforehand.

Oh, and if you can't work out who's the worst player at the table, it's you.

So, how exactly should you look when you're playing poker? What expression should you carry on your face? What should you wear? Just how thin should your pencil moustache be?

With most card games, it doesn't really matter what you wear or how you act (unless you're playing at a bridge club, which, frankly, I don't think you are), but poker is different. Because poker isn't just about the money, it's about theatre too, about showing off, which is why we like it so much.

Traditionally it was always accepted that you should try to act as inscrutable as possible, and always carry your 'poker face' (especially with strangers). You were meant to look as blank as possible, sometimes even a little confused, in the hope of throwing your opponents off the scent. But that doesn't wash any more, and while you might get away with behaving this way if English wasn't your first language – and I'm basically thinking Russian New Money here – in poker games these days you have to sing for your supper.

Which means drawing attention to yourself. Because if no one is looking at you then no one will notice when you try and intimidate them. You've got to be 'in' the game to win, and you don't do that by sitting back and being moody. Sit upright, talk the talk, and give the impression you know all there is to know about everything (even poker).

Trust me: it is vitally important. The reason there's much more bluffing with online gambling is that it's easier to bluff; and if you can't look into an opponent's eyes (or sunglasses), then you have no idea what he's up to. In real life, 'being there' is everything.

'Table image' is crucial, and while I wouldn't necessarily advocate the type of image used by poker player David 'Devilfish' Ulliot – sunglasses, leather jacket and a pair of brass knuckle-duster rings – you need to look distinctive. And here, you should dress for a marathon, not a sprint. You're going to be sitting there for a long time, so while you shouldn't dress like a tramp (which impresses no one, least of all tramps), you at least need to look smarter than the guy bringing you your drinks. Which, incidentally, doesn't mean sporting a pencil moustache, a three-piece chalkstripe suit (jacket off, tie loosened), and elasticated arm bands. If you want to look like an extra from *The Sting* then you shouldn't be playing cards.

Note: Poker is played with a standard deck of 52 playing cards (except for George Bush Poker, which is played with slightly less than a full deck). The cards are ranked from high to low in the following order: Ace, King, Queen, Jack, 10, 9, 8, 7, 6, 5, 4, 3, 2. Aces are ALWAYS high. Aces are worth more than Kings which are worth more than Queens which are worth more than Jacks, and so on. The cards are also separated into four suits. The suits are:

- Clubs

- Spades

- Hearts

- Diamonds

The suits are all of equal value, meaning that no suit is more valuable than another. It's a very democratic game.

There are many classic poker hands, so many that some have even been given nicknames – four Kings, the Four Horsemen of the Apocalypse; four Queens, the Village People; two fours, a Magnum (Colt .44); two Aces, Rehab; three 6s, the Beast or the Devil; four 2s, the World Cup Final (England 4, West Germany 2, Wembley, 1966); four Jacks, a Chicago Full House (House music, 'Jack Your Body', geddit?). One of the more famous is Deadman's Hand – two black Aces and two black 8s – the hand that Wild Bill Hickok, the murdering sheriff of Ellis County, was supposedly holding when he was shot by Jack McCall on 2 August 1876. 'As might be expected from such a legend, considerable dispute surrounds the composition of Hickok's hand, especially the identity of the fifth card or "kicker",' writes Ben Schott. 'Most sources agree that the "kicker" was the 8 of Hearts, but others assert the Jack of Spades, the 9 of Diamonds, or even the Queen of Spades.'

HOW TO SPREAD BET

It's a lot easier than you think

Trust me, spread betting is not complicated, or at least not as complicated as you think. Like driving a car, or eating lobster, many of us decide that it's too difficult without even giving it a try. In fact, once you've grasped the concept, it's extremely easy to understand. Easier than eating a lobster while driving, anyway.

The Internet has actually been an enormous boost for the spread betting fraternity, not just in making it easier to bet, but also in terms of education and clarification. Spend an afternoon online and you can see hundreds of betting permutations similar to the ones used below, and there are dozens of extremely well-crafted and hard-working websites devoted to little but explaining the minutiae of 'the deal'. Try either www.thegoodgambling guide.co.uk, or www.sports-index.co.uk.

So: the spread betting firm makes a prediction on a particular aspect of a sporting event, such as how many goals will be scored in a game of football, how many runs in a game of cricket, or – you get the picture. You simply decide whether that prediction is too high or too low. If you think they're spot on, you don't bet. It's that simple. If the bookmaker reckons England will score 150 runs, it's up to you to decide whether your spread bet is higher or lower than that figure (and where England are concerned, it's always better to bet lower). And, obviously, the amount you win or lose depends on the size of your stake multiplied by how correct or how wrong you are.

Got it? Let's say that the bookies predict there will be three goals in the game between Newcastle and Arsenal. You – like a lunatic – reckon there will be more, so you bet higher with a stake of £100 for every goal above three. If there were five goals in the game, you would have won £200 (5 minus 3 times your initial stake equals 2 x £100 = £200). If only two goals were scored, you would have lost £100 (3 minus 2 times your stake equals 1 x £100 = £100).

The reason spread betting took off in the City is that it's simply a basic version of market trading, and is the sort of thing many traders do all day anyway. Essentially, it's possible to speculate in the financial markets by making spread bets to profit from, for example, movements in the stock markets. On financials (with spread bets, anyway), there is still no capital gains tax, so for investment purposes it makes complete sense. As long as you appreciate the ramifications of losing, that is. It may be difficult for some to realise that they can lose vast amounts of money even if their initial bet is tiny, and yet they may obviously be seduced by the potentially massive rewards.

Basically, if you think a financial market or product will rise in value, then you'll want to 'go long' and buy it. If you think it'll fall, then you'll 'go short' and sell it.

Let's put it this way: imagine in the first days of March you had a hunch that the FTSE 100 index's value of around 6225 was too high and that share prices would fall over the following weeks. Then, having contacted City Index (www.cityindex.co.uk*), or some other spread

---

* Established in 1983, City Index provides access to thousands of instruments on the world's financial markets. Using one of the best online trading platforms in the market, they update prices in real time every second, so their clients always have a clear view of their positions. Predictably they're big in the City.

betting and 'Contracts for Difference'** provider, you're given a FTSE 100 price for the third week of April of 6145–6155. Based on that spread, you have two choices. You can bet on the Footsie falling below this level, by selling the index. Or bet it will be higher than this in April, by buying the index. Either way, you bet by staking a sum, say £100, per point. As you expect the Footsie to fall, you take the former option. Now imagine that on 14 April, the FTSE 100 actually closes at 6010, 135 points below the City Index spread. On this basis, your profit would be £13,500 – 135 times your £100 stake. In fact, you don't have to wait until 14 April to claim your profits. You can close your bets as soon as they become profitable. If the index had stood at 6040, say, on April Fool's Day, you could have closed out your bet by reversing it – buying points from City Index.

However, the downside of spread betting is that the potential for large gains is equalled by that for enormous losses. Imagine that you had bought, rather than sold, points from City Index in the example above. Your loss would have been a crippling £14,500 – £100 times the 145 points the Footsie finished below your opening spread. It's important to note that in spread betting gains and losses are geared. The more right you get a bet, the more you win. But the more wrong you are, the bigger your losses, baby.

Not surprisingly, spread betting brokers are wary about bad debts, and will only extend credit to investors who meet their losses. Expect calls for cash from your bookmaker if your bets move into the red. On the other hand, all the firms say that, unlike conventional bookmakers, they do not lose on winning bets, as they lay off risks in the underlying markets. Brokers, therefore, do not mind successful gamblers.

Which is nice.

** The CFD (Contracts for Difference) market is a way to trade shares without having to pay the full price of owning the stock. You can also profit by selling in anticipation of an expected fall in value, something you can't do easily with normal share trading.

The Single Index

This is by far the simplest form of spread betting. What defines this type of index is the fact that it's independent of all other scores and events. Take for example a cricket innings. England are playing Pakistan in a Test match and Batsman 1 is quoted at 85–90 for his two-innings combined run total. The final result (make-up) of this index will be his real combined two-innings total.

You think he is likely to score more than 90, so you buy at 90 for £5.

Here are two outcomes:

1 Batsman 1 scores 62 in the first innings and 68 in the second innings. His total (the make-up) is 68 plus 62 equals 130. Your result here is (130 minus 90) times £5, meaning you win £200.

2 Batsman 1 scores 18 in the first innings and 0 in the second innings. His total therefore is 18. Your result here is a loss because he scored less than 90 and so is (90 minus 18) times £5, meaning you lose £360.

The Heads-Up Index

With the Single Index, the make-up was determined by the actual result. With two player indices the bookmakers often like to spice things up by awarding points for a particular result. Imagine an 18-hole match-up between two golfers in a tournament. This is an index that is resolved in one day.

Buy: This obviously doesn't mean buy in the conventional sense. It means you're betting the higher value of a quote will be exceeded.

Imagine Batsman 2's innings runs 30–35. You buy at 35 in the belief that he's likely to score more than that. Your win is his final score minus 35. So if he scores 82 your result is a win of (82 minus 35) times your stake. If he was out for 28 your result is a loss of (35 minus 28) times your stake.

Sell: This means you're betting the lower value of a quote won't be reached. Imagine Batsman 2's innings runs 30–35. You think he's not going to make it, so you sell at 30. If he is out for 6 you win (30 minus 6) times your stake. But if he bats well and hits 77 then you lose (77 minus 30) times your stake.

Spread: The difference between the Buy and Sell prices – i.e. Boxer A knockout rounds 4–5. The spread is 1.

• You buy at one end of the spread and sell at the other, and if the spread moves far enough in the right direction between when you buy and when you sell, you make money. If it moves in the wrong direction you lose.

• The more right you are, the more money you make. The more wrong you are, the more money you lose.

• The size of your stake determines how much money you make per unit move.

• You never actually own the shares, commodity, bond or whatever else it is that's the subject of the bet.

• With spread betting you can make money whichever way the market is moving, be it rising or falling.

HOW TO GET TO GRIPS WITH GOLF

Learning to love clubs, wear Pringle sweaters and calculate your handicap

Tell people you're taking up golf and you normally get one of two reactions. Those who have already been converted give you a punch on the arm or a whack on the back and say, with no hint of irony (there is no irony in golf), 'Welcome to the clubhouse.' Those who aren't converts, and who never will be, look at you with the sort of withering, pitying sneer that Shrek always gives Eddie Murphy's Donkey. Don't be fooled by the converted, though, as they're not your friends. They can smell fresh blood, and are only waiting to get you out on to their favourite course and comprehensively thrash you.

But these days it doesn't matter what anyone thinks, because like many things that were hitherto barred from the Palace of Cool, golf is hip, and has been for some time. There are magazines aimed at golf punks, and clothes designed by everyone from Ralph Lauren and Tommy Hilfiger to Dunhill and Burberry. No longer is it the domain of ageing comedians and professional sportsmen who can't get insured to play anything else; these days the game is played by fashion designers, pop stars, porn stars, DJs, and all those flexi-time creatives who don't have much to do during the day.

When I first started learning to play I would sneak off to a base-
ment in Soho two or three lunchtimes a week to practise my swing.
There I would stand, arched over my feet, swearing at a huge video
screen as my balls careered off into the rough. I very quickly acknowledged the fact that if profanity had an influence on the flight of the
ball, the game would be played a lot better than it is, especially by
amateurs like me.

I became quite obsessed with the mythology of it all too, and could
be found listening intently to the most dreadful golf bores in bars
all over London. You soon learn there are so many mad stories that
surround the sport. For instance if you think your local course is busy,
just consider the nine-hole Aranda course, part of Singapore's Orchid
CC. In true life (as my seven-year-old daughter would say), the
fourth hole has its own traffic light. Since the drive from the fourth
tee is blind, obscured by a rather large hill, and you therefore can't
see when the game in front has moved out of range, you have to
wait for a green light before teeing off. Or take the sixth hole of
Green Zone Golf Club, which straddles the Swedish-Finnish border,
with the tee in Sweden and the hole in Finland. It's become famous
for being the only course in the world with a customs shed and
a scorecard with customs regulations on the back.

Obviously one of the most appealing aspects of
learning to play golf is acquiring the kit – the clubs,
clothes, bags, balls, shoes, hats, caps and all the other
stuff that proves to the world that you're really, really
taking it seriously. My first 'stick' was a putter – an Odyssey
2 ball, a good one – and I was told to invest in a set of Calloway
clubs, although for the first few weeks I was more concerned with
what I needed to wear.

Although the game was originally restricted to wealthy, overweight
Protestants, it's now open to anybody who owns hideous clothing
(Tiger Woods once said that golf is a sport for white men dressed
like black pimps); so one has to take care. While dress codes have

been substantially relaxed since the days when Wing Commander Huffton Tufton and his pals gathered around the nineteenth hole in their plus-fours and funny po-boy caps, you still need the right stuff. Stuff you can move in, that copes with the weather. Concentration is so paramount, so crucial to the whole idea of the game, that you don't want to have to worry about what you're wearing. You don't want something too extravagant or over-designed; nor do you want something too loose and casual. Like any sporting uniform, golf clothing is specific, exact. Although unlike any other sport, since inception the golf course has also been used as a catwalk, the only legitimate catwalk for men who don't work in the fashion industry or spend their leisure hours in nightclubs.

And I wanted to own that catwalk. So having first got the shoes (Ecco), I spent two weeks road-testing sack-loads of golfing schmutter – polo shirts by Pringle and Thomas Pink, jackets by Burberry and Dunhill, trousers by Tommy Hilfiger, and caps by everyone from M&S to Kangol. And after intense research (which mostly involved me poncing about in my office trying not to be caught by my PA), I discovered that, while everything I tried on has its virtues, probably the best golfing kit is made by J. Lindeberg, the Stockholm designer who specialises in funky golf gear and fashionable fairway apparel.

When you're learning to play, consistency is the name of the game, and the important question is not how good your good shots are – it's how bad your bad ones are (remember what A.A. Milne said: 'Golf is so popular because it's the best game in the world at which to be bad'). Initially you will probably find that your short game (putting) is relatively easy to master, as is your long game (teeing off); the difficult shots to learn are the ones in between, the pitching and the chipping. This is where you will discover if you are meant to be a golfer or not, and whether your temperament will allow you cope with the fact that for every brilliant, soaring, sweet-shot masterstroke, you will almost certainly hit twenty balls into the rough. Crucially, you must be able to keep up; you might not be the best player in the world, but if you can keep up, then you can play with anyone and, thanks to the handicap system, compete with anyone too.

Your grip needs to be identical every time you pick up a club, as does your swing. Dr Karl Morris is an expert in the field of golf psychology, and he advocates Zen-like repetition. 'Go through the same ritual for every shot you play,' he says. 'Create your own routine and stick with it. That keeps the mind in the present moment and doesn't allow it to wander. That's the single most important thing any club player can do.'

For Morris, psychology is everything. Consider the ten-yard line. 'This is something that Tiger Woods uses,' he says. 'Before a shot he sees a coloured line ten yards in front of the ball. He says to himself that whatever happens, he has to deal with it within that ten-yard area. So if he has to get mad after the shot, he'll get mad, but as soon as he walks over that line, that's it.'

As you develop you will need to calculate your handicap, and this is how you do it. Take the scores from the last five rounds of 18 holes you have played. For each of these scores look up the rating and slope for the course you played (this is usually printed on the score-card). Subtract the course rating from your score. Then multiply that number by 113. The resulting number is the differential. Then take the lowest of your five differentials and multiply it by 0.96, and you have your handicap. Anyone who has ever spent six hours filling in their VAT form will be able to do this.

HOW TO DANCE

Conquering 'Halston, Gucci, Fiorucci . . .'

The most important lesson to learn about dancing is this: no one is looking at you. The main obstacle to successful dancing is self-consciousness, and the fear that everyone else in the room is waiting for you to trip over your feet, fall on your face and generally begin to embarrass yourself. Trust me: no one cares. Not if you take things slowly, anyway.

Whether you're an inexperienced dancer, have never danced in your life before or have done and don't like it, there are two more important lessons to learn. Firstly, women expect a man to be able to dance, so if you can't, then stop being so wet and just get on with it. Secondly, you don't have to be good at everything. I can dance to most things, but whenever I hear the opening bars of 'I'm So Excited' by the Pointer Sisters, say, or 'Walking on Sunshine' by Katrina & the Waves, or indeed anything resembling drum and bass, I walk off the dancefloor. Not for taste reasons – although I could be forgiven for doing just that – but because I find them difficult to dance to; few people can dance to every song, to all types of music, and records that have a high bpm (beats per minute) or staccato rhythm, or that are simply too slow (e.g. the loping beat of the SOS Band's 'Just Be Good to Me') can easily be avoided by simply going to the bar. Don't like reggae? Then go to the loo. Find it difficult to take Coldplay seriously when you're trying to shake your tush? Sit down.

If you really can't dance and really need to, then you should begin tentatively. Don't move your feet and just work from the waist up, keeping your arms bent at the elbow, slowly twisting yourself in time to the music. It sounds simple, but then it's hardly rocket science. As you get bolder and more confident you'll start enhancing your movements, although the important thing is to keep everything in proportion. No one expects you to be John Travolta (least of all John Travolta, who was thoroughly choreographed though *Saturday Night Fever*), so just take things easy.

Just a couple of warnings: never dance to a slow song unless you're holding a woman; and never, ever attempt to emulate Bruce Springsteen in the 'Dancing in the Dark' video, or Kevin Bacon in *Footloose* by 'rock dancing' (lifting your legs and arms up and down at the same time like an uncoordinated or drunk puppet).

It is also advisable to learn a few traditional dances, like the Tango for instance. An easy dance to master is the Twist, which can be used for everything from old Chubby Checker records to George Michael's 'Faith'. For this you need to place one foot slightly in front of your body, and then start twisting your body using that foot as a pivot, putting particular emphasis on your hips. Then you begin twisting down to a crouch, almost to limbo level, always ensuring that you keep your back totally straight. Twist back up again, and then repeat.

For something even more traditional, try the Highland Fling. This involves holding the left arm up over your head, curving it over the top making a 'C'. Put the right hand on your right hip with the thumb pointing towards the ground and the fingers towards your back. Starting on the left foot, with the right foot fully extended to the right-hand side, do a quarter-turn hop. Bring the right foot in behind the left ankle, and then perform another quarter-turn hop on the left foot, again extending the right foot out to the right-hand side. Then do another quarter-turn hop, this time bringing the right foot in front of the left calf with the toe pointing down. Repeat the previous steps but with the arms and the legs in the opposite positions. When the song is over, end the dance with a slow and elegant bow, and a George Clooney smirk.

Please at all times remember this: there is a thin line between courage and recklessness.

HOW TO COPE ON THE SLOPES

Skiing, boarding and what to wear

Now, I am a simple man and I live by simple rules. One of the primary rules is this: if anyone ever invites you on to a private jet, say yes, regardless of where it's bound. Which is what I did one weekend a short while ago, flying to St Moritz for a weekend of white turf action.

I have to say that I am not the world's greatest skier, nor its most confident, not by any stretch of the imagination. And I will freely admit that Bode Miller and I do not come from the same gene pool. I have been skiing four times in my life – most embarrassingly at Klosters and Mirabel – and even spent a week at Steamboat in Colorado a few years ago with one of the state's best instructors in the hope of mastering the sport. But to little avail. Having tried to learn too late in life, I am simply overcome by fear. Flying down an icy mountain, on two thin pieces of bendy plastic? Without a safety harness? Are you crazy? Are you truly mad?

So as our friends had kindly invited us to share their jet to St Moritz, and as my wife wasn't about to let me say no, I decided to spend the weekend learning to snowboard. I must say snowboarding kit has improved vastly in the last few years. Back in the Nineties, if you went boarding you had to look like a renegade Swiss Liam Gallagher:

absurdly coloured jackets, horrible voluminous trousers and the kind
of hooded headgear that these days would invite a stop-and-search
if you were walking around a South London sink estate. Recently,
boarding seems to have finally grown up, and the silhouette has
changed from baggy and bulbous to narrow and streamlined. And if
you mix Prada, Peak Performance, Dolce & Gabbana and Moncler,
you'll look as good as you possibly can on the slopes.

Boarders and skiers now look more like each other than they ever
have, with salopettes only being worn today by ageing playboys and
provincial hairdressers (girls can still wear them, of course, but then
as far as fashion is concerned, girls can just about get away with
anything). Everything these days tends to come in a drifit fabric that
wicks away moisture, leaving your clothes completely dry. I was dressed
in a combination of Peak Performance, Nike and Prada, although if
I were seriously trying to make an impression on the slopes I would
probably opt for a red and white ski-suit by Anzi Besson, makers of
the uniforms for the Austrian ski team.

My wife rather unkindly suggested that all I cared about was looking
the part, although I would forgo any sartorial indulgences just to be
able to successfully negotiate a blue run without closing my eyes,
gritting my teeth and begging for divine intervention.

My instructor was called Ursina, which, she told me, means 'bear' in
her native tongue, the fourth language of Switzerland, Romansh. I
actually thought she said 'beer', which our party thought more than
ironic, particularly as I had spent the previous night trying to drink
as many Ursinas as humanly possible (in the end I managed eight).
At 9.40 a.m., as I fell over for the twentieth time, precisely forty
minutes since I had arrived on the slopes, I came to the conclusion
that trying to learn to snowboard with a black run hangover was
probably not exactly the best idea in the world.

Ursina – who, like all ski instructors, had thin lips, a chestnut
complexion and was 'looking forward to going to the Hard Rock

Café' – taught me as well as she could, and by lunch I had mastered the art of turning left and right in one movement. I was learning to attack the mountain, and to put all the pressure on the back of my board when facing the slope, and on the front of my board when facing the mountain. I kept falling over, but then everybody had told me that if you didn't fall over fifty times during the first day then you weren't doing it properly. I also learned that I never, ever want to hear James Blunt sing anything again, at least not on a mountaintop. Most ski resorts these days blare out music from the bubble-stops in the hope of attracting a younger clientele, but I'm not convinced that three hours of non-stop Blunt is the most successful way to entice people up on to the slopes. I would venture that it might actually have the opposite effect.

I returned from the mountains slightly earlier than everyone else, looking forward to a large glass of *Glühwein* and the delights of a bruise-soothing bath in our hotel (the Nolda, which, predictably, we had immediately rechristened the Noddy Holder). As I lay there, surrounded by Tyrolean splendour and a pile of technologically advanced drifit clothing, I wondered if I would ever become a down-hill racer, if I would ever go off-piste in search of thrills, spills and the legendary mountain restaurant where the waitresses serve *raclette* in technologically advanced lederhosen.

I've often thought that when we're born there should be some sort of tag attached to our umbilical cord containing salient information to help us through life. Mine would probably have read something like this: 'Dylan Jones, born Ely, Cambridgeshire. Will develop an unhealthy interest in expensive trousers, spend the bulk of his career cannibalising personal experience in pursuit of lifestyle journalism, and be bald by the time he's thirty. Does not ski.'

I will, however, persevere, which is what any man has to do if he wants to master the slopes. Next time I go skiing I'm going to attempt cross-country skiing, a far more demanding sport – you have to be extraordinarily fit – but at least you don't have to throw yourself off mountaintops every five minutes (it's also a far more authentic form of skiing – it's the old-fashioned way of getting from A to B).

One way or another, I will conquer skiing, and whether it's skiing, boarding, cross-country, even tobogganing – I shall find something I like. When you're learning to ski, the first thing you have to understand is that you are at a tremendous disadvantage compared with those who learned when they were kids. Watch children on the slopes and they zip about as if computerised – they have a low centre of gravity, can't fall very far, and treat the ice and snow as the most natural thing in the world. But learning as an adult is slightly different; you have to cope with fear, which, unfortunately, is innate.

One of the most important things about skiing is understanding that it isn't all about the lifestyle, that it isn't all about St Moritz and being photographed with the right people, wearing the right things, looking thin, tanned and generally gorgeous (or indeed, famous). Skiing can simply be about skiing, and there are so many resorts these days, that you don't have to think of the whole exercise as a fashion shoot. Yes, status is incredibly important where skiing is concerned, but it doesn't have to be. If you want to go to some little out-of-the-way Austrian resort to hone your skills, then so be it. Skiing is for everyone, not just the rich, the famous and the desperate. It is a totally legitimate leisure pursuit, and you should do anything you can to do it – because the longer you leave it, the more difficult it will become.

The fundamentals are as follows: start in a balanced stance, and place your feet shoulder width apart while slightly flexing your ankles, knees and hips towards the snow. Keep your weight evenly distributed over the centre of both skis by leaning forward into your boots. Initiate a run by steering both feet in the direction you want to turn. Place your downhill pole in front of your body and down the hill. Keep your upper body facing down the mountain at all times. Your upper body should remain stable while your lower body rotates independently with each turn. Take the weight off your skis at the end of a turn by pulling your ankles, knees and hips up. String a number of turns together. You are now skiing.

Here are some other tips:

• It's better to learn in North America, as the slopes are less busy than they are in Europe, and the instructors can be more indulgent – whereas a lot of French instructors just think you're useless for not being able to ski like a (French) god.

• Weighting and unweighting your skis is crucial, especially when you're skiing in powder (which is the most fun). This is performed by flexing and extending your lower body, and is the movement that enables a skier to float across the snow.

• Go pre- or post-season (the slopes will be empty).

• Always have one-on-one lessons so you can improve at your own speed.

• Hire an instructor who specialises in teaching children, as they tend to be more compassionate, more understanding, and less likely to fall about laughing when you fall over.

• Always, always take the opportunity if you can. Every time you go you will improve.

• It will take you approximately sixty hours to become proficient.

• Skiing is a contest between ability and fear.

• Try everything (skiing is like sex – there are lots of different types and you're bound to like one of them).

• Make sure you get the right kit, and dress in layers. If you're cold up there then you won't want to stay too long.

• Never, ever wear jeans on the slopes.

• It's crucial you learn to (a) parallel ski, (b) stop, and (c) get up without much fuss (you'll be doing it a lot).

• Explore everything else the resorts have to offer. It's totally possible to have a great mountain holiday without spending all your time on the slopes. Arranging where to have lunch, getting to lunch, and having lunch can take up the best part of the day.

• Get your own ski boots; your feet and ankles will begin to hurt as soon as you start practising, so you should try to take as much pressure off them as you can. It's worth going to bespoke ski boot technicians, who will mould special insoles, having photographed, measured, and then taken plastic jelly-moulds of your feet. By slipping these insoles inside your boots they produce a pair of boots that will give you as much support as possible.

• Don't give up, because if you do, you'll regret it.

HOW TO DRESS FOR THE BEACH

No pebbledash legs, tandoori tans or curtain-ring earrings

Just why are British men so badly dressed when they go abroad on holiday? Is it just that we look so bad in context, when compared to the Italians, the Spanish or the French? Or is our inability to look relaxed and well dressed in the sun simply innate? Admittedly, we're not quite as badly dressed as the Germans, but it's still a fairly close call.

Essentially, the generic sloppy Brit abroad looks as though he started dressing as if he were just off to the gym (trainers, fluffy socks, garish running shorts), and then lost interest and threw on a cheap summer shirt from a market stall. He will have fushcia, oven-done skin, an oversized singlet covered with brightly coloured go-faster stripes, goppingly awful fluorescent shorts and a pair of moon boot-esque training shoes. And these days he will no doubt also have two large gold(ish) earrings and some kind of pikey medallion. It is a look the British have made their own, largely because no one else has expressed any interest at all in acquiring it. It makes me think that if these men make the same sort of decisions about everything else in their lives as they do about their clothes, then it's no wonder they look so depressed.

One of their most heinous crimes is wearing football shirts, and while it's borderline acceptable for a Premiership player to do it (apparently former Liverpool superstriker Ian Rush was partial to this, and there is a famous story, perhaps apocryphal, about an Ipswich team who when holidaying together in Lanzarote never ventured into the local village without their away strip), for a civilian it's the height of bad taste.

But I'm being slightly unfair, as many more men nowadays make an effort not to be so disobliging. Before the consumer revolution, men's idea of dressing for the summer was taking their tie off, but at least the high street has made it easier for us not to look like third-rate children's entertainers when the days start getting longer.

One of the biggest mistakes men tend to make during the summer is wearing linen suits. As soon as the clocks change, we take it upon ourselves to embrace the summer even if frost is still on the ground. And one way we do this is by buying linen. We think it makes us look continental. Smooth. Sophisticated. Big mistake.

I remember an episode of *The Simpsons* in which Homer decides to shave. Having completed the task he turns to admire his freshly sculpted face in the mirror, only to have the stubble appear again – ping! – as soon as he leaves the bathroom. Linen suits are like that, only often they don't wait until you've left the room. One second you're looking sharp and smart, the next you're crumpled and crinkly. They also have the unfortunate effect of making some people look like extras in *Miami Vice*, where the likes of Don Johnson and Phil Collins would parade around in their brightly coloured crunchy linen suits, silk shirts and inopportune RUJs (rolled-up jacket sleeves), looking like gigantic packets of crisps.

If you're determined to look like a generic British Estuarial yobbo, then there's no hope for you, but if you're prepared to listen, then there are some simple sartorial rules that might help you this summer.

And they are as follows: Wear a strong-coloured plain shirt (by Ralph Lauren, for instance, in a purple, a navy or a bright orange), a long-sleeved T-shirt (by Richard James), or a bright white T-shirt from Topman or Zara; try a pair of knee-length Boss khaki shorts (complete with dozens of pockets for mobiles, BlackBerrys, tool kits, etc), and a pair of white Birkenstock sandals. I used to think that sandals were for backpacking relief teachers who drank half pints of real ale in ghastly country pubs surrounded by Ordnance Survey maps and home-made sandwiches. But how times change: as long as you don't wear them with socks, Birkys are the coolest things of all.

I would also heartily recommend a seersucker suit. For years seer-sucker was the uniform of the world-weary expat or battle- (or bottle-) weary foreign correspondent, usually worn with a pair of battered white canvas shoes, a pale linen shirt and a dishevelled tie. But not any longer. Wear one with pride, and if someone asks you for a choc-ice, just swear at them in Italian.

In addition to all this you will also need a couple of pairs of ridicu-lously expensive sunglasses, a villa on Ibiza and, most importantly of all, a fake tan (either walk-in or out of a bottle). To the untrained eye you might look as though you once drove through Essex, but at least you won't look German.

The Rules:

1   The unbuttoned shirt rule: one button undone for the day. Two for the night. Three, you're Jennifer Lopez. Five, you're David Hasselhoff.

2   Buy bright white T-shirts every summer and then throw them away come September.

3   Don't buy T-shirts with words on them, unless those words are, 'Got a sister?' Don't wear excessive jewellery.

4   You can't have enough white jeans.

5   Designer beach towels are extraordinarily chic (the louder the better).

6   Never take any socks on a beach holiday.

7   Always take a dark blue jacket, just in case.

8   Pack as many pairs of swimming trunks as you can, preferably all from Vilebrequin.

9   Take more suntan cream than you think you'll need, and always go for the higher numbers.

10   Pack a Panama hat, and don't worry about losing it (they're cheap and, like most beach clothes, should be bought on the understanding that they'll be thrown away at the end of the holiday).

11   Training shoes are for running in, and nothing else.

12   Wear a big, expensive, chunky watch (Tag Heuer, Panerai, Omega, Frank Muller, a Rolex Daytona, etc).

13   You can't beat a Gucci loafer. Invented in 1953, and resuscitated by Tom Ford in the 1990s, the Gucci moccasin is a veritable style classic, and looks just as good on the decking of your beachfront apartment as it does on the pavements of Fifth Avenue.

14   The only men who wear tucked-in short-sleeved shirts work for courier companies.

15   Cut-off jeans? Computer still says No.

16   Polo shirts work (John Smedley, Ralph Lauren, Thomas Pink).

17   Take a cashmere sweater for evening (Ermenegildo Zegna, Loro Piana, Land's End).

18   Sunglasses: Web, Ray-Bans, Tom Ford, Persol, YSL.

19 Don't treat your sunglasses so preciously. Persol shades all have two-way hinges, making them virtually unbreakable, no matter which way you bend them.

20 Brightly coloured JP Tod's driving shoes work.

21 If you wear spectacles or contacts, get some prescription sunglasses made; that way you won't always be squinting as you flick through the latest Dan Brown.

22 On no account wear your sunglasses after dark. Only Jack Nicholson could ever do this. If you follow suit, you will look like you should be holding a cane or following your dog.

23 Don't take your briefcase to the beach bar; buy a soft canvas bag from Bally, or a gym bag by Dunhill.

24 Drink Campari and soda, name brand vodka (Grey Goose, Belvedere) and tonic or good wine.

25 Drinking beer at midday is perfectly acceptable, just as long as your glass is never larger than a half pint.

26 Baggy surfing shorts are just about OK, although I'd rather you had IRONIC stencilled on your forehead.

27 Don't have IRONIC stencilled on your forehead, or indeed anywhere else.

28 Never wear short shorts.

29 Or skimpies (trust me on this one: no one wants to look at your penis).

30 Bizarrely, shorts with belts are now perfectly OK.

31 If you've got tattoos, keep them hidden (your name is not Robbie Williams. Unless, of course, you *are* Robbie Williams. In which case, Hello Robbie!).

32 Don't go naked: the only people who populate nudist beaches are those whose bodies the rest of us would rather not see.

33 Pack the Dunhill windcheater or the Belstaff biker's jacket just in case.

34 It's totally OK to have a white suit in your wardrobe, although I recommend you only wear it one day a year.

35 If you like flip-flops, don't buy any brand other than Havaianas.

36 If a stranger comes up to you on the beach and asks you something in English, pretend not to understand.

HOW TO BOWL A STRIKE

You too could be The Dude

Ten-pin bowling is one of those sports, like pool or shooting, that everyone can be quite good at without really trying. And ever since *The Big Lebowski*, the Coen Brothers' homage to Jeff 'The Dude' Dowd, the legendary bowling ace, the game has had an ironic allure (the film, the Coens' best, stars Jeff Bridges, Steve Buscemi, John Goodman, Philip Seymour Hoffman, John Turturro, Julianne Moore, Tara Reid and Ben Gazarra).

Of course anyone can learn to drink White Russians like The Dude, but how do you bowl a strike like him?

Well, the most important thing is getting as close to the ground as you can when you actually release the bowling ball, by bending the knee. Yes, you need to work out the number of steps you'll need in the run-up, and yes, you need to hold the ball properly (splay your fingers around it), and yes, your aim needs to be fairly accurate, but the most important element of the bowl is swinging your ball as low as possible. You should be taking four paces before sliding into the delivery, swinging the ball behind you and releasing it as your arm fully extends.

All bowling lanes are oiled, but what most punters don't realise is that the oil runs out just before the pins, allowing the ball to swerve left or right at the last second. So your bowl needs to be fast, it needs to be accurate (aiming for the 'one-three pocket', the space between the front pin and the second-row right – or the second-row left if you're left-handed), and it needs to travel along the wood for as long as possible. If it bounces, or spins, then you're doing it all wrong.

And a successful strike is always swiftly followed by a high-five . . . and a White Russian.

HOW TO APPRECIATE A CIGAR

. . . and smoke one properly

Cigar smoke is a lot like the smell of coffee in that it gives off such a powerful, exotic aroma that it's possible to enjoy it without actually enjoying smoking cigars yourself. Let's face it – cigars are alluring. As dear old Evelyn Waugh once wrote, 'The most futile and disastrous day seems well spent when it is reviewed through the blue fragrant smoke of a Havana cigar.'

The cigar is still the aromatic badge of the plutocrat, the internationally recognised symbol of the sybarite with money to burn. And as soon as you begin to smoke – *seriously* smoke – it turns into something of an obsession.

The trick with cigars is to make them *laaaaast*. 'If you are spending upwards of a tenner on a single tube of tobacco, which has travelled all the way from the tropics to wind up in your mouth, you don't want to rush the experience,' says Nick Foulkes, *GQ*'s erudite Luxury Editor, a man who smokes a decent cigar every day of his life. 'You want to have the time to cut its rounded end with care, to apply the flame from your match or cedar spill evenly over the cigar's end, to savour the first notes of the expertly blended and matured tobaccos dancing across the palate, and appreciate the concert of tastes and aromas building in intensity as more of the cigar is turned into ash.'

The only cigars worth smoking are rolled in either Cuba or the Dominican Republic, and both are sold with a government seal around the box, a greenish slip of paper that looks as if it might have fallen out of a Monopoly box.

There are five great cigar brands, three Cuban, two Dominican. In descending order of strength, the Cuban brands are Bolivar (the closest thing the island has to a weapon of mass destruction), Cohiba (still the trendiest cigar to smoke) and H. Upmann, a delicate smoke much favoured by JFK and named after a German banker who liked cigars so much he moved to Cuba and founded his own brand. The Dominican Republic brands are Davidoff (strong, and blue-blooded) and Avo (smooth, and named after a pianist who used to sell individual cigars from a jar on top of his piano).

The bands of the cigars obviously alert people to what brand you're smoking, however there is a vogue at the moment for unbanded cigars, as they are not only less likely to have been squashed by packing, but are suitably intriguing.

If you're keeping them at home you need a proper humidor to store them in, one regularly replenished with distilled water. The best are made by Davidoff, Griffin and Linley (who will make you one in the shape of your house for the price of your real house). My favourite is the Davidoff Zino perspex humidor, which not only costs around £100, but also allows you to see exactly how many smokes you have left. The temperature should be kept at 16–18ºC and 65–70% relative humidity.

If you're venturing out with your smokes then you'll need a leather cigar case. The best are to be found in any of the many leather shops in Florence but are also available in your local department store (if that department store happens to be Selfridges, that is). You'll also need a cigar cutter, either a small plastic and steel guillotine (for out and about) or something more extravagant like cigar scissors (for home).

Oh, and please remember: never, ever, under any circumstances light your smoke with a petrol lighter. Not only is it unspeakably common, but your cigar will taste of your local petrol station. Either use a lighter with odourless flames, a long match (once the phosphorus has burnt off) or, best of all, a strip of cedar wood.

The Size of Your Smoke

Panatella: 4 inches long, 26 ring gauge.
   Time to smoke: 15 minutes.

Tres Petit Corona: 4 inches, 40 ring gauge.
   Time to smoke: 20 minutes.

Petit Corona: 5.125 inches, 48 ring gauge.
   Time to smoke: 25 minutes.

Corona: 5.6 inches, 42 ring gauge.
   Time to smoke: 30 minutes.

Robusto: 4.9 inches, 50 ring gauge.
   Time to smoke: 40 minutes.

Lonsdale: 6 inches, 42 ring gauge.
   Time to smoke: 50 minutes.

Torpedo: 6.13 inches, 52 ring gauge.
   Time to smoke: 60 minutes.

Churchill: 7 inches, 47 ring gauge.
   Time to smoke: 70 minutes.

Double Corona: 7.6 inches, 49 ring gauge.
   Time to smoke: 90 minutes. And counting . . .

HOW TO SMELL

'That's an interesting top note. Gruyère?'

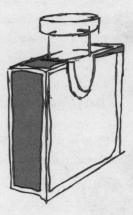

Traditionally, the first ten things about your appearance that a girl will check when she first meets you are as follows: 1) Shoes, 2) Crotch, 3) Waistline, 4) Clothes, 5) Chest, 6) Chin, 7) Teeth, 8) Nasal hair, 9) Complexion, and 10) Dandruff (swiftly followed by the crotch again).

Shoes first? Oh, yes. Recently a survey suggested that most women will check out the shine of your shoes before they check out the size of your, er, package. If your shoes are scuffed, or if they've fallen into disrepair, or even if you simply haven't polished them for a while, it's unlikely that that gal in front of you is going to allow her eyes to wander up your torso, because you obviously aren't worth it. Women now place enormous importance on how shiny men's shoes are, because it's supposed to be indicative of how they are liable to treat their women. A pair of brightly polished, positively gleaming black loafers will cause ladyfolk to dive into your arms expressing undying love and promising unbridled passion, whereas a pair of greying, cracked, unpolished brogues will cause any dame worth her sea salt to give you the full three-point body swerve.

If she actually bothers to talk to you (and that will all depend on how you have rated in the above ten areas), you will then be ranked on your conversation, your sense of humour, and then your smell.

Women aren't necessarily checking to see if you have body odour (because if you do the conversation will not get past 'Hello'), they're seeing what you have 'on'. Are you wearing a lemony designer fragrance, are you covered in the latest TV-advertised musk-based 'bulldozer' scent, or is there a whiff of Ye Olde Worlde England about you, a scent bought from one of those apothecaries you find in trendy little market towns?

What should a man smell like? Should he smell like himself – or should he smell like Giorgio Armani? Or Gianni Versace, Ralph Lauren or, perhaps, Calvin Klein? Today it's possible to buy any designer in a bottle, offering gorgeous smells, a hint of luxury lifestyle and usually a bit of inherited subliminal kudos along the way.

Buy a cologne and you become a Greek god, a Formula One racing driver, an androgynous lounge lizard or a mountaineer. In my time I've been all of these things, and more, but never for very long. The very worst cologne (well, all right, aftershave) I ever wore was, without a doubt, West by Fabergé, which was meant to make me feel like a cowboy, although I distinctly remember smelling more like a horse. West was made by the same people responsible for Brut, perhaps the naffest aftershave of all and – obviously – the first one I ever wore (it was the first aftershave every boy of my generation wore).

The trick with cologne is to steer clear of the pack, and find some-thing a little idiosyncratic, something that becomes part of you. The last thing you want to do is walk into a bar and have one of your friends turn round and say, 'Hey, you're wearing Noir Stud Sport. I wear that!' Because you should never smell like anyone else. Never. In fact if people ask what you're wearing, don't tell them. Be cool. Esoteric. A bit of a doofus. Keep it to yourself. Find something you like, something you've not smelt before – maybe an old classic, a 'vintage' cologne no less – and then make it your signature smell.

My favourite manufacturer is Creed, the 250-year-old Anglo-French company responsible for many bespoke fragrances (Prince Charles, Harrison Ford and Michael Jackson have all been customers), as well as dozens of ready-to-wear smells. Although the industry is trying to move away from citrus colognes (everybody does them these days), citrus is what Creed does best – particularly Green Irish Tweed, which is probably the chicest men's scent in Christendom; a bottled smell like no other, that will intimidate all the others in your bath-room cabinet. Despite being a *millésime* (roughly double the strength of a traditional *eau de toilette*), it is neither overpowering nor overbearing.*

If we are to believe the manufacturers of male deodorant, then men should smell exactly like their advertising. And though men have been taught how to buy boxer shorts and moisturiser, for some reason we are not considered sophisticated enough to want to buy a decent deodorant. Consequently it is always disguised with aggressive adver-tising and packaging. In fact it mirrors the packaging and advertising of tampons and sanitary towels; products that are considered so unseemly by their makers that they have to be disguised as some-thing – anything – else. That's why deodorants tend to be called things like Pine Action!, Blue Force Field!, G-r-r-r-rip!!!! – you get the drift (Blue Action Pine Drift!, if you must know).

The best men's deodorant is actually the unperfumed stuff (usually sold in a plain grey bottle) that can be found in the women's section of most chemists. It doesn't smell of anything – not even deodorant – and so doesn't clash with your own smell, or that of anything you're wearing. Most deodorants and anti-perspirants get a little stale after a few hours, and the sly, putrid smell will insidiously seep into your

---

* Always put your aftershave or cologne on *before* you put your clothes on, other-wise you'll end up with shirts and suits reeking of every designer smell you've ever worn (Giorgio Roberto Christian Jean Paul Hugo Ralph Tommy Versace).

clothes (all perfumed deodorants, regardless of their provenance, will, around six o'clock in the evening, start smelling like dead roses). Unperfumed deodorant doesn't have a big flash across the bottle, and it won't increase your pulling power, but at least you won't smell like a go-faster stripe.**

** My agent, the redoubtable Ed Victor, swears by Caswell-Massey's Jockey Club, probably the most traditional American men's fragrance there is. If you're ever in New York, check out the Caswell-Massey store at 518 Lexington Avenue.

HOW TO DO FANCY DRESS

Never, ever go as your boss

Fancy dress is God's way of mocking us. It's his way of telling us we should be happy as we are, rather than trying to pass ourselves off as Richard Gere in *An Officer and a Gentleman* or John Travolta in *Pulp Fiction*. We are made in his image, a perfectly reasonable image, and then we go and ruin it all by dressing up as Elvis. We squeeze into a much-worn, white studded jumpsuit with butterfly collar and nipped waist, a hot, sweaty wig that appears to be made from horsehair, and the sort of platform boots that haven't seen active service since 1974.

And trust me, it's nearly always Elvis. When I visited a hire shop recently in order to borrow something for our magazine conference, there were over thirty Elvis outfits in a room containing costumes for everyone from Sid Vicious and Ozzy Osbourne to Vicky Pollard and the Blues Brothers. Truly, in the kingdom of the kitsch, the King is still king.

It's always bad era Elvis too, never the snake-hipped country boy with the truck driver's hair and the pastel peg trousers, never the slack-jawed sex-god with the curled lip and the carnival sneer. Of course this is our way of semaphoring the fact that we don't actually think we look good dressed up as someone else, although all it really achieves is letting people know we are totally bereft of imagination.

And that's the problem with fancy dress. Whereas it used to be a celebration of glamour, an aspirational detour from the prosaic nature of everyday life, it's become a reductive way of telling each other that we're not as important – or as good-looking – as celebrities. In reality we're actually mocking ourselves.

I have, I must admit, been pretty good at this myself. Donkey's years ago – or in this case, ass's years ago – I went to a toga party in a part of London that I'm still not sure is actually on the *A-Z*. As I lived on the other side of town, this necessitated a ten-mile cab ride through the East End on a cold Saturday night in April. Which would have been fine. Had the cab not broken down. In the wilds of Bethnal Green. I'm not saying the staff laughed when I walked into Mile End Mini-Cabs at 9.30 that night with a very grumpy Cleopatra in tow, but if you close your eyes for a moment, you can probably still hear the guffaws echoing around certain parts of Essex.

I have even – on one occasion and one occasion only – dressed up as a woman, although it was over twenty years ago and I was at art school at the time. For whatever reason – immaturity, drunkenness, succumbing to latent cross-dressing tendencies – I had taken it upon myself to dress up as Marilyn Monroe, in a shimmering silver cock-tail dress complete with blonde wig, high heels and a fairly convincing shelf that was contained in a black lace bra. As if the sexual codes weren't confused enough, the only person that night to express any sexual interest in me was an unbelievably drunk girl from Solihull, who, in real life, had the misfortune to look like Marilyn herself. Only a really ugly version.

This was the first and last time I've ever dressed up as a woman, although in my defence I have to say I did have a 28-inch waist at the time.

This should have taught me what I later came to learn, that in the pantheon of dead celebrities (or living civilians), one should always

go for the obscure, the idiosyncratic and the unusual. Recognition
helps, but is by no means crucial; and if you want to dress up as 'that
weird bloke from Systems who looks like he wears a codpiece', then
so be it. Principally, you should not only try harder than usual, you
should put so much effort into it that you blow everyone else away.
Seriously, fancy dress is as much about competition as anything else.
Just think of it as a formative version of karaoke.

The best fancy dress outfit I've ever seen made an appearance at
our conference. This took place on Thanksgiving, so it was decided
that we should all dress up as famous Americans. Everyone put an
heroic amount of effort into it, spending weeks getting their outfits
together, and on the night we were treated to Stevie Wonder,
Barbie, Tippi Hedren in Hitchcock's *The Birds*, Marge and Bart
Simpson, Charlie's Angels, John McEnroe, Slash from Guns N'
Roses, Marilyn Manson and thirty other wonderful re-creations.
There was only ever going to be one winner, though. As we assembled in the banqueting hall of our country house hotel, slapping
each other on the back or tentatively asking, 'Er, I don't get it. Who
are you?', a porter arrived from the lobby pushing a trolley. On it
was our Deputy Art Director, strapped to a piece of board, head
shaved, dressed in blue overalls and a purpose-built (well, bought
on the Internet) brown mask. He received a standing ovation, some
fava beans, and a nice Chianti.

And if I needed any further evidence that, as far as possible, and as
far as I am concerned, fancy dress should be avoided, I was offered
some a few weeks later by someone at a party celebrating a mutual
friend's fortieth birthday. As this bizarrely dressed chap tried to move
round us in the crowd – wearing a multi-coloured high-necked shirt,
a velvet suit of indeterminate colour, and the sort of patent leather
shoes they could use to bounce sunlight into outer space – my wife
asked him who he had come as.

'Oh, do you like it? I've come as the editor of *GQ*.'

Some tips:

1   If you can, make the outfit yourself, rather than going to a hire shop. *Everybody* gets their stuff from a hire shop.

2   Look on the Internet for unusual costumes.

3   Ask someone to make it for you.

4   Don't choose an outfit that's too hot, or that you can't eat in.

5   Don't go as a woman unless you know you can carry it off. Seriously, how are your legs?

6   Wigs get hot.

7   Fancy dress is fundamentally unfair, as it encourages women to look overtly stupid, and men to look ridiculous. So come as Cary Grant or Clark Gable. And carry it off.

8   Have a sense of arrogance about you.

9   Think chic: the masked balls of yesteryear were incredibly sophisticated events; why make yours feel like a rugby club reunion?

10   No Nazi regalia, please. Not even royalty can get away with this.

11   If you're going to be wearing a moustache, don't make it too gay.

12   In fact, don't wear the moustache.

13   Choose a character and an outfit you can dance in. Does the Incredible Hulk dance? Does King Kong?

14   Can you pee easily?

15   Can you sit down in it?

16   Don't come to the party with a plastic penis strapped to your forehead, and announce to the assembled multitude that you've come as 'Dickhead'. Because 'Dickhead' is how you shall be known from now on.

17 There will be music at this party, and at some point in the evening some bright spark will decide to start playing records appropriate to the characters in the room. So if you've come as Travolta in *Saturday Night Fever*, make sure you can dance to 'Staying Alive'.

18 Ditto *The Blues Brothers*.

19 Ditto 'YMCA'.

Good Ideas: Tom Ford, Captain America, David Niven, Paul Simonen, Tom Wolfe, the 1995 spring/summer Gucci campaign, Robert DeNiro in *Taxi Driver*, Samuel L. Jackson in *Pulp Fiction*, Michael Caine in *The Ipcress File*, Lawrence Harvey, David Bowie circa *Young Americans*, James Blunt (you might get laid), Angelina Jolie, any outfit involving a military uniform or a white suit, and David Bowie again in *The Man Who Fell to Earth*.

Bad Ideas: Austin Powers, Meat Loaf, Pete Doherty, Cher, David Bowie circa *Labyrinth*, Van Morrison, Rod Stewart, Charlie Chaplin, David Beckham, Liam Gallagher, Barry White, any politician, anyone from a reality TV show, footballers, and anyone apart from the above who could conceivably be in Madame Tussaud's.

HOW TO HANDLE A CELEBRITY

Float like a butterfly or sting like a bee?

Many people in my industry love meeting celebs, and think that knowing them will make them better at their jobs, more famous, or closer to being celebrities themselves. And what sad people they are. I always shy away from meeting famous people if possible because it just looks as if you're brown-nosing, or sucking up to them in the most base way. And, frankly, anyone can do that. If I can become friends with A Famous Person on my own terms, without having to turn into a raging sycophant, then great. But I can't do it the other way.

However, as there are now so many famous people in the world – mainly due to the success of reality TV shows – it stands to reason that you're probably going to bump into one. Tomorrow. In your local Modern Ukrainian Tapas bar. So what do you do, and how do you handle them?

Well, the first and most important thing you have to understand is the fact that THEY HAVE A HUGE EGO. Such a huge ego, that they won't be particularly interested in talking about anything other than themselves. So anticipate having a fairly one-sided conversation. Genuflect. Laugh. Act like they are the funniest, most incisive person you've ever met. Because that's exactly what they expect. Yes, you can talk about yourself for a while, but make it snappy, so they can get back to talking about themselves.

And will they thank you for telling them you love them, adore their work, have followed them since you were a boy? Not really; they expect that from everyone.

I've spent over twenty years meeting celebrities, but only a handful have become proper friends. Mostly I've been in the position of meeting them for a particular purpose, usually interviewing them for whatever publication I was working for at the time. And while I realise that this isn't a situation that everyone finds themselves in, understanding the process of interviewing celebrities can come in handy when you're interviewing potential employees, or indeed anyone who needs prising open.

So how do you go about interviewing a famous person? The celebrity interview has been so devalued, so diminished by the extraordinary number of people who are now famous, that it's often difficult to think of them as anything other than glorified press releases.

Years ago, in the golden days of long-form journalism – when any new journalist worth his ink would spend the best part of six months with his subject before finally filing his copy – the celebrity interview was 'a very important thing'. But now, in a world in which TV's *Big Brother* makes celebrities out of nobodies, where fame is so homogenised, is conducting an interview still a skill?

Time and restrictions are hugely important to the success rate of the celebrity interview, and if you've only been allowed ten minutes or so, then it's best to go armed simply with twenty quick-fire questions that you can turn into a breezy Q&A (Q: You're trapped in a lift with Angelina Jolie, Kylie Minogue and Jodie Marsh. With a gun to your head, which one do you have sex with? Q: What colour is Tuesday?). Conversely, if you can convince your celeb to spend a few days with you, driving through the Hollywood Hills and hanging out at private views and film premieres, then so be it. This is obviously the best way to get to know your subject and, who knows, they might even become your new best friend. It's totally possible to build up a relationship with a celebrity over a period of time, and though they will expect you to treat them with slightly more decorum than they get from your bog-standard hack, the access afforded will, on occasion, counteract any sycophancy.

Any decent interview needs a certain amount of compromise; there needs to be a modicum of give and take. Ideally it should be an 'I win, you win' situation, with both parties coming away feeling as though their lives have been enriched – if only in a small way. Both parties need to give, and interviewees need to be generous with their time and anecdotes.

I once interviewed Gwyneth Paltrow on the set of *Shakespeare in Love* for the *Sunday Times Magazine* and she couldn't have been less interested. She offered nothing but monosyllabic answers, giving a good impression of someone who'd rather be picking skewers out of her eyeballs than talking to me. As for myself, it was an enervating experience, so, having not got what I needed, I proceeded to interview everyone else on set: the carpenters, the caterers, the sound guys, her chauffeur, the studio concierge, the make-up girls, the hairdressers – anyone I could find who had anything to do with her. I wasn't looking for a particularly negative story but, given Paltrow's unwillingness to talk to me, I had to get a story somehow. The feedback I got from those around her was not exactly positive. So, in the end, she got what she deserved, which is a shame – for her. I'm an easy person to charm, and if she had spent half an hour working her magic on me, no doubt I would have come away thinking Gwyneth Paltrow was a born-again Audrey Hepburn. But she didn't, so I didn't.

Probably my most open interview subject was Shirley MacLaine, who I interviewed around the same time, at her home in Malibu in

California. In her fifty-year career she has been interviewed by – I would guess – thousands of journalists, and was well past caring what any of them said about her. She didn't know who I was, and didn't care probably, but she had a project to puff and so was willing to spend two hours with me, talking about anything I wanted to – Sinatra, her brother Warren Beatty, JFK, the mob, whatever. She had been turned over by better people than me, and she was never going to read my piece so it didn't matter anyway – she had agreed to an interview and an interview was what she was going to give. She showed real class, not like some of the fifteen-minute celebs we get these days.

Journalists' techniques are fascinating. When A.A. Gill was interviewed by Lynn Barber a few years ago, he said it was like being interrogated by Columbo. 'Oh, Adrian. Just one more thing: you said you were wearing a cummerbund fashioned from yak gut and corduroy on the day in question. Where exactly did you say you bought it?'

Myself, I don't think I've ever been particularly good at it, even though I've interviewed hundreds of famous people in the past two decades. For years, I made the cardinal error of trying to impress the people in front of me; I wanted them to like me, wanted them to understand how bright I was, and how well-versed I was in their work. I wanted Paul McCartney to think I was the only person who really understood why he was the most talented Beatle, and wanted Keith Richards to think of me as a made man, a groovy young guy who never went to bed and had taken nearly as many drugs as he had. When I met George Bush in Dubai a few years ago, I tried, in the space of two minutes, to impress upon him that my view of the Gulf War was more incisive than anyone else's. I even tried to contradict Shirley MacLaine's anecdotes about Sinatra.

Fool. *Just shut up and let them talk*. That's what you've got to do. Ask a question, let the famous person start rambling, and then occasionally steer them in the direction of the place you want to end up. My biggest sin has probably been interrupting. You know, just as Nicole Kidman was about to tell me who she had been taking crack with last night (that's a joke, by the way: I know that Nicole Kidman doesn't take crack), I'd butt in with: 'That's great, Nicole, but tell me about that scene in *Eyes Wide Shut* where . . .'

My worst-ever interview, or at least the one I was least involved with (so it may actually have been one of my best), was in 1998, with Woody Allen in the Dorchester in London. As soon as I shook his hand I started thinking about Frank Sinatra's cock. Why? Well, Woody used to sleep with Mia Farrow, who, years before, used to sleep with Sinatra. So I instantly realised that I was only one sex organ away from Frank's Johnson. This thought preoccupied me throughout my chat with Woody. It may, as I say, have been a good thing indeed (I didn't keep interrupting him . . .).

In general, my problem was I couldn't bear for there to be any gaps in the conversation, and in that respect I'm probably like a lot of journalists. But the trick is to let the celebrity fill that space because, in reality, they're just as embarrassed by the silence as you. I know one journo who is a master at this: a man who thinks nothing of keeping silent for two, three, four minutes after his subject has temporarily stopped talking, thus forcing the star to start burbling about nothing in particular. Or, more pertinently, everything in particular.

Sometimes, with celebrities, you are told to adhere to ridiculous restrictions, so you're forced to resort to nonsensical methods. When David Bowie was involved with Tin Machine, he initially refused to do any interviews unless the rest of the band were present. This put a lot of people off, but when Tony Parsons interviewed them, he turned the situation to his advantage in the most obvious way: he ignored Bowie – for 45 minutes. In that time, he quizzed Bowie's backing band (which is essentially what they were) about stage dynamics, recording techniques and group compositions, until the 'Thin White Duchess' could take it no more. Bowie almost exploded into the conversation, falling over himself to tell Tony the reason for his solo volte-face, and his frustrations with the music industry. By ignoring him, Tony got an extraordinary interview.

Another way to avoid the dark tunnel of product-specific-questions is to confront the interviewee with 'the problem'.

'Hi, Tom. Your PR says that I can only ask questions about the film, but you don't mind talking about your sex life, do you? I mean, how does being gay affect your faith?'

'My PR said that? I don't mind at all. I've got some pictures on my phone of me having sex in church, if you'd like to see them.'

Of course, this won't always work but, as a journalist, you must assume that the PRs' restrictions are rarely imposed by the stars themselves. And even if they are, you can usually cajole your celeb into talking about the subject – if only in a defensive way.

With most famous people, there will be one question that is forever off-limits: one question that history has taught you to avoid. With Hugh Grant, it's his experience with Divine Brown; with Madonna, *Swept Away* (the shocking film directed by her husband Guy Ritchie); and as for Michael Jackson . . . Well, take your pick.

But you have to ask it. You just have to. Mark Ellen, the very brilliant former editor of *Smash Hits*, *Q* and now *The Word*, has a fail-safe way of asking 'the difficult question'. Throughout the interview he will say things like, 'Look, I know you won't want to talk about the thing, but I'm gonna bring it up later,' or 'That's all very well, but I must warn you that we're going to have a little bit of a fight later!' Mark says, 'It softens them up – lets them know you're going to ask something they don't especially want to answer. So by the time you get around to it, they're almost relieved.'

Once, many moons ago, when I worked on the *Observer*, we were offered an interview with Eddie Murphy who, at the time, was enjoying a second flush of fame. However, the product Eddie was pushing was a fairly useless rap record, and his Hollywood publicist told us that he would only answer questions relating to this particular project. Not only that, but we were only to be given forty minutes and it was to be in Los Angeles – not a cheap place at the best of times. Oh, and the PR had to sit in on the interview. Great! Just about the only thing they didn't demand was copy approval, but it was still a tall order. We ummed and aahed about it, and then decided it was too good an opportunity to miss; we'd have to find someone good enough to exploit the situation, to squeeze a few salacious drops from the over-wrung dishcloth. That person, we decided, was Hugh McIlvanney, the greatest sports writer the world has ever known (Scottish, gruff, then already in his sixties, known to like a drink).

Now, we could have picked someone whose job it was to interview celebs, or we could have chosen someone famous themselves (Lenny Henry? Stephen Fry?). We thought about a flirty female who could flutter her eyelashes and cross/recross her legs; we even considered the likes of Martin Amis (who was then writing for us). In the end we decided we needed someone with some very specific attributes: who wasn't going to be intimidated (by anyone), who knew nothing about hip-hop (thus eliminating the need for any protracted discussions about 'inspirations', 'motivations', choice of drum machines, choice of producers, etc), who was smart enough to sidestep the PR's restrictions, and clever enough to run rings around Eddie himself. And that person was obviously Hugh.

Boy, did we choose the right person. The interview Hugh came back with was remarkable, covering all aspects of the comedian's life: his movies, girlfriends, ambitions, race, politics, sex – the lot. Oh, and there was even stuff about the record (the awful, pitiful record). So how had Hugh done it? The tape of the interview did the rounds in the office for weeks afterwards, and it was almost a masterclass in the art of interviewing difficult, protected and self-protective celebrities. Stupidly, pathetically, I have since lost the tape, but I still remember Hugh's opening question as though he asked it only yesterday . . .

'So, Eddie. I must say that this new record of yours is quite a remarkable thing. I'm not an aficionado of this sort of music at all, but the way in which you paint yourself as the catalyst for this furore around you – the instigator – it strikes me that you are a man totally in charge of his destiny, if indeed that's what we can call it. How did the making of the record, of all the things you've done, affect the way you see yourself? How does this latest project redefine you as a man?'

Thinking about it now, the actual question was probably four times as long as this, but the convoluted way in which Hugh approached his subject – and the meandering way in which he asked the question – opened Eddie Murphy up like an oyster. And, for the next two hours, the comedian talked, and talked, and talked and talked. Which, after all, was the object of the exercise.

And the record? The pathetic rap record Eddie was so keen to puff? It wasn't a hit.

HOW TO CONQUER KARAOKE

Because it's not all about 'Angels', you know

Karaoke brings out the beast in all of us. It is not only a great leveller, but also tells us more about ourselves than we perhaps like to think. Shove a microphone under someone's nose and watch their true character emerge. Not slowly, but immediately, like a light switch. Or, more appropriately, a Kleig light.

In some ways karaoke is a less onanistic form of air guitar, and while running your fingers up and down an imaginary fretboard to the strains of 'Money for Nothing' or 'Sweet Child of Mine' is not exactly a dignified occupation, at least most men only do it in the privacy of their bedrooms (unless, of course, they're Mark Knopfler or Slash, who regularly do it front of hundreds of thousand of adoring fans). Singing 'Angels' in front of a room full of people you don't know is a totally different proposition altogether.

Even celebrities do it. Paul McCartney likes to tackle old Buddy Holly songs and early Beatles hits, Apple's Steve Jobs apparently likes a bit of Bob Dylan, and I know for a fact that – after a few shandies – James Nesbitt can sing Gilbert O'Sullivan's entire back catalogue without any encouragement at all.

I once interviewed the Conservative leader David Cameron, and as a parting shot I asked him what his default karaoke song was. His response, while hardly extraordinary, seemed totally genuine. After expressing a fondness for Pulp's 'Babies' ('It's a brilliant song to sing along to. When I'm falling asleep in the car when I'm driving, then I sing, as it's a really good way to stay awake') and for Bob Dylan's *Nashville Skyline* and *Blood on the Tracks*, he finally owned up.

'I've only ever done it overseas,' he said. 'I don't think it's something you want to do in your own country. I did once win a karaoke competition in Portland. I can't remember what it was. It was that terrible Chrissie Hynde, UB40 duet . . .'

'"I Got You, Babe"?'

'"I Got You, Babe" . . .'

Like I said, hardly extraordinary, but at least indicative of Cameron's willingness to share a stage. Which might come in handy if he ever has to form a coalition government.

In the same way that cocaine is God's way of telling you you've got too much money, so karaoke is God's way of letting you know you've drunk too much. Which is why you should be careful what you try to sing after drinking your bodyweight in cheap white wine. Default karaoke songs you are absolutely not allowed include the following: 'I Will Survive' (the default proclamation of secretaries who have just been dumped), 'Bohemian Rhapsody' (indicative of a misspent youth – i.e. you're a nerd), 'I Will Always Love You' (not even Whitney can sing like Whitney any more), 'Wonderwall' (every Swedish tourist's song of choice), 'Girls Just Wanna Have Fun' (sung by the dumped secretary after six drinks too many) or anything by Abba, Elvis or Bob Marley. And on no account ever attempt anything in too high a register, such as Michael Jackson, Justin Timberlake or the Bee Gees, because just as you're beginning to think you're doing OK, the key will shift up a few gears and you'll be left stranded, high and dry, trying to find a falsetto you almost certainly don't have.

To encourage an encore, eager karaoke singers tend to choose either magnificently overwrought ballads, or the sort of crowd-pleasers you hear buskers ruining outside underground stations. And that, essentially, is the problem: if, at any time, you think you could be mistaken for a busker, then you should quietly slip off stage, march straight to the door, and walk all the way home, never to darken a karaoke club again.

A friend of mine used to say that he knew it was time to go home when someone started singing 'American Pie', although the modern-day taxi-call has to be 'Angels', a song so regularly, wantonly ruined, it's become almost as embarrassing as 'My Way'. But beware of dismissing Sinatra completely. While I would never attempt his favourite valediction, I am a huge Frank fan, and if pushed on to a karaoke podium will gladly work my way through 'Summer Wind', 'Autumn Leaves', 'Learnin' the Blues' or 'Same Old Saturday Night'.

You see, for men, it's always best to croon. Great crooners tend to take leisurely walks through their songs, and whether you're trying to emulate Sinatra, Tony Bennett, Dean Martin or Nick Cave, you can usually get away with it as long as you focus on style and inflection, rather than simply trying to carry the tune. Successful crooners sing within a narrow register, and that makes it easier to follow their intonation. Sinatra used to say that he talked most of his songs, and if you analyse his records, you can see what he means. This is especially true of the later stuff he recorded when his voice couldn't jump up and down the way it used to.

So whether you're attempting to sing 'Fly Me to the Moon', 'More Than Words' or 'Drive-In Saturday' (and let me tell you that David Bowie is the best crooner still treading the boards), all you need is a snap-brimmed Fedora, a tumbler of Tennessee sipping whisky and a melancholy disposition. Everyone sounds good singing 'Love on the Rocks' (if you don't believe me, then I suggest you try it).

And if some drunken secretary climbs up on the stage, puts a sweaty arm around you and asks if you want to duet on 'Somethin' Stupid', then act like a man.

Ignore her.

Notes & quavers:

• Never sing a duet with someone you don't know, because they will – trust me on this – spill red wine all over your brand-new white suit (Have I forgiven her? Not yet . . .).

• Everybody has the childhood dream of pretending to be a singer and miming into a hairbrush, but be careful not to let this show. The trick, as with most leisure pursuits, is to be good at it without looking as if you spend every minute of your free time practising.

• Group singing is pointless, and being part of a gang of six blokes shouting 'Rebel Rebel', 'American Idiot' or 'The Boys Are Back in Town' will make you seem a little, well, immature.

• If you attempt a song that's too big for you, you'll look like an early, unsuccessful contestant on *X Factor* or *Pop Idol*.

• Never butt in on someone's performance when they're obviously taking it seriously, as you'll embarrass both of you. This is especially important in Japan, where karaoke originated. There they take it i-n-c-r-e-d-i-b-l-y seriously.

• Don't attempt songs with long instrumental passages (what are you going to do now?) or that have a broad register.

• Oh, and did I mention 'Angels'?

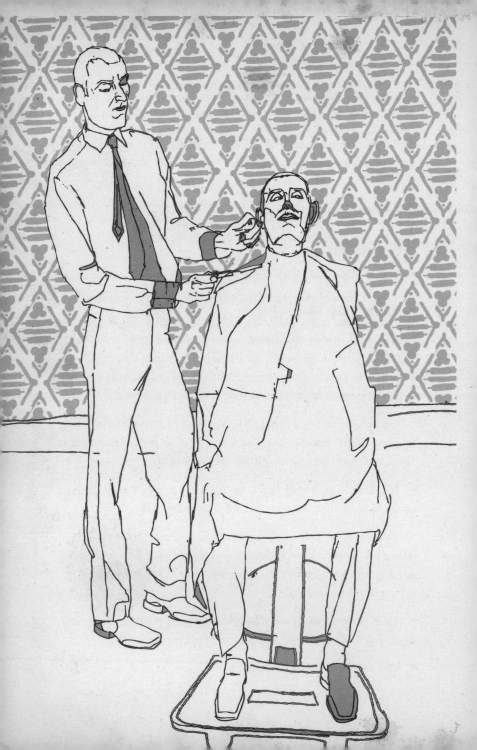

HEALTH
&
EFFICIENCY

HOW TO STOP SMOKING

Why cigarettes only look cool in old black and white photographs of dead movie stars

Be a man; just stop. Go cold turkey and stop being such a wuss. This is what I did. Smoking is a stupid habit and you should be able to kick it without making a fuss. Yes, you can read Alan Carr's book (it's worked for lots of people I know), or you can wear nicotine patches, or chew gum, or get yourself hypnotised. You can cut down until you eventually stop, or you can tell yourself you're only going to smoke in the evening, or only on certain days. You can do all of these things and more, although I'm not really sure why you need a crutch, or even an excuse really. Before I gave up I had never tried to stop, or even to cut down. I didn't because I really liked smoking – not all of the time, you realise, not when I woke up in the morning – I never reached for one on the bedside cabinet – but always with a glass of wine or after a meal. And take me to a bar and I'd hoover up twenty in a couple of hours.

But, like everyone else who has ever smoked, one day I realised it wasn't a very smart thing to do.

I decided to give up on New Year's Eve not long after I passed forty. We were having dinner with friends in Chantilly, near Paris, and I was the only guest out of twenty people who smoked. Every forty minutes or so I would disappear into the garden to have an illicit cigarette, naïvely hoping that no one would notice. But of course not only did they notice my absence, but the host knew exactly what I was doing. Why? Because I stank. When you eventually give up smoking your sense of smell suddenly returns like a long-lost friend, while cigarette smoke (or the remnants of) will cause you to gag. You will then feel yourself disappear into a deep, dark cloud of shame, knowing that for years non-smokers have been able to smell you coming. (Your clothes stank too.) You'll also soon find it impossible to sit in smoky pubs and soak up 'the atmosphere'.

That night, as soon as my host accused me of smoking, I knew I had to give up. The reasons were manifold: (1) Most people I knew had already stopped. (2) My children hated it (I told them it was a disgusting habit, so why was I doing it myself?). (3) I had smoked for far too long and didn't want to die. (4) I realised I was being appallingly anti-social (yes, I realise this was a long time coming, but at least I got there in the end – as I said, all smokers eventually do).

So I stopped, and immediately began to feel better. There are certain things you should do if you're going cold turkey, and they're relatively simple (simple compared to dying, that is). You might want to think about spending more time with people who don't smoke. It's all very well thinking that it doesn't matter whether or not your friends smoke, but it does. You should also start exercising; this will not only help prevent that thickening around the waist which can follow giving up, but it will also make you even more fervently anti-smoking.

The object of the exercise is to demonise the act itself, so you need to distance yourself from people and places associated with cigarettes. With the recent legislation concerning smoking in public places, this is obviously easier than it used to be, but you need to be vigilant. Throw all your cigarettes away, including the ones you once kept for emergencies, and even the foreign ones you've kept because of their strange, funny boxes. Throw away all your ashtrays, and make it known to your friends that you no longer want them smoking in your house. Usually, when you give up suddenly, the smell of cigarette smoke will be as enticing as the smell of freshly brewed coffee, but trust me, after a while the smell will, as I said, make you feel physically sick.

Was it easy to stop? Not especially, but I did it. You just have to make a pact with yourself. You need to make the decision and stick with it.

Rather foolishly, when I stopped I immediately decided to start smoking cigars, thinking this would (a) make me look cool and (b) satisfy any pangs I might have for cigarettes. Actually I don't think it did either, and really just put off the inevitable for a little longer. Smoking cigars is immensely enjoyable, but ex-smokers always think that they'll get a sly lung-full of smoke while telling anyone who will listen that they never, ever inhale. (And, of course, you've still got something to do with your hands.) So I gave up smoking cigars too, and now there is as much room in my life for smoking as there is room for contemporary dance, the recorded works of Dido or the novels of Barbara Cartland.

So just stop it, will you? Don't you feel ever so slightly embarrassed about being addicted to something that hasn't really been cool for over thirty years? James Dean and Steve McQueen are both dead, and even David Bowie (once the coolest smoker of them all) gave up eventually. Michael Caine stopped smoking cigars when he reached seventy because he felt enormously lucky to have lived so long and didn't want to tempt fate. And the rest of us have given up because we don't want to die either. So why don't you do it?

Smoking was considered cool in the 1950s and 1960s, when it was still thought to be rebellious and anti-establishment. Back then, smoking meant cowboy hats, jazz, black and white poster boys, boxes of Winston poking out of cap-sleeved T-shirts, and bespoke gangsters in velvet-lined cocktail bars sipping exotic martinis and wooing inappropriate women. But not any more. Today, smoking is associated with the underclass, with the poor, undernourished, overburdened, ill-educated single mother of four living in a condemned sink estate with nothing to look forward to other than the next Lambert & Butler.

You, on the other hand, have absolutely no excuse not to quit.

Go on, be a man.

HOW TO LOOK AFTER YOUR SKIN (WITHOUT FEELING LIKE A GIRL)

Super-action-hyper-age-defying-active-sex-mud

How do you take care of yourself without looking like a powder-puffed metrosexual? Is there a pumped-up beauty regime out there for men like you? Will cleansing lotion really put lead in your pencil?

Are you man or mousse?

Time was, back in the day, when real men didn't mess with this stuff. No moisturiser, no maximum hydrator, no alcohol-free toner. Back in the 1970s, women were lucky if their men even used deodorant, let alone something as exotic as aftershave. If cleanliness really is next to Godliness, then any man who reached adolescence during the Decade That Taste Forgot looked more like a heathen.

And until about ten years ago I was one of them. I shaved, brushed my teeth, used moisturiser occasionally and wore a cologne – Creed's Green Irish Tweed, which I still like – but I didn't feel the need to smother myself in essential oils and wonder creams, and my comfort zone was replete without refirming complexes, real peels, dusting powders, tightening gels, visibly revitalising masks and all the other beauty products aimed at the postwhatever man.

Until recently there weren't men's sections in chemists, there weren't even men's products, because the whole idea of men's grooming products was anathema to heterosexual men, as well as a lot of gay men. British men just didn't understand the idea of keeping themselves fresh, clean or attractive. Even ten years ago the notion of spending more than a few minutes 'getting yourself together in the morning' was considered effeminate, or even gay. Men only became well-groomed, ponced-up, slicked-back gods in the 1990s.

The market for men's toiletries has risen in the UK by 20 per cent in the last six years. This has gone hand in hand with the growth in advertising. And it seems to be working. We spent £6.47 billion on fashion and accessories in 1999 and £7.33 billion in 2004.

And this is one area where men's magazines have helped the beauty industry enormously. We have, particularly at the posh broadsheet end of the market, encouraged our readers to experiment with grooming products, and to understand that it's no longer enough to throw on a fancy suit and splash on some aftershave in the hope of seducing the object of your dreams – you have to wash, clean your skin, smell nice, pluck your eyebrows, look after your fingernails, look toned, tanned, and less like the traditional British playboys of old.

In the interests of research, I once spent a weekend road-testing a bathroom cabinet full of potions, lotions and cream-coloured notions. I tried age-defying formulas, high-potency serums, eye contour gels, crystal deodorants, terracotta bronzants and a type of active mud – a jar of anchovy-tinted greeny-brown gunk that unnervingly resembled a pasta sauce I'd made some days before (after a thorough application, I looked as though I were going on manoeuvres). It wasn't the most successful weekend as I found most of the products disappointing. Not only did they fail to do what they claimed they'd do, but they used such extraordinarily convoluted language not to do so.

One of the products actually did more than it promised, far, far more – unfortunately. The Atomic Hi-Intensity Gonzo Bronzer was definitely not for me; possibly because it was basically a brown blusher for blokes, possibly because I've never wanted the sort of tandoori tan enjoyed by George Hamilton and George Michael, but more probably because my wife said it made me look like an organic carrot with thyroid problems.

Another, a hair product, was meant to give my 'thatch' extra vitality and body. Soon after applying it, my wife – who was having something of a field day – remarked that I looked as if I'd covered my head with olive oil, which is a look I gave up years ago. I washed out the olive oil with a Philip Kingsley shampoo, something of a novelty because it was one of the few products I tried all weekend that actually did what I expected it to. In this case, it stopped me smelling like a cheap Italian restaurant.

The highlight of my two-day quest for inner personal grooming, however, was something called an 'early morning mask', which was meant to give me a 'unique facial experience'. Sadly, I could only assume this meant making me feel as though I had just covered my face in chilli-flavoured toothpaste. And is it not superfluous to have 'Not to be taken internally' printed on the bottle? Surely this is about as useful as having a sign on the dashboard of your car saying 'Do not drive underwater'.

But in the last few years I've become something of a convert, and have embraced this brave new world of men's grooming with vigour. Having been lucky enough to work in an office where I've been bombarded by inordinate amounts of royal oils and cream dreams, I've had plenty of time to experiment, and I now cleanse, scrub, tweak, tease, spray, peel and wipe with the authority of a professional beauty therapist. Face masks are a breeze, super serums no longer give me the willies, and astringents make me positively glow. Beauty products actually do work, and all it takes to understand them is a bit of education.

There's a revolution happening out there, guys, and it's happening whether you like it or not. So if I were you, I'd grab some fruit-acid serums, a few hydromineral scrubs and a super antioxidant complex and get in line.

You're in the aftershave balmy now.

Does an interest in grooming diminish a man's masculinity? Only if they're insecure. And as you're not, here is what you need – the essentials:

1 Cleanser: removes dirt and grime from your skin. Use it twice a day with cotton wool.

2 Moisturiser: keeps the skin in good condition, and helps stop wrinkles. Rub it on in the morning after you shave and then again after washing your face at night. A good moisturiser should contain antioxidant cream, be fragrance free, and have a high SPF factor (to protect you from winter and summer sun).

3 Exfoliating scrub: removes dead skin from the face. Use it once a week and be careful not to do it too near the eyes.

4 Eye cream: helps slow down the ageing process around the eyes.

5 Drink at least a litre of water a day – it really will do wonders for your skin.

6 Foods that will benefit your skin include salmon, carrots, nuts, sunflower seeds, spinach and avocado.

7 If you have particularly oily skin, try using a skin toner or an astringent. These will help close unsightly large pores.

8 If you have problem or acutely sensitive skin, then be careful which products you use. And if you're suffering from undue redness on the face, then try visiting a Chinese herbalist. A lot of skin problems are caused by bad diet, irregular ablutions, or stress, and Chinese medicine is especially well-equipped to deal with this.

9   Always carry a lip-balm, as your lips get cracked far more than you realise.

10 If you're still unsure about buying beauty products, or want to experiment with more products, visit a department store; increasingly these are displaying products according to function rather than brand. Their assistants are also trained to help you. Sure, they're principally there to sell you stuff, but they know that men are only going to become repeat customers if they like the results. So indulge yourself a little. As Kyan Douglas from *Queer Eye for the Straight Guy* says, 'Your skin is your armour and also your weakest link. Nothing else is as vulnerable to life's elements, and yet nothing is as easily ignored by men as the health and well-being of the skin they're in.'

HOW TO WET SHAVE

Because in the end it's all about technique

The mistake made by men who complain about getting five o'clock shadow just after lunch is shaving too soon after they wake up. The hair follicles on your face take at least half an hour to fully expand after you awake, so you should re-order your morning routine and start shaving only after half an hour.

Then, wash your face quickly with warm water, and cover your stubble with whatever shaving foam or cream you use. Then take your razor and begin shaving. New products and new razors are launched every month, and while they all endeavour to supersede all the products and razors that went before them, they're all so sophisticated nowadays that you should really only concern yourself with technique.

First, using a downward stroke, cut a horizontal line across the side-burns, making sure it's the same height on both sides. Always cut them quite close to the top of the ear, because if you cut them lower, everyone – and I really do mean everyone – will think you're trying to make a statement, and why would anyone be so dumb as to try and make a statement by the length of their sideburns?

Then, begin shaving, always from the bottom of the neck, and always with upward strokes. As you pull the blade up, finish the sweep by lifting it away from the skin. Do it methodically, shaving each part of your neck completely before moving on. Start with the lower neck, then the chin and the sides of your face, and finish with the upper lip, to which you obviously need to pay close attention. Always shave this area with upward strokes; if you use downward strokes, you run the risk of only partially cutting the hair, and thus making it more difficult to cut when you try again.

Make sure you finish shaving before you begin washing the cream off; it's when you go back to clean up after you've done this – with a shave here and a shave there – that a lot of cuts happen (because you're shaving directly on to the skin, without cream). Get to know the contours of your face, and learn how to shave quickly without cutting yourself. Frankly, coming into work with a face covered in blood is embarrassing.

If shaving irritates your skin, then try a medicated cream (although they all claim to be medicated in one way or another), and if it continues to hurt afterwards, then maybe you need to start using an electric razor (millions of men do).

After you've finished, leave it a few minutes before putting on aftershave or cologne, because it'll sting. And if it stings too much, or you want to smooth your skin afterwards, then use a perfumed aftershave balm (most designer colognes now come in a balm).

The Rules:

1   Use a magnifying shaving mirror, as they're the only way of guaranteeing you do the job properly. You really don't want to be sitting in a meeting, composing your response to something or other, and, in the process of running your hand around your neck and face, find a clump of hair you've missed. It's not the end of the world, but if the meeting's not going well, the irritation will grow exponentially.

2   Shave before you go out in the evening.

3   Most cuts to the face are caused by blunt razors.

4   If you find yourself without shaving foam, lather some soap.

5   The more stubble you have, the closer your shave will be. It's easier to shave longer hair – the closest shave you will ever have will be when you shave off your beard (which, by rights, you shouldn't really have had in the first place).

HOW TO CHECK IF YOUR BREATH SMELLS

Don't wait for someone to offer you some gum

First, make damn sure no one is watching. Then lick your wrist from the back of your tongue to the very tip. Let it dry for about ten seconds, and then sniff. If you don't like what you smell, it's guaranteed that no one else will either. Then you can go and buy your own gum. Note: it sounds almost too obvious to mention, but if you've ever had bad breath (and that's everyone reading this book), by rights you should aim to brush your teeth, use mouthwash or chew gum before any serious meeting where you're going to be in close proximity to somebody else. You have to believe that deals get scuppered because of bad breath (I've avoided people because of their bad breath, or turned away from them at dinner). Having bad breath doesn't make you a bad person, so check it – regularly (especially if you drink a lot of coffee).

HOW TO GIVE MOUTH-TO-MOUTH RESUSCITATION

Finally, it's time to kiss a man

For reasons beyond your ken, there is suddenly a casualty on the floor in front of you who appears to be unconscious, and who appears not to be breathing. Which means you – yes, you – have to start giving him mouth-to-mouth.

MTM, or CPR (cardiopulmonary resuscitation – a combination of rescue breathing and chest compression) is important in providing ventilation during cardiac arrest and is the primary resuscitation technique for children with respiratory arrest, as well as drowning and drug overdose. These days it's even more important that you're able to perform it, as the fear of contracting HIV continues to deter people – even professionals – from doing it themselves.

This is how you do it:

1 Quickly loosen their clothing and make sure they're not constricted by anything like a tie or a belt.

2 Now open the airway by lying the casualty on his back on a flat surface, opening his mouth and tilting the head back so his chin is elevated.

3 Clamp the victim's nostrils shut with your fingers, making an airtight seal over his mouth with yours, and start breathing into it with gusto. You should blow hard every five seconds.

4 Start checking the carotid arteries (the large blood vessels on either side of the voice box) for a pulse.

5 If there is still no pulse, then you need to start the chest compressions, pushing down on his chest with both hands, one on top of the other. You need to get into a fairly furious rhythm for this, as you need to press down about eighty times a minute. Continue giving breaths at the rate of about ten to twelve each minute, alternating with chest compressions. Do this until the casualty starts to breathe on his own, until a qualified person relieves you, or until you become too tired to continue (in which case, let someone else have a go).

HOW TO STOP A NOSEBLEED

Because sometimes you'll have to

Nosebleeds are often associated with children but, make no mistake, they affect adults all the time. They can be caused by almost anything – congestion, infection, common colds, blowing your nose too much (the usual reason), hypertension or, more obviously, simply being punched in the face. These days, they occur when people have been doing bucket-loads of cocaine (nosebleeds happen when the membranes tear, and this accelerates it like nothing else). Bizarrely, they can also be caused by air-conditioning, by sneezing too much, and – whisper this, in case you're passing it on – by actually picking your nose too much.

Now, if a nosebleed happens at home, you just end up with a stained carpet and a dirty tea towel. But if it happens at work, then suddenly you are the centre of attention. Just what have you been doing to warrant such an attack?

So the best thing to do is to get rid of it without delay.

1   Take your shirt off. Quickly.

2   First you need to pinch your nose between your thumb and forefinger and gently apply pressure to the septum – that thin piece

of bone that separates your nostrils that is usually the first thing to disappear if you've been taking too much cocaine over a prolonged period. Hold them there for fifteen minutes.

3 The most common mistake people make when they have a nosebleed is leaning their head backwards. It feels natural, so we do it, but it's wrong. You must *lean your head forwards, not backwards*, so the blood doesn't drip down your throat. Not only will this stop you swallowing a lot of blood, it will also stop you gagging. Important, this. Besides, the object is not to divert the flow of blood but to block it, so that it clots.

4 Breathe through your mouth.

5 After the fifteen minutes is up, apply a soft, cold compress around your nose as you continue to hold it with your thumb and forefinger.

6 Once the bleeding has stopped, on no account lie down, and try to keep your nose above your heart.

7 Send someone out for some petroleum jelly (who has this lying around the house, let alone the office?), and then dab some into each nostril. This should prevent any bloody encores. Then stick some rolled-up tissue paper or cotton wool up each nostril.

8 Avoid blowing your nose for as long as possible – at least twelve hours.

9 Avoid exercise or lifting heavy objects.

10 If you keep getting nosebleeds, buy a humidifier.

Oh, and dry-clean your shirt.

HOW TO PERFORM THE HEIMLICH MANOEUVRE

Saving a life the easy way

As recently as 1974, choking on food was the sixth most common cause of accidental death in America. For fifty years it had been assumed that the thing to do with a choking victim was to slap them on the back, even though every study showed that this only served to force the choking object further down into the airway. Then, in the mid 1970s, Dr Henry Heimlich developed a sure-fire technique that drove food out of the mouth. Long used to help choking victims, the technique is now also used to help save the lives of drowning victims by expelling water from their lungs.

A choking victim can't speak or breathe and needs your help immediately. And here is the correct way to do it:

1   From behind, wrap your arms around the victim's waist.

2   Make a fist and place the thumb side of your fist against the victim's upper abdomen, below the rib-cage and above the navel.

3   Grasp your fist with your other hand and press into their upper abdomen with a quick upward thrust. Do not squeeze the rib-cage; confine the force of the thrust to your hands.

4   Repeat until the object is expelled. Note: Never slap the victim's back. (This could make matters worse.)

If the victim is unconscious, or if you can't reach around him:

1   Place the victim on his back.

2   Facing him, kneel astride the victim's hips.

3   With one of your hands on top of the other, place the heel of your bottom hand on the upper abdomen below the rib-cage and above the navel.

4   Use your body weight to press into the victim's upper abdomen with a quick upward thrust.

5   Repeat until the object is expelled.

HOW TO BEAT JET-LAG

Avoiding the schoolboy errors

The best way to beat jet-lag is by sleeping through your flight, either naturally, or with sleeping pills or Melatonin.

It all depends how easy you find it to catnap. Even if you're lucky enough to be lying down it can be pretty difficult to sleep when you're flying, especially during turbulence. I've travelled with some people who will optimise any available free time, who can close their eyes and doze for ten minutes regardless of where they are (flying Economy in a bad seat, in the back of a cab, waiting to board, wherever). I can never do this, and need a darkened room, a bed and plenty of silence to have any hope of falling asleep. I find it almost impossible to sleep sitting down, and this is before the idiot sitting in front of me has jammed his seat back into my face, sending my congealed scrambled egg flying all over my shoes.*

---

*If someone does this repeatedly, don't confront him (waste of time), don't complain to the flight attendant (ditto), and don't retaliate by doing the same thing and taking it out on the poor soul behind you (you should rise above such behaviour). If you're feeling vindictive – and with nothing to occupy your mind for the next nine hours other than six films you've never had any intention of watching, and a book you wish you hadn't bought – then you can get back at the person in front of you as you can (an apple works wonders), blow gently on the back of his head (he'll think his air spout is malfunctioning) and whenever you get up to go to the loo, grab the headrest in front with the sort of vigour you usually reserve for the chest-press in the gym. There's no way that bastard's going to sleep now.

If you're travelling Economy on a long-haul flight, try to pick an unpopular flight, ask for a seat in the central block and you may be able to lie across four seats after take-off. Remembering, of course, not to have any caffeine before you do so.

While you fly you should drink as much still water as possible (buy a litre bottle at the airport to take with you), and avoid alcohol, as it will dehydrate you. Don't eat too much, and if you have to eat, try to stagger your intake. The trick is to get into the local time pattern as quickly as possible (you should set your watch to your new time as soon as you board), and if you're full and bloated from the journey, this will make it more difficult to acclimatise. Some say you should try a little gentle readjustment to your new time zone a few days before, by slightly altering your sleep patterns, although I've never met anyone who actually does this (it sounds feeble to me).

The way I do it is this: it doesn't matter if I'm flying east or west (forwards or backwards in time), or whether I'm flying to or from home, I make it a policy to stay up for as long as possible when I land, and not to go to bed until at least 11 p.m. local time. I expect to get around 3–4 hours' sleep for the first night, 4–5 on the second, and 5–6 on the third. By the fourth night I'm sleeping 6+ hours a night, which is normal.

I know men who regularly fly long-haul on business a couple of times a week, whose policy is to always stay on London time, and to fit their meals and their sleep pattern around this. Of course this is fine if you're travelling alone or with colleagues, but doesn't work at all if you're going to be spending time with other people.

One of the best ways to beat jet-lag when you're flying back from New York is also one of the easiest. Instead of taking the red-eye, which will leave between six and eleven in the evening, take a day flight. This means you'll take off in the morning, land at night and go straight to bed. You'll 'lose' a day, but your body clock will get back in sync a lot quicker.

And the very best way to beat jet-lag? Travel Business or First Class.

HOW TO KEEP COOL UNDER PRESSURE

'Don't panic, Mr Mainwaring!'

You will not be considered to be an ultra, or an alpha male, until you can handle yourself under pressure, unless you can show 'grace under pressure'. To enable yourself to do this you need to be able to understand your own emotions, and be able to cope with yourself when you begin to panic.

I've had panic attacks, and they're not nice. As I've said earlier, I remember beating my fists on the floor of my room in the Watergate Hotel in Washington back in the early 1990s, as I was about to exchange on a flat I wasn't really sure about. For twenty minutes I was a basket case; having had almost no sleep in two days, and worried that my life was going in the wrong direction, I smoked myself stupid as I beat my fists against the floor. I calmed down – obviously – but I was scared it was going to happen again. And it did, once, but since then I've learned to cope with this sort of thing.

The way I did it was to break the cycle. When you begin to feel like this – and the feeling is often caused by suddenly realising you've made a cataclysmic error, whether it be work or romance related – you have to stop yourself spiralling downwards. You need to pull yourself together, and let your emotions flood out . . . but then you need to stop. Stand up. Talk to yourself aloud. Tell yourself to act like a man, not a baby. Even if you're crying.

Then, when you've convinced yourself to stop dwelling on the awful thing you've just done, make a mental list of all the potential outcomes. You need to analyse what can go wrong, and then work out ways of limiting the damage in each case.

If you're in an office, or a situation where you are surrounded by other people, then you need to take yourself away and do this in private. Quickly. If you're alone you can do what the hell you like, but if you've got company then you need to sort yourself out quickly, or else you will forever be labelled a wet mess. So go to the loo, sit down and calm yourself down. Take a walk outside. Drink a glass of water. But sort yourself out. Urgently.

If you're in your office, then open the windows, loosen your tie and try not to sweat. Stay off the coffee, stay off the cigarettes, and don't be tempted to have a drink as you'll only feel worse (alcohol exacerbates mood). You must now compartmentalise your problem, and convince yourself that it isn't the end of the world (because it isn't).

And whatever you do, don't start stammering, because not only will you start to appear weak, but you won't be able to stop. A nervous reaction like this can become something of a default mechanism, and the last thing you want is to start stammering whenever you feel yourself starting to panic. If you do, however, you can do something about it. Having stammered quite badly for the best part of thirty years, in my early thirties I went to see a speech therapist. Strangely – stupidly, perhaps – it was only being asked to write an article about stammering that spurred me to do this; I suppose previously I had accepted my stammer as part of my life.

I went to see a consultant in west London, a charming woman in her mid thirties with immaculate diction. 'There's no absolute answer to stammering, and even some of the best teachers repeat the mantra

"Once a stammerer, always a stammerer," but the best way to attack it is through practice, lots and lots of practice,' she said.

'Having said that, people's reaction to stammering generally is not as negative as most stammerers think, and one of the easiest ways of coping with it is to just say to yourself, "To hell with it," and carry on regardless. People really are more tolerant than you might think.'

As with tennis tuition, speech therapy tends to make you worse before you start getting better, as you unlearn all your bad habits. However, my condition was – technically speaking – 'mild' (I was only faltering on a few consonants); and the tutor seemed to think I would improve relatively easily. The first thing I learned was to run up to words using something called 'easy onset', which is basically breathing in and partially breathing out before you attempt a difficult word or letter (in my case, ironically, 'D'). Speech is all about air flow from the lungs to the mouth, and understanding how to breathe properly is a fundamental part of the learning curve.

The second thing I learned was that all my problems revolved around sounds which were caused by blocking this air flow with the tongue (try saying 'D', 'G', or 'B'), so consequently I learned to tap my tongue on the roof of my mouth instead of allowing it to linger.

'Learning to speak more slowly is often the answer to everything,' my teacher added, and this was what I was urged to do. 'It gives you more time to think. It allows you not to get so pressurised and not to fall over yourself in trying to spit something out. You have to smooth things out and then remove them.'

The tuition proved to be a fascinating process, and, with practice, I slowly began to feel myself getting better (I am now almost free of it). But while my stammer improved, I was still not overly fond of dedicate, didactic, determinate, desultory, divot, Dixie, dynasty or dunnock, though thankfully dunnock is a word I have very little cause to use. Curiously, dodecahedron is a word I've never had any problems with; unfortunately I probably use it as much as dunnock.

So, you've learned to control your panic attacks, taught yourself how to cope with unprecedented amounts of stress, and stopped yourself stammering. What do you do now? Well, when everything is over, and you've bodyswerved disaster, and you're sitting in some leather sofa in the far corner of the bar, having a celebratory libation, think ahead to the problems around the corner. Think who you're going to need on your side to make sure this sort of thing doesn't happen again. Who are you going to hire?

Well, just remember the one question that Napoleon used to ask when deciding whether to promote a promising young general to his chosen band of marshals: 'Is he lucky?'

Because luck you're going to need.

HOW TO COPE WITH FAILURE

Because one day you will fail

Failure happens in everyone's life, and if you're lucky, it will happen earlier in your career, rather than later. If you never experience failure, then you'll think you're immune, think it's never going to happen. And then, when it does hit you, it will hit you like an express train. You'll recover – of course you will – but it will take much, much longer if you've never experienced it before. We all need failure in our lives, every one of us; otherwise we won't know what to do when disaster eventually comes. And trust me, it will come.

Mine came in my mid-thirties, after a decade of what I thought was fairly consistent, incremental success. But, one day in the middle of 1993, along with practically everyone else in my office, I was suddenly made redundant, at the tender age of 33. One minute I was on top of the world, smug as a bug in a rug . . . and the next I was just another unemployed hack, at the mercy of lackadaisical commissioning editors and absent-minded accounts departments. It was a massive, massive shock, especially as I had walked into the new editor's office expecting to be promoted. I thought I was immune to this sort of thing, thought things like this happened to other people. But apparently not; bad things obviously happened to everyone.

And they do. Every day. Even to you.*

But when bad things happen, you only need to remember this: failing is not falling down; failing is staying down. What we all need is the ability to bounce back. And to do it with style, and a smile. You've lost your job, got divorced, suffered from ill-health, or been told that your lease extension is going to cost you £150,000 more than you thought it would . . . You can let it unduly affect your life, and your demeanour can change accordingly, but unless you deal with it, and push it to the back of your mind, it will have a seriously, *seriously* debilitating effect on the way you operate. So you've been fired – so what? Big deal! What makes you so goddamn special? Sit yourself down, have a long, hard talk with yourself and, as Tory *compassionista* Norman Tebbit once said, on the subject of jobs, get on your bike and go and look for another one. Brush yourself down, sit yourself up, and start all over again. (Graft works: when Take That were trying to break into the British charts in the early 1990s, they spent over a year relentlessly touring the UK. On any given weekday they would play a school in the morning, another one in the afternoon, a youth club in the evening, a concert hall two hours later, and the day would be topped off with a personal appearance at a gay club in the early hours of the following morning. Now that's graft.)

---

* My career cloud did, however, have a rather heavily polished silver lining. The newspaper I had just joined (the *Observer*, then owned by Lonhro), had been rumoured to be up for sale when I joined it twelve months previously, and because of this I had negotiated an especially advantageous notice period. This meant that when I was whacked, the company buying us (the *Guardian*, itself owned by the Scott Trust), had to give me enough money to buy a house. Which I did, along with a lot of other people in the office. Whenever I hear someone use the term 'mixed emotions', I always think of the day I turned up at the *Guardian* to pick up my (largely tax-free) redundancy cheque, walking the long Walk of Shame through the newsroom, only to have a hatchet-faced virago reluctantly, resentfully hand it over. Bittersweet, yes, but rather sweeter for me than for her.

If you have a problem at work, it might simply be because of a personality clash. And if your boss doesn't like you, or has made life difficult for you, then it's probably best that you move on. I've worked for enough people to know that if your boss doesn't like you, then you should change jobs as soon as you can. Because you're going nowhere; not only that, but it's going to be a rocky old road while you're (not) getting there.

But then again: so what? If one person doesn't like you, just think of all the dozens that do (the ones who gave you work before). This person's problem with you isn't going to be resolved overnight, so leave and go somewhere you're appreciated. And if it's not expedient to do so, then put your problem in a box. I once worked for someone who obviously didn't like me, and when I finally understood this (it took me three or four months to come to the realisation that the reason I wasn't enjoying work was because for some reason – jealousy, insecurity, general loathing, whatever – she just didn't get on with me), every decision I made was made with this knowledge. It made life a lot easier, let me tell you.

Being fired, or experiencing a flop, is not the end of the world. It's just a blip, an erroneous smudge on your career chart, a descender in a world of fluorescent pen ascenders. Don't beat yourself up about it. It's how you bounce back that's important. Imagine you're Michael Caine, a man who has appeared in a hundred-odd movies (and some of them are very odd indeed). Did he give up making films after allowing himself to be cast in *The Swarm*, *The Hand*, *Blame It On Rio* or *Jaws: The Revenge*? Did he crawl back to southeast London with a cockle in his pocket, a cackle in his throat and a chip on his shoulder? No, he went on to make *California Suite*, *Educating Rita*, *Hannah and Her Sisters* and *Little Voice*. Did he worry that he was continually lampooned for having wayward quality control? No, he just made more movies. When Tom Hanks read the reviews for *The Bonfire of the Vanities* – 'A strained social farce in which the gap between intent and achievement is yawningly apparent' was *Variety*'s humble opinion – did he crawl back to Concord, California, where he was born? No, he went on to make *Forrest Gump*, *Philadelphia* and *Apollo 13*.

Remember: destiny isn't bound by the rules of probability. And sometimes when it calls, it calls somewhere else. It's crucial to understand that failure isn't finite, but then neither is success. Everything changes, all the time, and you need to know that if you're in a bad place right now, it won't last for ever. In fact things could change tomorrow. And let's assume they're going to.

HOW TO STOP A FIGHT

A fist full of diplomacy

So, you've just come out of a bar, and you accidentally bump into someone walking in. And instead of shrugging it off when you apologise, this other guy starts making trouble. Calling you names. Asking you why you couldn't look where you were f****** going.

Houston, you have a problem. He's on his own, but he's big, and he's had a few drinks. Not a lot, you understand, but enough to think that he can knock seven bells out of you.

And what do you do? You apologise, profusely, again, and start walking away. But he's not having any of that. He wants his pound of flesh, and he's going to stand around until he gets it. You're unsure as to whether he wants a proper fistfight or whether he just wants to humiliate you in front of a bar full of early evening drinkers. And you don't want to make a mistake, either way.

So you try and talk him down, by telling him that it's no big deal while apologising again. Act surprised and apologetic, but don't smile. Be sure not to patronise him, and don't touch him. If you put your arm on him as you're trying to reason with him, then you are acknowledging the fact that the argument has moved to another stage. If you put your arm around his shoulders in a conspiratorial act of friendship, he will react in one of two ways: 1) He will shrug you off and attack you. And as you're in close proximity he won't be able to throw a proper punch at you so it will be messy, and if he's bigger than you then you're in trouble. 2) Or he will do nothing, which will indicate that you have won, and that he isn't going to do anything violent.

If he puts his arm around you, then you have to consider what action you want to take, because now he's taking the reins. If your ego can take it, I'd put your hand on his other shoulder, nod your head and walk off. He will think he's won, but at least you haven't had to punch anyone.

You didn't want to hit him, did you? 'Although the better angels of our nature recoil from the concept of being hard, this territory is not alien to any man alive,' says Tony Parsons, who has written on this subject a lot. 'When we are boys, we admire hardness in other boys, and we never truly get over it.

'The cruel rules shout what we dare not whisper. All men want – need, crave, yearn – to be hard. And secretly fear that they will never be quite hard enough . . . The entire business of being hard is absolutely terrifying. Because the cruel rules state that no matter how hard you are, there is always someone harder.'

But you don't necessarily need to be hard in order to know how to throw a punch. You just need the emotional and technical prowess. When we're young, what we often fail to understand is that the person who takes the initiative, or who acts first, usually stands a much better chance of winning. This is true whether you're thinking of chatting up a girl, approaching a potential employer, applying for a job, or indeed, hitting someone. The guy in the playground who went around as though he owned the place, he wasn't necessarily the best fighter – not initially, anyway – but he had bigger balls than anyone else. Maybe he had less to lose, maybe he was less inhibited, less educated, who knows. But he had what you probably didn't have, which is the natural instinct to act fast. Which is what you've got to learn to do. Just do it. Evaluate the situation and then go for it.

If you are going to punch someone, then learn how to do it properly. You can only do this if you think you're going to have any effect. If the chap you're thinking of lamping is six foot four and built like a brick shithouse, then you've probably only got one shot at this, because even if he's not a very good fighter, his sheer size will overpower you one way or another. So choose your course of action carefully (i.e. only pick fights you think you can win).

But if you are going to hit him, you've got to catch him unawares, and make sure you give him everything you've got. Your punch needs to be quick, firm and powerful. Most men would avoid a fight if they possibly could, so even if he's had a couple of drinks, the confrontation will have sobered him up enough to make him think he probably doesn't want to get involved in a fight. So act quickly, as hesitation is the quickest way to lose a fight. You can't miss, or trip, or punch him with anything less than total conviction. Because if you don't hit him properly, he's going to come at you like a train, so you'd better know how to defend yourself and fight back. If you haven't punched him properly, he will eat you alive, principally because he is no longer scared of you. Fear plays an important psychological part in any duel, and if your opponent has suddenly realised that you can't punch, then any fear he had will evaporate.

So learn how to punch. If you're right-handed, stand in a twenty-past-ten position with your legs slightly bent and your feet the width of your shoulders apart. Put your left hand slightly in front of you and snap your right hand out from your shoulder while lifting up on the balls of your feet. Now push your right fist into his jaw, twisting your arm as you go, so that by the time your fist has connected with his face, your knuckles will arrive first. The whole movement of the arm should be horizontal, or parallel with the ground (i.e. don't swing up from your waist).

This is the punch used by security guards when they're trying to get rid of you, a punch that, if delivered properly and with enough force, will have your oppo gasping for air on the floor. 'Your punch has to be lightning fast, so that when his head snaps to the side, it cuts out his central nervous system, affects his breathing, prevents oxygen going to his brain and he hits the floor,' says super-middleweight boxer Joe Calzaghe. 'It's the quick punches you don't see that take your lights out.' He should know.

J.P. Donleavy in *The Unexpurgated Code* is of a similar mind: 'It is therefore advisable to deliver one clean blow to start with and if your opponent is clearly not of the old school, clean out his teeth with your elbow as he falls and give him a belly full of your boot when he reaches the ground. Of course, should he be armed, run in a ducking zig zag fashion.'

HOW TO COPE WITH GRIEF

. . . and escape the cycle of depression

The five stages of grief, as identified by Elisabeth Kubler-Ross, the psychiatrist who wrote *On Death and Dying* as well as *On Grief and Grieving*, are . . . 1) Denial ('This is definitely not happening to me'), 2) Anger ('Why is this happening to *me*?'), 3) Bargaining ('I promise to be a better person if . . .'), 4) Depression ('I do not care any more'), and 5) Acceptance ('I am ready for whatever comes').

The trick, I would venture, is to move to stage five as quickly as humanly possible.

Grief is not just an expression of mourning, or a process of mourning. More important than that, it is a healing process, one that helps us to deal with the loss of a loved one. As Kubler-Ross writes, 'Grief does not have a clear beginning or clear end to it. Rather, it is a reflection of feelings surrounding the loss. Grief will ebb and flow throughout our life after a loss. We don't get over the loss of someone, but we learn to live with that loss. We also will eventually remember and honour our loved one without feeling pain. We will grieve as long as we need to.'

Don't expect the pain to go, because it won't. You need to get used to it being there, and then push it to the back of your mind. It will lessen, eventually, as everything does, but it will never completely go. You need to compartmentalise it, just as you do if you dislike or hate someone.

You don't think about that person all the time, in fact you probably rarely think about them, but your feelings towards them sit, quietly, in some dark recess of your mind, waiting to be called upon when needed. Grief should be compartmentalised in the same way. Essentially you need to be able to cope with the aftermath of a tragedy, one that could, conceivably, and in some form or other, last a lifetime. Don't worry that you might not have enough inner strength, because everyone does; the problem for a lot of people is that they don't know how to channel it.

Never forget that a lot of grief is self-serving, and that we are often being selfish and simply feeling sorry for ourselves because that person is no longer around. We are now unhappy and we're blaming that person for our unhappiness. This is natural, but not something you should dwell on for too long. Keep moving.

One of the ways we cope with grief is through denial, by filling our lives till they can't possibly be filled any more. They say that happiness is a by-product of absorption, and there's no reason why this can't come into play. Sometimes this works – for a while – and if you can keep this up, through work, socialising, or, no – let's face it – simply more work, then you should at least occasionally allow yourself some time to think. As Kubler-Ross says, 'Learn to get in touch with the silence within yourself and know that everything in this life has a purpose.' If the pain is excruciating, and you're finding it impossible to cope with, then allow yourself an hour a week in which to let it all out. Just walk into another room, sit down, and allow yourself to explode (or implode) with grief. Use this as a valve, a tap.

During a period of grief, I once embarked upon a course of Transcendental Meditation, thinking this would help me come to terms with not only my loss, but also where I was at that stage of my life. I hated it, and thought the whole process preposterous. Sitting in a room, repeating a mantra over and over again with a bunch of strangers, just felt like an irrelevance. In fact I felt vaguely ridiculous. But as I sat there, trying to empty my head, everything came rushing in, as though an emotional dam had just burst. And while it wasn't exactly a day at the beach, it taught me that even small periods of time alone, just quietly thinking, allow you to analyse your feelings in ways you would never have considered if you hadn't stopped to think in the first place. Not only that – and while it might sound callous, I think this is crucial – after a while you become desperate to shake yourself out of your mood, and long to move on. So by actually forcing yourself to grieve and to wallow in your own sadness, you're also moving towards the other side – 'Get me out of here!'

Often, people will just sit and be, while others read relevant texts, or pore over old photographs and cards. I've always found the best way to fast-track my catharsis is through music, either by playing something specific to a memory (the music that we were listening to during a particular point in our lives), or by playing a record guaranteed to have me convulsed by tears. For me those records are 'Being Boring' by the Pet Shop Boys, 'Somewhere Down The Line' by an old pop group called Rogue that you've probably never heard of, Chopin's 'Etudes' and the Beach Boys' maudlin, self-regarding 'Till I Die'. And every one of them works.

In essence, it's important to keep developing, but it's crucial to keep moving. And while it's true that a little suffering is good for the soul, if you want to be happy, don't ever ask yourself if you actually are.*

---

* If someone you know has just suffered a loss, and is experiencing grief, don't offer to help – actually do things without them asking you to. Don't go out of your way to make grand gestures about your willingness to help; the best thing you can do is to actually make a list of ways you can help that person out, and then do them, unasked. If they are a true friend, they won't mind you interfering – and if they do, they'll soon tell you. Trust me, this is the best thing to do, because people experiencing grief are not good at asking their friends and relations to help them out. It's a mixture of pride, guilt, and our natural propensity for wallowing in our own misfortune. So don't ask if you can do the shopping/service the car/organise and pay for a weekend spa/recommend a solicitor, etc – just do it.

ELBOW GREASE
&
SKYHOOKS

HOW TO BUILD A BACHELOR PAD

Your crib says more about you than you know

The first rule is, live alone. It doesn't matter what age you are, no woman wants to find that her date shares his living quarters. The second rule is, accept that your apartment is a work in progress. Sure, you can buy the Dualit toaster, the Philippe Starck lemon juicer, the Eames chairs, the Artemide Tizio lamp and the A2 dual cavity Smeg range cooker (you know the one – in anthracite or stainless steel, with two electric ovens and a six-burner gas hob with automatic ignition and cast-iron pan stands). Sure, you can cover the walls with Jamie Reid prints and Alma Tadema lithographs, and the floors with Paul Smith rugs and Italian white plastic floor lamps, but taste is something you can buy from magazines. What your flat needs is individuality, the sort of individuality that invites criticism and that is open to change.

Women like vulnerability, and they want to know that they can inflict themselves upon you. To them, you are a project, and if they begin making headway with you, then they will want to start altering your apartment. And you must let them do it. If you look too settled in your surroundings, you're toast.

Finding a woman to love isn't that difficult, but luring her into love is another matter altogether. She may let you buy her a few drinks, even dinner, and she may even let you pay for the cab back to your place. But once there, you can't rely on your charm to keep yourself in her favour; you have to rely on your previous lifestyle decisions. You hope she likes your neighbourhood, your apartment, and, above all, your bedroom.

Your bedroom says more about you than your haircut or your Audi. It's more revealing than the Meat Loaf CD in the attic or the huge stack of *Playboys* under the sink. You spend a third of your life in your bedroom, and it is the place where you are most naked (literally) and usually completely alone, unencumbered by designer suits, shiny shoes and flashy neckties. It is where you can lie in bed scratching your backside and reading the sports pages. It is where you can be called a pig and offer no plausible defence whatsoever.

You'd be surprised by the number of presentable, relatively successful, and supposedly sophisticated men whose bedrooms make them look as if they never left college. But I'm sure you wouldn't be surprised by the number of women who have run for their lives after being coaxed there from the dining-room. Which brings us to the central thrust: how do you make your bedroom more attractive to a woman?

Because single men have a tendency to let the housework slide, the answer really is a catalogue of don'ts – which probably means you're going to have to evacuate your boudoir and begin again. But don't worry: once you've done a little bedroom pruning, no self-respecting female should be able to find a reason not to spend the night. With you.

A single man interested in making his sleeping quarters more attractive to the opposite sex should avoid having a bed that's too big (it looks too pushy, not to say ostentatious), expensive stereo equipment (music in the bedroom is cheap and tacky – so much better to have a suitably discreet iPod dock), pin-up posters or ironic erotic art (particularly if they look as though they were tacked up with one hand), camera equipment or cuddly toys and lingerie (which your guest will assume – correctly – have been left there by previous conquests).

In fact, there should be nothing visible to remind her of your ex-lovers, such as sex toys, ornaments (single men don't own ornaments), sex toys, dried flowers, sex toys, drapes, cute duvet covers, sex toys, and particularly photographs of other girls (you can tell her they're your sisters but she'll never believe you).

You should also conceal anything that even hints at deviant sexual practices (she'll find out soon enough), e.g. claw marks on the wall, hand-cuffs dangling from bedposts (even pink fluffy ones from one of those high-street sex stores), digital camcorders, leather girdles, strap-ons and girlie magazines (especially *Hustler*). Did I mention sex toys? Other no-no's include exercise equipment, half-eaten pizza, crusty towels, empty beer cans, full beer cans, sculptures made out of beer cans, football paraphernalia, Led Zeppelin or System of a Down paraphernalia, Bruce Weber or Iraki photo books, car magazines, firearms, drum kits, and copies of *American Psycho* or *101 Things to Do to a Hooker on a Stag Weekend*. Anything, in truth, that defines you as a man.

I have also found that it's not a good idea to leave clothes lying around your bedroom, as women may want to try them on, or at least waste precious minutes (sometimes hours) asking why you bought that pair of orange suede chinos or how many times you wore that bomber jacket, oh and by the way do you still want it.

In general your bedroom should not look like a regulation-issue state-of-the-art love nest. Women do not appreciate red lightbulbs, the collected works of Nelly, mirrored ceilings, water beds, deep-pile shag rugs, or bottles of cheap champagne – either strewn around like cheap champagne bottles or standing expectantly in silver ice buckets. Remember: a bedroom isn't the right place for seduction, it's the right place for sex.

After quizzing a few of my female friends on the subject, I discovered that women like to see the following in a man's bedroom: rows of polished shoes (it indicates order), clean white cotton sheets (cleanliness), classical instruments such as tubas, mandolins or harps (breeding, refinement), pictures of your parents (aah), expensive cotton pyjamas (for her, not you), and candles (as long as they're not in the shape of male sexual organs). Every woman likes a candle, especially in a man's apartment. It shows you have a soul, apparently. Not surprisingly, all the women (bar one) said that what they'd most like to see in a man's bedroom is Brad Pitt. The other one wanted James Blunt.

One woman was even more specific. 'The first thing I look for is a packet of condoms. Once I've seen them, I can relax. Then I can ignore everything else and just get on with things. I like a boy who takes precautions – that's a very good sign. Either that or a ceiling loosely wallpapered with fifty-pound notes.'

Ideally, the most important room in the house should be as empty as possible. Do all your showing off in the other rooms in the house – let the designer strip-lighting and the furniture and the iPod playlists and the kitchen knives and the art and the wine alert her to the sort of person you think might be to her liking. When you get to the bedroom it should be as empty and as simple as possible. I always thought the old Rothko room in London's Tate Britain would have made the perfect bedroom – with the whiteness of *2001: A Space Odyssey*, and four big purple and black paintings on the wall. And one, perfectly normal double bed sitting right in the middle. This, I think, is the effect you should be going for.

With a rug, of course. For what feels like forever, but is only probably about seven or eight years, the quintessential bachelor pad accessory has been the man-sized cowhide rug, oh-so-casually strewn across your interior decking, summoning you to the great outdoors, all brown and white and luxe.

For a while there, it seemed as though cowhide was in danger of taking over our lives, a talisman of rural luxury in a world overloaded with ergonomic plastic, plasma screens, laptops, trendy Italian Anglepoise lamps and customised iPods. First it was rugs, then bedspreads, then headboards, cushions, wall-hangings, chairs, sideboards and side tables – there didn't seem to be any artefact or household item that couldn't be randomly wrapped in cowhide, or something that looked quite like it. A few years ago I even saw an entire wall of the stuff in a hotel lobby in Los Angeles, confirmation – in case any were still needed – that cowhide had replaced leopardskin as the loungecore fabric *du jour*.

Now it has become an interior design staple, and if you check into one of these trendy feels-like-London rural retreats (formerly known as upscale country house hotels), a gargantuan cowhide rug in reception guarantees that you'll be able to get the sort of holistic spa treatments, organic room service menus and in-house porn that you can in any hotel in Paris, London or New York. In a way, cowhide has the same effect that halogen lights had in the Eighties, making you feel fantastically pleased with yourself for being somewhere that has them. And you could do a lot worse than buy one. A big one.

For extra measure I would recommend a selection of suitably highbrow books nestled on the bedside table – modern classics, or collections of short stories by contemporary women authors (make no attempt to actually read these, as they are interminably dull and will send you into an emotional tailspin).

While décor and ambience are all well and good, basically – truthfully – once the object of your dreams is actually in your bedroom, you're almost home. And if you still have any doubt about the particulars of the setting, remember: you can always turn off the light.

Let joy be unconfined.

HOW TO BUILD SHELVES

Any Domestic God should be able to do this

I have to admit that my own interpretation of DIY usually involves a telephone. It's called GABI (Get A Bloke In), and I've been doing it for years. Having been tangentially involved in the reconfiguration of three London houses, the Jones household address book now includes the much sought-after, highly prized and rarely given-out numbers of various exemplary craftsmen, including builders, carpenters, electricians, plasterers, labourers, plumbers, etc (OK, not plumbers – no one knows a good plumber). However, there are some things that you shouldn't really need to get a man in to do. And building shelves is just one of those things. Sure, if you want the sort of professional, double-width, floor-to-ceiling shelves you find in museum bookshops – the sort built from the type of reconstituted wood and industrial-strength glue you only find in unlisted, impossible-to-find hardware stores, then you (or I) call Ian the carpenter. But if you want the sort of bookshelves you're going to put in the garage or what you laughingly call a study, possibly to house that collection of *GQ* that you can't bear to throw away, then you should be able to do it yourself.

How to Keep House: The Lost Art of Being a Man, has some sound, no-nonsense advice on this: 'The more shelves you have, the more space you have to store and organise your stuff. There are the wall-hung bracketed kind, the freestanding metal kind [which the Jones household was formerly very fond of] or the complex wooden kind made from dados and mortises. One easy way to build a sturdy set of freestanding wooden shelves is to use cleats – small pieces of wood upon which the shelving boards can rest.'

They advocate the following method, for which you'll need the following bits and pieces: two 180 x 2.5 x 25cm boards; twelve 22 x 2.5 x 2.5cm cleats (or oblong sticks); six 100 x 2.5 x 25cm boards; a 180 x 100cm sheet of 5mm plywood; six 100 x 2.5 x 5cm 'lips' (thin strips of wood); a tape measure and a sharp pencil; an electric drill; a packet (get 100, just in case) of 3.5cm flathead wood screws; an expensive retractable screwdriver; and a bloody big power saw.

Lay out the two 180cm boards on the ground. Starting at what will eventually be the bottom of the bookcase, measure up 2.5cm (about one inch) and mark the spot with a pencil. From there, measure every 35cm (14 inches) and make pencil marks at those spots. The bottom of each of the horizontal shelves will rest at these points.

At every pencil mark – and flush with the back of each board – screw in a 2.5 x 2.5cm (one inch x one inch) cleat, lining up its top with the pencil mark. To make sure the cleat won't split when fastened to the sides, drill three evenly spaced pilot holes into each one, then push the screws through the cleat face (see Fig. A).

Done that? Right, once you've attached all the cleats, get one of the shelves and put it in place on top of the bottom cleat and screw in two screws, equally spaced (in case you didn't realise), through the face of the 180cm board into the end of the shelf. Now lay the unit on its side and screw the other end of the shelf to the opposite board (see Fig. B).

Leave the unit lying on its side while you secure the top shelf, then the rest of the shelves. Now measure and cut the sheet of plywood to fit snugly on the back of the shelving unit. Fasten it with the screws, evenly spaced every 25cm around its perimeter (see Fig. C). To finish the mission, attach a 'lip' to the front of the unit, under each shelf. Make sure it is flush with the bottom of the shelf and drive one screw into each end through the outer face of the bookshelf sides (see Fig. D).

Then stand back, admire, open a cold can of Cobra and – if it looks like I think it probably does – Get A Bloke In. *How to Keep House* is full of other neat household tips such as repointing brick walls, servicing gutters and replacing an asphalt roof tile, and I heartily recommend you get a copy. Just make sure you avoid the chapter on the textile labelling code.

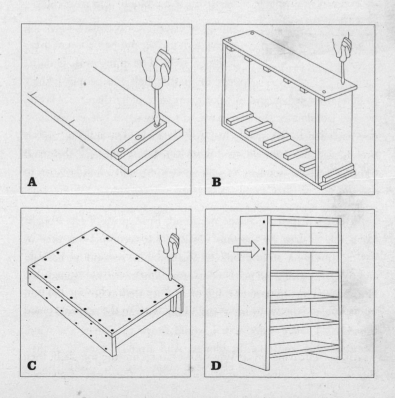

HOW TO DRIVE

The time is right for racing in the street . . .

It would have been embarrassing if it hadn't been so ludicrous. There I was, at 29, a fast-lane virgin, unable to drive – unable to negotiate a gear stick, a steering wheel, foot pedals and half a ton of over-designed steel. The thing was, it didn't seem to matter; half the people I knew couldn't drive either, and most of them were older than me. Having lived in London for thirteen years, I'd simply never got around to it, never needed to. I'd always had friends with cars, and had always been ferried about abroad. And there were buses and taxis, tubes and trains. There was nowhere to park anyway. So why on earth learn to drive?

Four things helped to change my mind. First, pride: I felt I ought to be able to drive by the time I was thirty; second, I was tired of having to rely on other people to chauffeur me around on holiday; and third, my girlfriend persisted in reminding me of my inadequacy. Fourth, the most important thing of all, I wanted to be able to listen to the Eagles' 'Already Gone' at maximum volume as I rocketed down the A303. I made a decision: I would throw caution to the wind, bite the bullet, and take the plunge. And after I'd done all of that, I told myself (and anyone else who would listen), I would finally learn to drive.

I called the London School of Motoring, and was assigned an instructor, a man called R.G. Moyse. Friends had warned me that driving instructors were the very worst thing about learning to drive, that they had invariably been bullied at school, and now made any pupil's life a misery. But this wasn't the case with RG, who turned out to be the perfect teacher – firm, but friendly.

My first lesson was a nightmare, but then I suppose it couldn't have been any other way. At midday one Wednesday in the middle of July, when a tube strike was bringing London to a standstill, RG told me to drive down the Edgware Road, one of the busiest roads in the capital, to Marble Arch. It was a veritable baptism of fire, but succeeded in teaching me never to be scared of traffic, in much the same way – I imagine – that throwing someone out of an aeroplane will cure their vertigo. The strangest thing about my first lesson was that I assumed my instructor would drive me around a bit first to show me the ropes; but he didn't, he just sat me down and told me to drive. So drive is what I did. If I started learning now, I would spend several lessons on a simulator, teaching my arms and legs to interact with the car just like they do if you're learning to fly a plane or a helicopter. But nothing beats actually getting out on to the road.

I soon discovered how tolerant most drivers are of learners – mainly because they want to stay as far away from them as possible. In six months of driving I only received one piece of serious verbal abuse, and that was from a ratty-looking would-be taxi driver, careering round a roundabout on his moped, doing the Knowledge and brushing up on his vocabulary. 'Watch where you're going you blind c***,' he said, as he cut me up with consummate ease. I've no doubt he has turned into an exemplary cab driver.

If you can come to terms with the fact that You Know Nothing, and The Instructor Knows Everything, then it shouldn't take you too long to learn. My first day was hell, but after that I grew to enjoy the sessions. As I got better, I'd forget I was a learner, and we'd be

deep in conversation – inflation, property, football, road works, etc
– when Mr Moyse would apply some hard-shoulder tactics in order
to remind me of my lowly, licence-free status: 'Fourth gear,' 'Signal
left,' 'Pull over,' or 'You do realise you're going well over thirty, don't
you?' He had a way with words, did RG.

It took me about six months – with one or two lessons a week – to
tame the beast. I drove around Kilburn, Marylebone, Paddington and
Brondesbury Park, coping with sluggish London traffic, absurd one-
way systems and old men in hats driving cars that went out of
production sixty years ago. And as I grew in confidence, so my toler-
ance levels dropped. I started swearing at other drivers, cursing them,
like a veteran, under my breath whenever they crossed my path. In
other words I started to become a proper driver, a Mad Max in penny
loafers, a road warrior in an Emporio Armani suit. My Nissan hot-
hatchback became a Lotus Elan, my horn a Magnum .44; I was ready
for anything, so everything had better be ready. It was true, I thought,
there really were no liberals behind the steering wheel. I gradually
began to understand the stress and strain suffered by my driving
friends: so *this* was what they meant when they talked about driving
in London. Actually it was the best place to learn, and all those boy
racers who learn to drive in the country may well be more adept at
negotiating country lanes, but are completely unable to handle the
traffic around Hyde Park Corner at rush hour.

Taking the test was less painful than I imagined. I studied the Highway
Code, even watched the video, and practised my three-point turns
until I could do them blindfold. (Perversely, night-driving and parallel
parking, two things which are fundamental to the driving experience, are not considered important enough to be taught in any great
detail.) As the test was at 8.40 a.m. I was too tired to be really
nervous, and by the time I woke up it was over. My instructor told
me that it was almost impossible to tell if someone was going to pass
– examiners will only pass a certain proportion of drivers (they will

be examined themselves if they pass too many or too few), so it was best not to worry.

The practical test was fine (I was atypically calm and considerate); it was the Highway Code I wasn't so sure about. People had told me that if you pass the practical, then it doesn't matter how bad you are at the theory, but it didn't make me feel any easier. I shouldn't have worried, though. After showing me some rudimentary road signs – 30mph, humpback bridge, etc – he showed me a 'Stop' sign. Did I know what it meant? 'Stop?' I offered, trying to divest my voice of irony. After this I knew I was all right.

Passing the test first time still doesn't make up for the fact that I should have taken it twelve years earlier, but it has at least given me some of the arrogance which you need on the roads today. The learning was actually quite easy, and while you may think that you have more than enough information bouncing around your skull without needing or being able to take in any more, the trick is to learn muscle memory. As soon as you've achieved this, your body starts making the manoeuvres for you, which is what driving is essentially all about.

And, as with most things which require a certain amount of teaching, making the decision to do something isn't the hard part; it's *deciding* to make the decision. Once you've done that, once you've acclimatised, it's easy.

The Rules:

1 Don't drive an automatic for a while, because if you do you'll soon get out of the habit of changing gears, and it will make you – long term – a worse driver. Also, trust me, being able to drive 'stickshift' in the US proves to be a great aphrodisiac.

2 When you park your car, leave it in gear and set the parking brake. That way, it won't start rolling as soon as you put it in neutral to start again.

3   Whenever you take your new car out for the first time, spend twenty minutes learning where certain things are: the spare, the boot release, the bonnet release and the petrol lock.

4   Avoid coasting with the clutch all the way down (always referred to as 'riding the clutch'), as this will cause needless wear and tear on the clutch. When stopped at a traffic light, don't sit with the clutch engaged. Put the gearshift into the neutral position and release the clutch.

5   When learning to drive, if you can find a disused airfield to practise in, do it.

6   There is no great shame in being unable to drive stick-shift, as the Americans call it, but why be half a driver?

7   Before you choose a car, test as many as you can.

8   It's no longer OK to simply drive a Mercedes because they are sexy and reliable. Are they still?

9   Toyotas are making some interesting cars too.

10   As are lots of other companies.

11   Many cars these days tell you exactly how many miles you have left in your tank. You should test this when you first get the car, because one day you'll really need to know.

12   Your rear-view mirror will have a switch on it, allowing you to flip to a night-time driving mirror, in order to cut out glare (it only took me three years to find it on my current car).

13   Braking too hard uses as much petrol as extreme acceleration.

14   Don't worry if you write your first car off. I did.

HOW TO IRON A SHIRT

Because sometimes you have to be a house-husband

Frankly, I would have thought a man in your position would have had someone to do this for you, either a 'little woman' or – look away, *Guardian* subscribers – a wife or a girlfriend. Either that, or a cheap, reliable dry-cleaners round the corner who will wash and hang them for you (if you take in at least seven or eight a week, it's not going to cost you much per shirt).

But if you want to do it yourself, make sure you have a sturdy, state-of-the-art board and steam iron (topped-up with distilled water). First select the right temperature (you are listening, aren't you?), and fold the shirt flat over the end of the board, with the outside back facing up. Iron the back first, as this is the part of your shirt people will probably see least. Then iron the sleeves, with a sharp crease from the shoulder to the cuff. Next iron the shoulders, fitting the armholes over the very end of the board. Most men miss these bits, but a shirt looks terrible if they aren't done.

Then open up the cuffs and do them on both sides, before finally doing the front of the body, and then the collar. This is the most important part of the shirt, the one that will be seen by most people (especially if you're not wearing a tie), and so you need to iron carefully, in slow, deliberate movements. Beware: if you iron a crease into your collar, it's almost impossible to totally get it out. Also please, please don't forget to take your collar stays out first – and to put them back afterwards. (A lot of bunk is talked about stays, and to my mind they can be metal, bone *or* plastic; no one ever sees them anyway.)

Even with a steam iron, I always use a small spray bottle filled with water (the sort you'd use for potted plants), as it will get rid of tough wrinkles before ironing. Be liberal, but watch the paintwork.

If you've bought the right steam iron, it should last for a good few years, although here are some tips in case it's playing up. If it's spluttering too much when it heats up, you've either over-filled it (idiot), or the steam holes could be clogged with dirt or minerals. If this happens you should empty the iron and fill it full of white vinegar. Then turn it to the hottest setting and lay it face down on the metal rack at the base of the board and allow the steam to pour out. Once all the vinegar has gone, you can then use a toothpick to clean out the individual steam holes. The reason the holes got bunged-up in the first place is probably that you've been using tap water, which obviously contains a lot of minerals.

If the iron has got burn marks or burned-on matter on its plate, then heat it up and – again using white vinegar – clean it off with a scourer or some steel wool.

If you have any more complicated problems, then buy a new iron.

HOW TO START A FIRE

The essential wilderness survival trick

If you need to start a fire and you don't have two Boy Scouts to rub together, then what you do is this: carry matches or a lighter in a waterproof container. Alternatively, always carry a flint-and-steel set, because they still work after being soaked. And if you've packed none of these things, then try and find some flint or sharp stone and rub it against any exposed piece of metal on your backpack or belt – or, if you're carrying one, a penknife – to produce sparks.

Getting appropriate tinder and kindling is half the battle; cedar and birch shavings work well, as do dying grass and twigs. If you're trying to light a fire in the rain, use dead branches off trees rather than from the ground, as they will be less wet – or else crumbly dead wood from the inside of an old fallen branch. You could also pack some cotton wool dipped in Vaseline or lighter fuel into a film canister.

As for igniting your tinder, on a sunny day, you can always try using your spectacles, or even a glass bottle, to focus the sun's rays on it (a magnifying glass will work better, but I think we all know that you're unlikely to be carrying one). If you're carrying a gun, you could try removing a bullet from its cartridge and pour half the powder over your tinder. Put the half-empty cartridge back in the gun (minus the bullet), and fire it at the tinder.

The traditional way of starting a fire without any matches is to rub two sticks together, but you need such a lot of friction that you could be doing it for hours without achieving anything. It also requires a lot of practice (which, obviously, you might just get). This is known as the hand-drill method and is without doubt the most difficult option. When an outdoorsman becomes proficient in this method, it can be one of the fastest ways to create a fire – but you're not an outdoorsman, are you? You'll need some cedar bark to act as your nest-shaped spark catcher, as well as a straight and strong yucca stem (however this tends to be found only in the western United States and desert locations). Break your stem into two pieces. You will need to use the straightest part of the yucca stem for the 'drill'. You can use a knife or sharp rock to slightly sharpen the end. Next prepare the second half of the stem to create your 'block'. Make a small hole and cut a small hole in the side. The hole is where the ashes will fall to create the ember. Put the two ends together and rub them rapidly while pushing downwards. Continue doing this until it starts to fit together well. This is done to get the block and drill working together.

Use a small piece of bark to put under the block where the hole is, to catch the ash where the ember will be created. At this point, continue hand-drilling until the ashes have collected into an ember and it's (hopefully) glowing. Spitting on your hands will make it easier. You'll need to keep the movements rapid and the pressure intense to obtain results, and when you're first learning you can expect a combination of blisters and disappointment. However, it is possible to make a good ember this way, and after placing it in the nest and gently blowing on it, to build a successful fire.

But the best advice, if you're going down to the woods today, is to take a lighter. Or a mobile. Or both.

HOW TO HANG A PICTURE

It's not just books that furnish a room

Surprisingly, there are few things that highlight quite so appositely the difference between being a boy and a man. Owning poorly framed, poorly chosen art is one of those things that marks us down as an overgrown adolescent, as someone who hasn't quite escaped the bachelor pad sensibility of 'make do' interior design. The right picture, properly framed, can lift a room in the same way as the right light, the right piece of furniture or the right wall colour. Don't underestimate its importance, or its ability to transform your living quarters.

This is the third stage of an extremely idiosyncratic and personal process. The first stage involved you buying the picture in question (print, photograph, painting, film poster, magazine cover, cowhide, etc); the second involved you framing it (one piece of advice: get this done professionally), while the third involves you actually putting it in your home.

Which is what we're doing now.* And these are the steps:

_____

* If at all possible, try to hang pictures without asking your girlfriend or spouse to help. Putting up pictures is one of those things – like driving, parking and shopping in supermarkets – that will cause you to row like fury.

1   First, decide where you're going to hang the picture. Don't be rash about this, as there are many different ways of making the picture work with the environment. You may want one big picture isolated on a huge expanse of wall, you may want it to extend the lines of the furniture, or you may want it to be grouped with several other pictures. The best thing to do is to leave the picture on the floor for a while, leaning against the wall below where you intend hanging it, to see whether you like it there or not.

2   Check that whatever you're about to knock a hole into can actually take the strain – i.e. make sure the wall isn't just wallboard. Ideally you'll need a stud wall, a brick wall or a beam.

3   Also, make sure there isn't a cable running vertically from a power point on the skirting board, as you don't really want to electrocute yourself by banging a nail into it.

4   Make sure you check the way your picture has been wired. What you don't want is a wire that is so long that you'll be able to see it above the picture when it's hung. If it's too long, undo it, shorten it and re-tie it, using pliers.

5   Work out where you want the picture, and then measure *exactly* where it should go, using a tape measure. Measure vertically and horizontally – and accurately.

6   Now hold the picture in front of where you want it, making sure that you allow for the wire at the back being as taut as possible (if it has one, that is – it may just have a hanging tab).

7   Mark the spot where the nail is going to go with a soft pencil.

8   Choose an appropriate hook. You'll either want a single nail-and-hook, a double nail-and-hook for heavier pictures, or, for really heavy ones, wall plugs and screws.

9   Partially bang in your nail(s).

10 Stand back and inspect. If everything is straight, take the picture off the hooks and nail them in completely.

11 If you're putting up a big picture, maybe one that involves using two nail-and-hooks, use a spirit level to make sure it's perfectly horizontal, and if necessary adjust one of the hooks.

12 To keep your pictures permanently straight, take a piece of mounting putty and put it in one corner of the picture between the picture and the wall.

13 When you're grouping frames together, make sure they are at least two inches apart.

HOW TO JUMP START A CAR

'I'm on the A1, on the hard shoulder just north of junction 9 . . . You can't miss me. I'm wearing Cavalli'

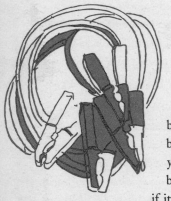

If you change your car regularly (every three or four years), or if you're the lucky beneficiary of a company car (which should be changed around the same time), then you'll probably never experience a flat battery, but if your car's more than ten years old, or if it's a 'classic car' (old, rare, expensive to run and a pig to drive), or if you're stupid enough to park your Mercedes on the top of a chalk valley in Wiltshire on Bonfire Night, putting your lights on full beam so you can see where exactly to light the fireworks (I know, I won't be doing it again), then you'll need to know all about this.

Firstly, make sure the ignition is turned off, along with the radio, the CD player, the heater, the lights and anything else that uses electricity.

Get the other car to park as close to yours as possible, preferably bonnet-to-bonnet, but if necessary side by side, having noted which side of each car's engine the battery is located. Open said bonnets. Take out your jump leads and attach one red cable to the positive red battery head of your car (the car that needs to be jump started)*. Attach the other red end to the other car's positive red battery head. Attach one black cable to the other car's negative black battery head. Attach the other end of the black cable to the unpainted frame or a metal part of the engine block on your car. Don't attach it anywhere near or on the battery. This is the grounding end of the connection.

Start the other car (the assisting car, the one that isn't yours), and then gently rev its engine. Wait a few minutes, and then, without disconnecting anything, try starting the dead car (yours). It should start immediately; if it doesn't, turn it off and wait a few minutes before trying again. After a while it should start, but if it hasn't done after about ten minutes then it's probably not going to, and you need to call one of the emergency services.

If it does start, keep the engine running and remove the cables in reverse order: the grounding end, the other black end, the red cable on the other car, and then the red on yours. Drive around for at least 15 minutes to give the battery the chance to recharge itself (enough to restart) and do not turn off the engine for at least 45 minutes, even if it's stationary. And the next time you decide to let off some fireworks in the middle of nowhere, plan ahead: buy a torch.

(If you have to call the AA to come out and do it for you, for God's sake tip the guy when he's finished – £10 minimum.)

---

* Always make sure you carry jump leads in the boot; along with a spare tyre, a jack, (all of) the correct tools for the car, and the phone number of the AA or RAC and/or your insurer.

HOW TO CHANGE A TYRE

First, make sure you've got a spare

If the tyre blows while you're driving, don't slam on the brakes. Hear me? Don't slam on the brakes. Use them sparingly, carefully tapping up and down, and steer the car over to the next safe bit of kerb. Park, turn off the ignition, and put on the hand brake. If you're in a dangerous or exposed part of the road, put your hazard lights on. Now lift the spare out of the boot, or wherever it's kept (and one of the first things you should do when you buy or rent a car is find out where it is), and take out the jack and the lug wrench. If the owner's manual is still in the car – it's best to keep it in the glove compartment, along with your girlfriend's parking tickets and those hip-hop CDs you don't play any more – have a look in it to see where the jack should go (these days manufacturers often build a special dock on the underside of the car). If, like most men, you've consigned the owner's manual to history or that special place at home where you keep every form, manual or catalogue of importance (stereo, dishwasher, phone, etc), then use common sense and put the jack underneath the car, under something that looks solid, probably about a foot from the flat tyre, and a couple of inches in. The jack should always be on the same side as the flat, between the wheel arches. Then proceed as follows:

1 Remove the hubcap, using either a large flathead screwdriver or your fingers.

2 Loosen the lug nuts, unscrewing each one a little in turn. On some cars these will need to be unlocked, so make sure you know where the key is. You should really keep it, along with all the tools, in the compartment under the boot where the spare is kept. Hopefully it will be free of old parking tickets and hip-hop CDs.

3 Start jacking the car up until there is room to remove the wheel (the jack will usually have a winch which you will wind, in an alliterative fashion).

4 Remove the lug nuts in an alternating order and put them in the hubcap, where you can find them.

5 Wiggle the wheel off and put it to one side.

6 Jack the car up a bit more, high enough to put the new wheel on.

7 Take the new wheel out of the boot, align the holes in the wheel with the threaded shafts and slide it on.

8 Screw the lug nuts back on, again in an alternating order.

9 Tighten the lug nuts, and then tighten some more.

10 Lower the jack and put it back in the boot.

11 Tighten the lug nuts as far as they will go.

12 Put the flat and any remaining tools back in the boot.

13 If you don't have a foot pump, drive to the next petrol station and pump up the new tyre to the same pressure as the corresponding tyre on the other side of the car.

14 Buy a new spare as soon as possible.

Alternatively, when you've attempted stage **7** and discovered you don't actually have a spare, call the AA, the RAC or the leasing company you rent the car from. Steel yourself and try to suppress any guilty feelings as well as any embarrassment in your voice. Who was to know you didn't have a spare!

HOW TO BUY A SECONDHAND CAR

'Smoke shouldn't be coming out of there, should it? It should?'

I've bought enough secondhand cars in my time – three, and let me tell you, it's enough – to know what I'm talking about. The first one, a Citroën BX, I bought in a bit of a rush (I was young, stupid, and wanted to show it off to my girlfriend), and consequently it turned out to be a lemon. So much of a lemon, in fact, that it broke down exactly two miles from the inauspicious garage in north London I'd bought it from. Smoke began pouring out from under the bonnet, it wouldn't move up through the gears, and gradually grunted to a halt outside an undertakers (true story). This from a dealer, too.

The next time I bought a car – having written the first one off, skidding into a line of traffic as I drove to Heathrow *en route* to Italy to watch AC Milan at the San Siro* – I went to a dealer

---

* Not only did I write off my car that weekend, but the inconsiderate Italians had changed the date of the Milan game, pushing it forward to the Saturday. I only found this out as I walked past a TV shop, as the game was on every screen. At the time I had just arrived in Milan and was actually looking for somewhere to have a coffee, but after this I decided to go for a very large Negroni instead.

related to a friend of mine, in a far more salubrious part of town (Chelsea, as opposed to Wanstead). I bought a BMW and it never went wrong. Later, when that was stolen (from outside the Victoria & Albert Museum on a Sunday afternoon), I bought a Mercedes from the same dealer. Which I kept until I got given my first company car.

My experience taught me all I needed to know about buying an old car. Namely . . .

1   Take as much time as you can when buying a lemon (sorry, secondhand motor vehicle).

2   Never buy an old Citroën.

3   Always buy German.

4   Get your car from someone you don't mind calling when it falls to bits (if it doesn't fall to bits, bits will fall off it).

5   Change your mind: buy a new one instead.

So why are you buying a car? What are you going to use it for? Is it a first car? A second car? Or a vintage car? What are you going to do with it? Drive to work? Go to France or Cornwall every other weekend? Race it? Stick it in a garage? If you know why you're buying the car, everything else should fall into place.

Work out how much you want to spend before going to look at anything, and then stick to that amount. Decide which questions you're going to ask when you see it – it doesn't matter if these are written down, as most sellers now expect you to have had some contact with one of the emergency car services. You can even write the answers down and then ask the seller to sign the piece of paper (although this does suggest that you might have an inkling that they're not entirely trustworthy). In fact one of the most useful tricks is to hire someone from the AA or RAC to come with you, to give the car a once-over. If you're buying a classic car, either take someone who collects them, or a vintage dealer you can trust.

Ask whether the car has been involved in an accident, or whether it was imported. Check the mileage: does the condition of the car match it? Ask the owner whether the mileage is correct and take careful note of his answer (if he says, 'I think so' no further questions are necessary). Obvious signs that the car may have been 'clocked' include misaligned digits on the odometer (although with newer, digital displays it is more difficult to tell), or the mileage shown not being consistent with entries in the service history. And then check that the engine and chassis numbers match the documentation provided, and make sure that the insurance is in place.

If you can, buy from a reputable dealer, or from someone you know. If it's a private seller, ask them why they're selling. What's wrong with it? 'Don't you like it? Isn't this good enough for you? What's so great about your new car?' And make sure it's not too cheap – if it's less than it should be, there must be something wrong with it (there are no bargains in this world). And make sure they're not trying to sell too hastily. Be wary if they try to close the deal too quickly.

Take note of the colour, too. Silver and black cars tend to be safest, being involved in 50 per cent less accidents than – you guessed it – white cars. Yellow and brown cars are also dangerous, but then you wouldn't buy a yellow car, would you? (FYI: according to insurance histories, Ford Fiesta owners are probably called Gareth or Dennis; Ford Escort drivers are called Wayne and Darren; Gavins and Nigels prefer Renault Meganes; and VW Golfs are more likely to be owned by someone named Jonathan, Daniel or Nicholas.)

There are hard and fast rules concerning what you should and shouldn't do before buying, and here is the RAC's advice:

• Check the car's log-book or registration document to validate its age and ownership. Don't rely on the MOT as evidence.

• Make sure the model badge matches the specification on the registration document.

• Is there any evidence of repaired accident damage to the body panels?

• Do the colour and texture of the paintwork match all over?

• Check the bodywork with a magnet to discover any dents touched up with body filler.

• Check beneath the bonnet or under the boot for bad welds, untidy seams or any other evidence of accident repairs.

• Check for rust and paint bubbles, particularly on the sills, wheel arches, seams, door bottoms and suspension mountings.

• Check headlights, dashboard and warning lights.

• Remember to check the hazard lights, windscreen wipers and the horn.

• 'Under the hood', look for oil leaks, defective or damaged hoses and drive belts.

• Check oil and coolants for low levels or signs of contamination.

• If the engine is reconditioned, ask for evidence, e.g. a bill or a warranty.

• Make sure the seatbelts show no sign of damage or wear.

• Check the doors, the windows and the sun roof seals for leaks.

• When taking it for a test drive, try a variety of conditions and situations: hills, stop-start driving and open roads.

• Listen for any noises from the engine or the suspension.

• Test the steering, the brakes and the clutch.

- Let the engine idle and check under the bonnet for oil or water leaks.

- Check the tyres, including the spare, for tread depth and damage. The grooves of the tread must be at least 1.6mm throughout a band comprising the central three-quarters of the breadth of the tread, and round the outer circumference of the tyre.

- Check for bulges or cuts in the tyre wall to guard against blow-outs.

You should take as much care as you can, as you'd be amazed at what dealers and sellers will do to a car just to make it look nice. From a dealer's point of view, the most important aspect of the car will be its appearance (i.e. they've given it a wash, a wax and a valet), and you must not be distracted by this. Keep reminding yourself that you're not just looking to buy a clean car.

Most mistakes can be avoided by taking a professional with you, so call the AA or the RAC and hire an expert.

Lastly, check to see what CDs the seller's been playing. Would you buy a car from a man who listens to nothing but Marilyn Manson, Black Sabbath and the Darkness? (What do you mean, you listen to nothing else?)

And don't kick the tyres, not even in jest (it isn't funny).

FOOD
&
DRINK

HOW TO HOST A FORMAL DINNER PARTY

'Elton, you sit there, and Nelson, why don't you sit over there, that's right, by Bono . . .'

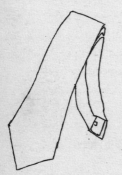

Most of us have fairly informal dinner parties these days, but if you actually want to do something that involves a bit of effort, for whatever reason, then here is what you do . . .

Invitations

You should invite people at least three weeks in advance, either by card or by phone. If it's a drinks party you're having, then invite at least half as many people again as you'd like to have come, as you'll be surprised how many won't be able to.

At a push it's fine to ask the day before ('Hi, look, I know it's short notice, but we've decided to have a few people round tomorrow and we wondered . . .'), although it's a bit much to emulate the hostess in Evelyn Waugh's *A Handful of Dust*, who always invited poor John Beaver at the last minute, 'Occasionally even later, when he had already begun to eat a solitary meal from a tray . . . "John, darling, there's been a muddle and Sonia has arrived without Reggie. Could you be an angel and help me out? Only be quick because we're going in now . . .'" One famous old hostess, when she was asked what she most valued in a friend, used to like to say, rather bluntly, 'availability'.

You yourself ought to have an excuse at hand, should you get invited to something you'd rather not go to. I've always found a hesitant, 'Now, I think I'm doing something that night. But let me firm up and I'll get back to you' works adequately well (I always get back to them and I always firm up). Peter Cook, on the other hand, didn't give a fig for this type of convention. David Frost called him up one night and said, 'Prince Andrew is coming to dinner with Fergie, the lovely girl he is going to marry, and they are both tremendous fans. Could you come to dinner? They would really love it because they really want to meet you. Be super if you could make it Wednesday the twelfth.' At which point Cook ambles off to check his diary. After a while he comes back to the phone and says, 'Oh dear, I find I'm watching television that night.'

Table Plan

Eight o'clock means 8.30, but six o'clock cocktails means six o'clock cocktails. Make sure you always do a *placement*, and carefully choose who to put next to each other. By rights it should be boy-girl-boy-girl. Don't seat couples together, nor people who know each other well; the whole point of a dinner party is to mix people up, and give everyone a new experience. As host you should normally sit at the head, although you might want to occupy a chair that allows you easy access to the kitchen. Just use common sense.

Laying the Table

If your napkins can't be changed or washed after every meal, it's far better to place a box of paper napkins on the table. If the plates are going to be on the table when your guests sit down, put the napkins on the left of the plates, to the left of the cutlery.

When laying the cutlery, the first things you're going to use should be on the outside – first course fork, main course fork on the left; and first course knife, main course knife on the right (with the blades facing the plate). When eating, work from the outside in. The dessert fork and spoon are placed above the plate, the spoon on top facing left, and the fork underneath with tines facing right. (The only exception is a seafood fork, which should be sitting on the extreme right of the knives.)

You should really have different glasses for each wine – a regular-sized wine glass for white, a larger one for red, some sort of tumbler for water, and a much smaller one for pudding wine. These should sit to the right of the plate, above the knives, and can be arranged in any order. If you're going to be using the champagne glasses again at the end of the dinner (you might be having a celebratory cake), then wash them before refilling them.

If you get up from the table half-way through eating, put your fork down on the left-hand side of your plate, with the tines facing down, and the knife on the right, with the sharp edge facing in. And put your napkin on the seat, never the table.

Food

Always give your guests plenty of hors d'oeuvres, if only to soak up the booze. For twelve people you need roughly eighty pieces, as well as crisps, nuts, breadsticks, and whatever the finger food *du jour* is (although personally I don't think you can beat the mini sausage).

As for the dinner, don't be pretentious, and don't attempt anything beyond the ordinary limitations of your kitchen. Even if you're having it catered, it should be food that you could plausibly cook yourself. And don't wing it. As *Queer Eye for the Straight Guy*'s Ted Allen says, 'Allow yourself plenty of time; dinner guests, like feral animals, can smell panic, and it makes them uncomfortable.' Give your guests four courses: starter or salad, main (meat), cheese, and then dessert. Try not to buy the dessert, as no matter how good it is, this shows rather a lack of imagination. If you're stuck for ideas, or worry that your guests have grown tired of your repertoire, then open one of your books: Jamie Oliver, Nigel Slater, Nigella Lawson, Simon Hopkinson, The River Café, etc (the only problem with serving French food is that, three or four days later, you're hungry again). Plan in advance, but don't get too anal about it. Alternatively you could lay on an ad hoc buffet, and eat in the kitchen.

Notes:

1 Leaving food on your plate is not a sign of bad manners, but leaving food you've served yourself is.

2 Always try to warm the plates before serving; put them in the oven for two or three minutes at the lowest setting.

3 And serve from the left.

Drink

Serve champagne before dinner, or a limited number of specific drinks. Either pour people champagne as they arrive (giving them no choice), or offer a specific selection: white, red, water or beer. If you're offering vodka and tonics, then make everyone one, and if you're only serving white wine or prosecco, don't apologise. Remember this too: an aperitif is something you drink before drinking something else, so although you should get everyone loosened up, don't get everyone so drunk that they won't enjoy the food.

Then, when you sit down, serve white first, then red, then dessert wine. You should allow one bottle of white and one bottle of red for each person, because although most people drink red, until they sit down you never actually know exactly what they'll be drinking (and neither do they). If it's a very formal dinner you can stop serving white after a while and move on to red for the main course, but it's usual these days to offer both from the off. And even if it is formal, some people will just choose to drink a specific wine all evening. It is important to serve the same wines throughout – you don't want to be continually moving backwards and forwards between Fleurie and Barolo. White wine is poured from the bottle, whereas red should be decanted, around twenty minutes before you intend to drink it. When you're decanting wine, make sure there is a candle or a light behind the neck of the bottle when you pour; that way you can stop pouring when the sediment appears.

As for still water (and everyone wants still water at dinners nowadays), you can either have half a dozen plastic litre bottles of Evian or Vittel (the two best types) sitting on the table, or decant same into large glass jugs.

Conversation

• Good talk is usually slow in getting started and long in winding up.

• Don't listen to people just so you can come up with a smart alec retort. *Really* listen.

• Don't interrupt.

• Don't argue to win, don't argue for argument's sake and don't be unnecessarily polite. Get involved, but don't become demonstrative.

• Don't disagree until you fully understand what you're disagreeing with.

• Don't go on for ever.

• And don't bang on about the difficulties, the fabulousness and the minutiae of your job. Trust me: we don't really care. A little, yes; but not a lot.

• Don't allow yourself to be monopolised. Some people are like chewing gum and won't leave you alone. Be firm but polite and switch to the person on the other side of you. This is a tremendously important thing to do, and you need to be able to switch off at some point. If there isn't a natural break in the conversation you're having with the person sitting to your left, it's quite OK to abruptly start talking to the person on your right when the next course arrives.

Moving

Don't encourage people to switch places – 'jump ship' – until all courses have been served. If you're at a big event, then it might be OK to go and perch on someone's chair, or sit down in an empty space to talk to someone you know, but if you're at a dinner with less than twelve people, it's not on.

Music

If you're in any doubt as to what sort of music to play at your dinner, just imagine you're in a restaurant. In all my years of going out to eat, I can't recall any dining experience that would have been improved by having a musical accompaniment. Not one. On the other hand, I can think of many dinners that would have been exponentially improved by turning the stereo off. Frankly, music in restaurants is not necessary; never has been, never will be.

It is used, fundamentally, for one of two reasons: to create 'atmosphere', and to hurry people up, like bright overhead lights in fast food restaurants. To be blunt, any establishment that needs artificial 'atmosphere', that can't rely on its food, décor or staff, is doomed from the off. What makes owners think that we're going to forget the undercooked fish or overcooked vegetables just because they've rushed out to HMV and bought the collected works of Dido, Moby or Mylo? Will we be prepared to ignore the fact that we're eating in an unheated aircraft hangar, or pretend not to notice that we haven't seen a waiter for twenty minutes, just because we're listening to a chill-out CD? The only time it's acceptable to listen to chill-out CDs, ambient music or neo-classical background sounds is when you're getting a massage and actually wouldn't mind falling asleep for a bit; not when you're about to work your way through a plate of suckling pig.

The other sort of music you hear in restaurants is LOUD music, the sort that will encourage you to drink more, eat quickly, and not care too much about what you're putting in your mouth. However, the only time I can actually recall having enjoyed hearing 'The Boys Are Back in Town' by Thin Lizzy as I was eating a burger was the first and only time I went to the Hard Rock Café. Which, I think you'll agree, while being an adolescent rite of passage, is not exactly a culinary hotspot.

If you're intent on having music, then make it instrumental, so your guests don't start singing along, or picking up on particular lyrics. This is the perfect way to decontextualise the event. No emotions. No instructions. No localisation. Move from 1960s movie soundtracks to 1990s Japanese loungecore, from 1970s folk to 1980s alt country and beyond, via prog, space age pop, and chill-out with consummate ease. For three hours of failsafe 'background' noise, you could do worse than use the following (it's important not to let the music repeat itself, as then your guests will begin to think they've been there too long):

1   'The Ipcress File' by John Barry

2   'The Nearest Faraway Place' by the Beach Boys

3   'Std 0632' by Alan Hull

4   'Song of Innocence' by David Axelrod

5   'Watermelon Man' by Herbie Hancock

6   'Harlem River Drive' by Bobbi Humphrey

7   'Man Alive' by Tony Hatch

8　'Samba Pa Ti' by Santana

9　'Follow Your Bliss' by the B-52s

10　'International' (the original 1978 version) by Thomas Leer

11　'Mouthful of Grass' by Free

12　'Peaches En Regalia' by Frank Zappa

13　'Casino Royale' by Herb Alpert

14　'Mas Que Nada' by Sergio Mendes & Brasil '66 (although it contains vocals, I doubt that anyone at your party will actually know what he's on about)

15　Ennio Moricone's *Once Upon a Time in America* (all of it)

16　*Ocean's Twelve* by David Holmes

17　'A Man and a Woman' by Francis Lai

18　'A Shot in the Dark' by Jimmie Haskell

19　'Adagio' by William Orbit

20　'Girl in a Sportscar' by Alan Hawkshaw

21　'That's Nice' by Alan Moorehouse

22　'Robinson Crusoe' by the Art Of Noise

23　'Slow Hot Wind' by Block 16

24　'Pacific Coast Highway' by Burt Bacharach

25　'Wives and Lovers' by the Dieter Reith Trio

26　'Reveries' by Dimitri from Paris

27　'Sentimental Journey' by Esquivel

28 *Betty Blue* by Gabriel Yared

29 'Belgravia' by Workshop

30 'Nice Work If You Can Get It' by Thelonious Monk

31 'Alpine Crossing' by Swing Out Sister

32 'Rose Rouge' by St Germain

33 'Man of Mystery' by the Shadows

34 'So Easy' by Royksopp

35 'The Girl from U.N.C.L.E.' by Teddy Randazzo

36 'Soul Bossa Nova' by Quincy Jones

37 'Lolita Ya Ya' by Nelson Riddle

38 'Blue in Green' by Miles Davis

39 'Générique' by Michel Legrand

40 'Harlem Nocturne' by Martin Denny

41 'Nude' by Karel Velebny

42 'Lady in Cement' by Hugo Montenegro

43 'Everyone's a VIP' by the Go! Team

44 'Roda' by Gilberto Gil

45 *The Family Way* by the George Martin Orchestra

46 'On Her Majesty's Secret Service' by David Arnold

47 'A Night in Tunisia' by Art Blakey

48 'Goodbye Pork Pie Hat' by Charles Mingus

49 'Body & Soul' by Coleman Hawkins

50 'Blue Rondo à la Turk' by the Dave Brubeck Quartet

51 'Manha De Carnaval' by Dexter Gordon

52 'Not for Nothin'' by the Dave Holland Quintet

53 'Song For My Father' by Horace Silver

54 'Children' by Robert Miles

55 'Sadness' by Enigma

56 'Open Your Mind' by Gerardo Frisina

57 'East St Louis Toodle-Oo' by Steely Dan

58 *Talk to Her* by Alberto Iglesias

59 'Alone in Kyoto' by Air

60 'Little Bird' by the Elsie Bianchi Trio.

All this should be on a playlist on your iPod, played through a Bose iPod dock and speaker system.

The Clincher

In the end, it's less about the food or the music or the booze and all about the company. When asked by an interviewer in 1982 what his most pleasurable, memorable meal was, John Updike said, 'My most memorable meal was a lunch with Alfred Knopf [the distinguished publisher], who took me to La Côte Basque [the once famous New York restaurant] when it was still owned by Henri Soule [the eminent French chef]. I can't remember what we ate, but . . .'

HOW TO ORDER WINE

'Have you got anything, you know, cheaper?'

Wine, like golf, women and life itself, is one of those things it might take you your entire time on Earth to understand. And even then I wouldn't bank on it. And like certain types of those women, wine is deep, dark and unfathomable.

But we all have to learn, and there's no better time than the present. The moment you begin being more interested in wine is usually the moment you can afford to (it's a lot like voting Tory). After all, it's all very well knowing a lot about wine, but if you're seventeen you probably won't be able to afford to do anything about it. And a passion for wine also starts stirring when you begin to swap quantity for quality. Because not only does good wine taste better, it's also better for you. One of the things people rarely mention about wine is its effect on your hangovers – i.e. if you drink very good wine then you won't experience the same sort of hangovers as you will with the cheap stuff. I once went to a David Bowie concert at Wembley Arena and stupidly ordered a small plastic bottle of white wine from the bar (we had been drinking white wine in the pub beforehand and I thought it made sense to carry on in this vein). But what a mistake: approximately five seconds after swallowing some I got a migraine right above my left eye, one that continued until Bowie encored with 'I'm

Afraid of Americans' (or, as I immediately rechristened it, 'I'm Afraid of Cheap Australian Chardonnay in Disposable Plastic Bottles').

Wine is about as subjective a subject as it's possible to bring up in mixed company, although it's safe to say that red wine these days is considered to be slightly more sophisticated than white. Red wine is a slower drink, a more considered drink, while white wine has become the default alternative to beer. And can you drink red wine with fish? Of course. Don't bother about the old Ian Fleming way of looking at the world – whenever we have Sunday lunch in our house, we nearly always drink red, regardless of what we're eating (and regardless of whether we're eating).

You also need to be aware of the mark-up. Restaurants don't source their wines from the same supermarkets as the rest of us, but their bulk deals are rarely passed on to the customer. So expect a mark-up of between 65 and 75 per cent on each bottle sold. This means you pay around three times what it cost wholesale, plus VAT. Because of this, don't necessarily think that the house wine will be better value. Often it's the cheaper wines that have the heaviest mark-up, while the more expensive wines are less aggressively priced (in the hope that people might actually buy them). The price of wine is largely determined by its reputation, although cheap wine isn't necessarily bad and expensive wine isn't necessarily good. But on the whole expensive wine is expensive because it's good and in demand.

And if you're ever in any doubt as to what you should spend, seeing that your finances are almost certainly finite, then take this advice from *GQ*'s wine correspondent Robert Sandall: 'Calculate what the food bill for one will come to and then select a bottle of wine priced in the same range. Drink it and repeat to taste.'

So, what will you order? Traditionally you'd match bigger, bolder red wines with big, rich, grilled and roasted meats. For example, a California Cabernet Sauvignon or a Rhône Valley Crozes-Hermitage will go very nicely with roast beef, prime rib or steak. For even bigger beefy dishes, or incredibly rich food, then you should opt for a Syrah/Shiraz, Zinfandel, Barolo (a great, great wine), Barbaresco, Brunello di Montalcino, Tempranillo or Super Tuscans (overpriced but hearty Italian wines). For lighter meat dishes – grilled chicken, liver, etc – then try Montepulciano d'Abruzzo, Chianti or Valpolicella.

According to www.bullz-eye.com/wine, if you're eating Italian, especially pasta, then you can choose any wine that ends in a vowel, specifically Bardolino, Valpolicella, Chianti, Gattinara, Dolcetto or Barbera for red-sauced dishes. For white-sauce pasta dishes, or fish, try Gavi, Orvieto or Trebbiano.

You should try to avoid the obvious wines, like Merlot or Chardonnay. Merlot has become something of a cliché, and ever since the film *Sideways* (2004) it has become a naff default wine . . . while Chardonnay is usually too overoaked and sweet to accompany food (it's basically for single girls who want to get drunk quickly). Pinot Noir is very fashionable now, mainly due to the success of *Sideways*, although the grape is supposedly the favourite tipple of Michael Jackson. Allegedly he used to swig it from soft-drink cans so that his drinking habits could go undetected.

Sideways has become something of a cult, and has generated the type of affection it usually takes years to develop. It also has an extremely popular website, on which you'll find the following 'Snob-free guide to wine', designed to help you order the best wine for your meal. To paraphrase:

1 Sauvignon Blanc and Riesling are good to accompany fish, salads, vegetables, and food that has been poached or steamed, or prepared with lemon glaze, rosemary, cinnamon, dill or garlic. They are also good with blue cheese, goat's cheese and Gorgonzola.

2 Sangiovese, Pinot Noir, Merlot and Chardonnay are good with pork, poultry, veal and roasted, baked and sautéed food, along with

Mozzarella, Feta, Cheddar, Gruyère, Ricotta and Pecorino. Perfect to accompany cream and butter sauces, as well as oregano, mustard, cloves, sage and ginger.

3   Zinfandel, Cabernet Sauvignon and Syrah work with braised and grilled red meat in wine-based or meat sauces, as well as parsley, nutmeg, anise, Brie and Camembert. I assume you're not meant to mix all these things together, but it doesn't say . . .

If it's an important meal, it's a good idea to get to the restaurant early and ask the sommelier's advice on what to order with what. Also, some restaurants now put their wine list on their website, so you can acclimatise yourself well in advance.

You should never be afraid to ask the sommelier's advice. There's nothing wrong with saying, 'I like New World Sauvignon Blanc but wouldn't mind trying something different.' Believe it or not, sommeliers actually like punters who engage with them and ask their advice. And if you can't pronounce the name of the wine, then don't. Just tell the sommelier the number, as you would in a Chinese restaurant. There's nothing gauche about it; your guests will probably think you're being discreet in not announcing to the table what extravagant wine you're ordering. And if the sommelier says, 'The 1999 Brunello Montifitadorino di Tulio Santidorino?' don't get intimidated. After all, he's paid to pronounce stuff like that. And if you've asked the sommelier to suggest something, but actually don't like it, then send it back. *Never be embarrassed to send wine back.*

And by all means be led by your inclination. If you like a wine, then there's absolutely no reason why you shouldn't order it, or at least something like it. You're the ones who have got to drink it, after all. However, if you're going to go off-piste, then you should be mindful of those fateful words uttered in Wagner's gloomy 'masterpiece', *The Flying Dutchman*: 'If you trust the wind, you trust in Satan's mercy.'

When the waiter presents the bottle to you, always look at the label, as sometimes waiters make (deliberate) mistakes, and try and fob you off with a similar vintage or a less good wine. After he's poured a little into your glass for you to taste, you should swirl the wine around, and then smell it. As you get more accustomed to this you'll rarely need to taste it, but it's always better for novices to taste the wine, just to build up an idea of what various wines actually taste like. Don't, however, smell the cork, as all you'll smell is cork, and this will identify you as a boy in a man's body.

If, after tasting the wine, you think there's something wrong with it, then ask the sommelier to taste it too. Corked wine will smell of vinegar and taste of cheese (or, occasionally, the other way round), and you'll probably be able to tell it's corked without actually tasting it. And don't expect to get balloon glasses if you're only ordering half-decent wines. These are usually reserved for people ordering older, expensive wines that need to breathe.

Of course there's no substitute for actually knowing what you're talking about, and there's no reason why you shouldn't go on a few wine courses. At the very least you'll be able to compile a cheater's guide to ordering wine, and it's always good to know the rules before you break them.

Sometimes, however, your knowledge of wines will not be needed, perhaps because you've made an unfortunate choice of venue. Some years ago I was involved in a reality TV show and, as a member of the four-man judging panel, had to attend auditions all over the country, in London, Birmingham, Manchester, Cardiff, etc. We descended upon Newcastle late one Sunday afternoon and after unpacking I went down to the bar to join the crew for a drink.

After a while I managed to attract the waitress's attention.

'Do you have a wine list?' I asked.

'No,' she said, not a smile in sight.

'Do you serve wine then?'

'Oh yes.'

'Er, what sort?'

'Both. Large or small.'

'Oh, I see. I'll have a Beck's, please.'

Some Good Vintages of Wines to Drink Now:

Alsace: 1973, 1976, 1983, 1985, 1988, 1989, 1990, 1995, 1996, 1997.

Barolo: 1989, 1990, 1996.

Bordeaux (claret): 1970, 1975, 1978, 1982, 1983, 1985, 1986, 1988, 1989, 1990, 1995, 1996, 1998, 1999, 2000, 2001, 2002, 2004.

Bordeaux (white): 1970, 1975, 1978, 1983, 1985, 1988, 1989, 1990.

Burgundy (red): 1985, 1989, 1990, 1994, 1995.

Burgundy (white): 1979, 1985, 1988, 1989, 1990, 1995.

California (red): 1985, 1994, 1995, 1996, 1997.

California (white): 1986, 1990, 1994, 1995, 1996, 1998, 1999, 2000.

Mosel: 1990, 1995, 1999.

New South Wales: 1983, 1985, 1986, 1998, 1999.

Rhine: 1988, 1989, 1990, 1995, 2001.

Ribera del Duero: 1989, 1990, 1996.

Rioja: 1983, 1989, 1990, 1994, 1995, 1996.

Rhone (red): 1982, 1983, 1985, 1988, 1989, 1990, 1994, 1995, 1997.

Rhone (white): 1989, 1990, 1997.

South Australia: 1982, 1986, 1988, 1994, 1996.

Veneto: 1985, 1988, 1990, 1997.

Western Australia: 1985, 1986, 1988, 1994, 1995, 1996, 1997, 1998, 1999.

HOW TO NAVIGATE THE MODERN RESTAURANT

Sit down and order with impunity: here you are the King

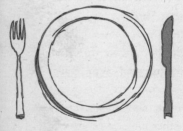

There are many things I find irritating about eating in smart restaurants. And while I will never tire of eating at truly great places – The Ivy, Le Caprice, The Wolseley and Pied à Terre obviously spring to mind, restaurants where the customers are the stars, rather than the staff – I fail to understand why going to a fancy restaurant these days still has to be such a bloody performance.

And though the culprits obviously pride themselves on the food they serve, many of them forget that what most people want from an evening out is great service, followed by some great service, and finished off with some, yes, you guessed it, more great service.

It's a universally acknowledged truth that if you don't want a waiter he'll be there, at your shoulder, hovering like Uriah Heep and pouring the wine into your glass after every sip; and that if you do want one (you might think it's time to, say, order something, or – God forbid – pay your bill), he will dematerialise as though he were never there. There used to be a girl in the café underneath our office who was so pathetically useless at her job that we started calling her Halley's Waitress.

Why, whenever I hear the words 'May I tell you about our specials this evening, sir?' do I always think I'm about to be fobbed off with something the chef has over-ordered and now can't get rid of? Do I want to hear about the specials? Well, no actually, and could you just bring the wine I ordered twenty minutes ago? When waiters used to recite the seemingly exponential list of elaborate specials at New York's ultra-cool cool SoHo restaurant Odeon, it took so long that regulars started calling it 'The Knight's Tale'.

I'm also completely uninterested in their internal hierarchies. Once, in Terence Conran's Sartoria in Savile Row (where the service was, and still is, unbelievably slow), I asked a waiter for some bread, only to be told that he would 'go and let the bread waiter know'. Like I cared! Later during the meal, when I made the mistake of asking the 'bread waiter' for some water, he looked at me as though I'd just asked if I could sleep with his younger sister. I don't care who brings the water, the wine or the waffles, nor do I care how many conversations the waiters have to have with each other in order to achieve this – just do it!

My second greatest restaurant irritation is when you turn up at a c-o-m-p-l-e-t-e-l-y empty restaurant, only to have the maître d' tediously and oh-so-slowly scan his list of bookings before asking you if you've booked. 'Yes, but would it actually have made any difference if I hadn't? Forgive my impertinence, but you don't exactly seem to be overburdened by customers right now. And could we sit over there, by the window, right next to the tumbleweed?'

But my ultimate dining bugbear is the soliloquies given by the waiters as they're finally bringing the food to the table. I will never understand why my food has to be explained to me – again, laboriously, ad nauseam – once it's actually in front of me. 'Sir,' they'll announce, as they puff out their chests and begin gesticulating with their hands, 'here we have a riot of seared grain-fed baby chicken breast, brine tomolives and whisked avocado on toast points with faux tuna niçoise sprinkled with burnt garlic, bruised thyme and supermarket cheese string. And for you, madam – what a wonderful choice – the avalanche of sunbaked aubergine spaghetti with kumquat and pepper vodka consommé served with slightly overcooked crab cakes and peppermint mash.'

What do they expect you to say? Oh, thanks, I'd forgotten. Surely if you've gone to the trouble of mentally ploughing your way through an exhaustive – and exhausting – menu that contains the likes of pan-fried Anjou pigeon with celery and beetroot or lime-marinated ceviche of scallops and clams, then you're surely not going to fail to remember you ordered the braised alligator turtle with bacon bits and marmalade ice-cream.

In a bid to compete with the gastro-capitals of the world, London has, I fear, become rather too preoccupied with style at the expense of service. I don't mind paying for haute couture food as long as I get bespoke service. Not obsequious service (think Petrus), not offhand service (think Cipriani, probably the worst 'good' restaurant in London), but good old-fashioned polite and non-invasive service (think J. Sheekey's, definitely the best fish restaurant in Britain).

But all this is nothing when compared with the treatment you get in Hollywood restaurants. Californians are not only pathological about their own drinking habits (basically they don't), but incredibly suspicious about other people's. A few years ago, when a few of us were in LA on business, we took a writer out to dinner at a trendy little Hollywood trat called Little Door. The four of us were going out afterwards, so we took it easy, splitting two bottles of red between us. But when we ordered the second bottle the waitress looked at us like we'd just asked for a gram of cocaine.

We forgot about this until we got up to leave about an hour later. As we did so we spied her hastily scooping the bottles from the table.

Caught in the act, she said, without a hint of irony, 'Just destroying the evidence.'

My advice on navigating the convoluted etiquette of the modern restaurant is simple: as you are the customer and the customer is king, do not worry – about anything. Be courteous, treat the staff like colleagues, and tip properly. But don't be intimidated, don't be subservient, and make sure you get *exactly* what you want. Restaurants offer a service, and without customers they do not technically exist. The democratisation of eating out has made the restaurant culture far more inclusive, and with choice comes the inevitable raising of standards. It is a meritocracy worth celebrating, and if you don't feel like a celebration then you very quickly vote with your feet. Food should be a celebration, and these days there are thousands of places where you can celebrate, so if you don't like the service in X then you simply pop down to Y.

HOW TO DRINK WHISKY

Always go for the single malts . . .

. . . because the blended whiskies are just *soo* naff.

The days are over when whisky was emblematic of a certain kind of hipster cool, yet the gentle sipping of a single malt – sitting on a Chesterfield stool, alone at a circular baize table, secreted in the dimly lit corner of some West End bar – still evinces proper outsider status. Remember: whisky is no substitute for a decent education. And vice versa.

You're listening to Donald Fagen, maybe, at least in your head, and you're wearing a one-button navy two-piece from Richard James, with a smoking scarf round your neck (one of those little silk things you can wear indoors without feeling too self-conscious).

But what are you drinking? Well, you're probably drinking a single malt Scottish whisky.* You could be sipping Glenmorangie (the biggest selling malt in Scotland), Glenfiddich (the biggest selling malt in the world), or Glenlivet or Lagavulin (simply very good single

---

* Irish whisky is spelt 'whiskey', and if you're going down this road, drink Jameson's.

malts). But what you should be drinking is ten-year-old Laphroaig, the most richly flavoured of all the single malts (full of traces of peat and smoke). Hailing from the Islay region of Scotland (one of the four main regions of Scotch distillation – the others being Campbeltown, Highland and Lowland), it has all the history, all the taste, and exactly the right sort of kudos.

Those who despise cocktails say that if you can't taste the alcohol, you won't respect the drink. This has never been a problem with whisky, which is one of the reasons you should really drink it neat. Yes, you can have it with ice – if you insist – and yes, you can splash it into a glass of Coke if you're trying to stay up, but the only proper mixer is lukewarm water (because of the high alcohol content of many single malts, potency levels are quite high). The only things that have been known to improve the taste of Scotch – as accompaniments – are strong coffee and dark chocolate.

Like fine wine, single malt Scotch does improve with age, although many plateau around the 25-year mark. Each region and distillery has distinctive production methods, ranging from the type of barley, water or yeast used, to whether the casks are made of Madeira or Sherry oloroso wood, and whether or not a layer of peat has been added to the barley. It's long been acknowledged that it's this bizarre marriage of art and science that makes really good single malt.

HOW TO MAKE THE PERFECT MARTINI

. . . and the only four other cocktails you'll ever need to master

These days men don't need to be the dextrous mixologists they needed to be forty years ago – women don't necessarily see it as a compulsory skill – yet it's still something you should master. Being able to make a martini is one of those things that you should be able to do with a minimum of fuss and without any fanfare. It should be no big deal, just one of those things that you acknowledge once separated the men from the boys. After all, your woman should understand that you have a deep and thorough knowledge of the intricacies of the surface smarts that make or made men great. As H.L. Mencken once said, the martini is 'the only American invention as perfect as a sonnet'.

Personally I've never been fond of them, for the same reason that I don't inject myself often with rocket fuel: I find them too strong (with booze I like to go from nought to sixty in the time it takes to finish a bottle of wine, although I appreciate that some men like to do it in the time it takes to move through the gears). Our relationship with alcoholic drinks is traditionally based on our first teenage experience of them, usually because we got so drunk on something when we were thirteen that we haven't been able to touch one since. In my case I have never been able to drink vodka and lime or rum and black, although as these are two of the most disgusting drinks ever to have been invented, this has not been any great loss.

Embarrassingly, I had a similar experience with martinis; embarrassing because (a) I drank four on an empty stomach, and (b) I was thirty at the time. I hope you will already have heard of the analogy between drinking martinis and women's breasts: one is not enough but three is too many; four, I would submit, is almost suicidal. I had arranged to meet friends in Duke's Hotel, just behind The Ritz in London, whose barmen are generally regarded as the purveyors of the best martinis in Europe. I was a martini virgin and – stupidly, ridiculously, pathetically – drank four big ones having only had a light lunch. The rush you get from martinis is the same sort of rush you get from good cocaine (which is why they were so popular in New York in the 1980s and in London during the 1990s), a rush that can only be maintained by ordering more, or stopped by falling over. True to form, I did both, and still have no recollection of getting home, or what her name was.

So for me they will for ever be tainted, although I realise that increasingly they have become a cocktail party staple. We will never drink them again the way they used to in the days of screwball comedies and Noël Coward plays, when trussed-up socialites appeared to knock back four or five before going in to dinner; nor will we ever return to what New Yorkers used to call the three martini lunch (Wall Street and Evian put paid to that), but you still need to be able to make one.

This is what you do to make the standard dry martini: take two or three parts dry gin (or, increasingly, vodka), one part dry vermouth, and pour them over ice in a cocktail shaker. Stir, and then strain into a chilled martini glass, accompanied by a dash of orange bitters (optional) and a twist of lemon peel. The proportions vary from bar to bar and from so-called expert to so-called expert. Hemingway was always a fan of the Montgomery martini, fifteen parts gin to one part vermouth (the odds Monty gave on the battlefield), Richard Nixon preferred seven to one, and Doors troubadour Jim Morrison liked them any way they came. Famously, Luis Buñuel thought it enough to hold up a full glass of gin next to a bottle of vermouth and let a beam of sunlight pass through.

As to whether the drink is shaken or stirred, shaking makes for a colder drink (Ian Fleming's preference), while most modern bartenders adhere to Somerset Maugham's old adage: 'A martini should always be stirred, not shaken, so that the molecules lie sensuously on top of one another.'

The traditional garnish is the green olive, although what you should really have these days is a tomolive, a small green tomato pickled like an olive. I first discovered these in the bar of the Bel Air Hotel in Los Angeles, and frankly have never looked back. It is perfect in vodka and tonic, gin and tonic, and any other drink that requires a spherical verdant vegetable.

Four other cocktails you should be able to make:

1   Caipirinha: mash half a lime with a teaspoonful of sugar in the bottom of a glass and then add a shot of cachaca before filling the tumbler with crushed ice.

2   Seabreeze: two parts vodka, two parts cranberry juice and one part grapefruit juice. Shake and then strain over ice in a tall glass.

3   Mojito: grind some fresh mint into a tall glass with a teaspoon of sugar syrup before adding the juice from half a lime. Fill the glass with white rum and soda, according to taste.

4   Negroni: one part gin, one part sweet vermouth, one part Campari, mixed in a large glass and then topped up with soda and garnished with a slice of orange. Serve and then stand back.

HOW TO CURE
A HANGOVER

The most useful advice you'll ever get

As many of you will recall, in September 2005, England gloriously wrested back the Ashes from Shane Warne's ugly mob of Antipodean interlopers. While most of us can recall the final innings of the last Test, surely what no one will ever forget is Andrew Flintoff's magnificent victory celebration; not just one of the greatest drinking binges in British sporting history, but also one of the most gleefully reported.

Freddie started the evening at 6.30, enthusiastically knocking back a couple of bottles of chilled champagne and quaffing a few beers with team-mate Steve Harmison before spending the night in the hotel bar. He becomes so drunk he announces, to no one in particular, 'I'm ugly, I'm overweight, but I'm happy. I'd never make a decent celebrity.'

Then, at 6.30 a.m., after twelve long hours on the pop, he has a gin and tonic and a vodka and cranberry juice to wake himself up. At 8.30 a.m. he joins another champagne reception at the hotel, surprising himself – and the press – by being the only team member to make it. At 9.45 a.m., a little more beer, followed at 10.30 a.m. by some more chilled champagne, this time drunk straight from the bottle on the open-top bus on the victory parade through Trafalgar Square (a difficult thing to do in his condition, even at five miles per hour). Then, at 1.30 p.m. at Downing Street, after being offered a variety of inappropriate and frankly unwanted soft drinks, Flintoff bravely orders a beer. By 3 p.m. he's drinking more champagne at Lord's, where he stays until staggering off to the long-awaited but hardly needed victory dinner. Finally, around 2 a.m. the next day, a full 32 hours since that first glass of sparkling pop, the mighty Flintoff calls it a day, crawling off to bed (albeit with 'Tw*t' scribbled on his forehead, courtesy of Harmison).

Now, though there are many who might say that he let the side down by failing to sneak in a cheeky beer between leaving Lord's and arriving at dinner, it's still a fairly impressive display, a display that in Flintoff's case didn't require any sort of 'adjustment' the following day. Flintoff is young enough not to have to worry too much about hangovers, and if he occasionally has cause to, will simply just drink himself through it.

This is the solution favoured by many, especially as they get older, and a very small hair of a very large dog is often the best remedy. A Bloody Mary is the most popular solution, but one not appreciated by me. Not only do I not like the smell of napalm in the morning, I don't appreciate the taste of vodka either, and if I'm going down the 'dog' route (what I always refer to as the 'bitch'), would prefer to wait until lunch and then knock back two glasses of champagne (I would avoid, however, 'the sergeant major', which is a glass of champagne with two raw eggs plopped in it; not only does it not work, but has the capacity to make you feel as though you're on a reality TV show, albeit a quite upmarket one).

Before that I will have woken up, bleary-eyed and bloated, and then drunk a half-litre of bottled water. Then I'll have a cup of tea, some sort of dissolvable vitamin drink and a couple of pieces of brown toast. An hour later, at work, instead of coffee I'll have a red ambulance (full fat Coca-Cola), and then drink a litre of water until lunch.

When you're in this condition, lunch is the most important time of the day, as you need to decide whether you're going to try and make it through to the evening, knowing that you're going to feel increasingly bad; or whether you're going to climb back on the horse and have a little snifter. Personally I would advocate a quick drink at lunch and then calling it a day.

There are hundreds of amateur hangover 'cures', most of which only have a slim chance of working. They include 'the doctor' (raw egg, brandy, sugar and milk), 'the Lazenby' (hot water with ginger, cloves and honey) and 'the Gazza' (two beers for breakfast). But the wrath of grapes (thank you, Jeffrey Bernard) should be circumnavigated, not tended to afterwards. I would suggest making an effort the night before, rather than the morning after, either by drinking very good wine (the best that you can afford), or by also drinking a hell of a lot of water. People like to suggest that you drink a litre of still water before you got to sleep; this is good advice (doubling the amount won't kill you), and especially successful if you've been spending all night drinking a glass of water after every glass of booze. At dinner parties this is relatively easy to do, but slightly trickier when you're out drinking. In this case, instead of alternating between water and alcoholic drinks at the bar, just order or ask for both every time.

Oh, and if you really want to feel better when you wake up after a night on the sauce, stop smoking. When I quit, my hangovers improved by approximately fifty per cent.

HOW TO OPEN A BOTTLE OF CHAMPAGNE

Avoiding the bubbly blush

Being asked to open a bottle of champers is one of those little things – like, perhaps, being asked to hold a strange and unfamiliar baby – with which some men are still not completely happy. It's not the act itself (only a baby would worry about that), it's the dread of what *might* happen: a high-decibel tantrum in the middle of your local supermarket on a busy Saturday afternoon, or a shower of poo (that's champoo) covering your father-in-law's three-piece suite. It's only ignorance that causes this fear, and negotiating a bottle of bubbly should be as easy as winning the trust of a six-month-old.

To begin with, be sure your bottle is well chilled by putting it in the bottom of the fridge for at least two hours before you intend drinking it. Either that or put it in an ice bucket (full of ice, dopey) for twenty minutes. Champagne should be drunk at 8–10ºC, and if it's too cold it can lose flavour. There was a time when champagne was always served in a saucer-shaped glass (also known as a 'coupe', and apparently modelled on the breasts of Marie Antoinette), but the wide mouth actually causes the effervescence to dissipate, so it is now almost always served in a chilled flute or tulip glass (unless you're a student, obviously, in which case you drink it from a dirty tea cup, a traffic cone, or anything else that happens to be lying around the flat). The mouth of the glass should be narrower than its centre, to concentrate the bouquet and prevent the bubbles from escaping too quickly. You should always hold the glass by the stem, because if you wrap your hand around the glass it will warm up the liquid inside. Champagne cascades can only be achieved using saucer-shaped glasses, and the optimum ratio in which to stack them is as follows: bottom tier – 60; first tier – 30; second tier – 10; third tier – 4; fourth tier – 1. Good luck.

There are no hard-and-fast rules concerning what is actually the best champagne house; essentially you should drink what you like and what you can afford, though the more you pay, the better the poo. If you are giving a drinks party, and don't mind a slightly sweeter champagne taste, then you should choose a good prosecco, the Italian sparkling wine that is a lot, lot cheaper than champagne, and tastes especially good mixed with fruit juice (Bellinis etc). Prosecco is perfect for summer weddings, although a good champagne should really be used for any toasts during dinner. If you're going down this route, choose your prosecco carefully, as some are too sweet and can be rather flat . . . but a good one is a great party drink.

Good champagne continues to mature after bottling, although non-vintage wine can soften remarkably if stored too long. In ideal cellar conditions (around 10ºC) some fine champagnes will keep for twenty or thirty years, but otherwise your timescale is very limited. The Champenois say that you should not keep champagne for longer than it was cellared originally, so that means up to two years for a non-vintage and up to three years for a vintage. The following are good vintages: '71, '82, '85, '88, '89, '90, '93, '96 and '02, with the best being found in the brut category. Also, the bigger the bottle, the better the wine.

It is generally considered to be the only wine which can be drunk at any time of the day or night, and before, during and after meals, as well as on its own. The most famous quote regarding champagne is attributed to Madame Lilly Bollinger: 'I drink it when I am happy, and when I am sad. Sometimes I drink it when I am alone. When I have company, I consider it obligatory. I trifle with it if I am not hungry, and drink it when I am. Otherwise I never touch it – unless I am thirsty.' As a fitting epigram it is almost perfect, only tarnished by the fact that these days you could apply its sentiments to everything from beer to vodka.

Now to the important part: to open your bottle, wrap it in a towel or dishcloth, and remove the wire and the foil that surrounds the cork (never let go of the cork once the muzzle of wire is removed). Point the bottle away from any guests, pets or six-month-old babies at an angle of 45 degrees. Then, while firmly holding the cork with one hand, gently twist the *bottle* in a clockwise direction with the other, slowly pulling it towards you until the cork quietly pops out. This is called a soft-pop, although the 'pop' can be increased by speeding up the process. The champagne pop is part of the drink's iconography, and has become a nouveau yob ritual, a cheap and deliberately gauche spectacle perpetuated by the antics of triumphant racing drivers. Much better to let the cork escape quietly and discreetly. When pouring, fill the glass one-third full. When the bubbles subside, add another third. Italian waiters are taught to just pour the first third, and I know from experience that the only way to get them to pour more is by demanding it: 'More please. I'm English.' Accompanied by a smile, of course, albeit a rather thin one.

Oh, and you should never keep champagne, either by resting a teaspoon in the neck or by using a stopper, no matter how air-tight. Please don't be a ponce or a tightwad: drink it or throw it away.

HOW TO SKIN A RABBIT

Because one day you'll have to

First, check your (dead) rabbit's eyes. If they're milky, then throw it away as it's probably diseased. Then pinch the skin at the loose part of the lower belly, and cut a small hole in it (being careful not to puncture the stomach lining). Pull the skin from the body, towards the head. You can tear and cut as you go, as long as you don't cut the animal. Now pull the skin extremely hard in both directions until the front and back of the legs are free of the skin. Take a sharp breath and cut off the head, and then quickly snap the lower part of all four legs to remove the feet. Then cut through the groin and remove the waste tube, and cut a substantial 'V' into the flesh and lop off the tail. Being careful not to cut into the intestines, cut the stomach lining and remove all the innards. Check the internal organs, especially the liver, for signs of white patches or spots (and if you find any, ditch the animal). Now wash it under the tap and soak it in salt water, to improve the taste and texture.

Your rabbit is now ready for cooking.

HOW TO CARVE

En garde! How to get your bird (etc)

As far as men are concerned, carving used to be something of a rite, as 'absolutely essential a part of his education as a knowledge of horsemanship, swordsmanship, and dancing' according to one twentieth-century etiquette guide. And while swordsmanship has certainly vanished from the societal landscape – when was the last time you needed to challenge someone to a brunchtime duel? – knowing how to carve is crucial if a man is to convince people he hasn't spent his youth eating cold pizza and drinking warm beer.

First you will need a good knife and fork. The knife should have a blade about nine or ten inches long with some depth at the heel (two inches at least); the blade needs to be slightly curved and should taper to a point (never use a knife with a serrated edge as it will tear the meat). The fork should have large curved prongs (i.e. it needs to be a proper carving fork – you can't really get away with anything else). You should also have an industrial-strength knife sharpener.

Before carving your bird, let it stand at room temperature for twenty minutes to allow the juices to saturate the meat. Then transfer the bird from the roasting pan to a carving board. Now cut through any trussing with scissors or your knife, making sure you remove all of the string. To prepare the bird for carving you sink the fork a couple of inches behind the point of the breast bone, with one prong on either side of the bone. Once you've done it a few times you'll realise that there is a special place for it, which was apparently designed to accommodate really big forks. Slip the knife under the right wing and cut upwards to release the joint that holds the wing to the chicken or turkey. Do the same on the left. Then cut off both thighs, cutting through the joint, not the bone, wiggling the drumstick to locate the joint (if you pick it up and twist it, it should now come off). Next, slice open the neck cavity with an oval incision that allows you to remove the stuffing while leaving the skin intact. Use a long-handled spoon to scoop out all the stuffing from the bird, and then transfer it to a serving dish. Then cut an inch above the parson's nose, pushing as far as you can. Then make the same cut underneath and separate it from the bird.

Now you are ready to carve. Put the fork into the bird in exactly the same place as you did first, and – if you can – turn it on its side so it looks as if it's lying down (poor thing). Start carving the breast into slices, leaving them on top of each other on the bird. You can carve meat standing up, but when chicken or turkey falls the meat can sometimes crumble. It's not imperative that you do this, but it looks impressive. (Don't carve the drumsticks; it's silly.)

Ducks are carved in the same way, as are geese, although you should remember than most people much prefer goose breast, rather than the other bits and pieces. When carving a partridge, cut along the top of the breast bone and divide it into two equal parts (half a partridge is a fair portion for one person).

When carving red meat, always cut across the grain, unless you're carving saddle of mutton, of course; this is always carved at right angles to the rib bones, in slices running parallel with the grain of the meat. If you're carving a suckling pig (the prince of pork), the pig should be served with the head separated from the body. The pig is then sent to the table with the body separated in half, lengthways. Now cut away the shoulders and then the legs, and you can carve away to your heart's content.

HOW TO FRY THE 'SECRET' EGG

A culinary gift for the starter-pack chef

Perhaps unsurprisingly, hardly any reputable cookbooks tell you how to properly fry an egg. After boiling an egg, frying one is meant to be the simplest kitchen exercise there is, a task ranked alongside drinking a glass of water or walking up and down the stairs without falling over. But it too has its secrets.

The Perfect Egg . . . and other secrets was written by the Italian architect and essayist Aldo Buzzi in 1979, and is a playful and idiosyncratic tribute to the profound pleasures of cooking and eating. While quoting Alexandre Dumas, Franz Kafka and Raymond Chandler, Buzzi pontificates on the joys of gnocchi, salsa verde, stuffed pigeon and *farfalle alla matriciana* as well as the humble sandwich. He also – almost in passing – explains how you cook the 'perfect' fried egg. It is short, to the point, and it works: 'You cook it on a low heat; you don't put it into the pan directly from its shell but from a cup: only the white to begin with, holding the yolk back with a spoon; then, when the white starts to set, you sprinkle it with salt and pepper and pour the yolk on top of it, right in the middle, and thus avoid too direct and searing a contact with the bottom of the pan. The cooking is completed with the lid on the pan; that way the egg cooks (just a little) on its upper side.

'Once it's ready you transfer it on to a warm plate to avoid it over-cooking in the heat of the pan. It is possible to add a little of the olive oil or butter (frothy) in which it was cooked. But if the egg is being cooked with bacon it has to be picked up with a spatula so that whatever it is cooked in drains off, and it is placed dry on the warm plate.'

I would suggest using duck eggs, as they're bigger. Serve with toast (never *on* toast), with strong coffee (espresso, if you have the machine) and, if you're technically making brunch (i.e. after 11 a.m.), or have a hangover (or both), also with champagne or beer.

This is a breakfast to be eaten by men and their best friends when their wives or girlfriends are away for the weekend at some ludicrously overpriced spa. It celebrates fastidiousness and a certain attention to detail without taking any time or needing preparation. Eat it quickly while reading the papers and planning the day ahead (which will hopefully involve watching sport on television, drinking moderately and preparing dinner). Don't cook another, as it will take away the novelty. You are, however, allowed one more beer.

Gentlemen, you owe it to yourselves.

HOW TO MAKE A THREE-EGG OMELETTE

Because you can't make one without breaking the other

Controversy rages in the kitchen: milk, or no milk? Most chefs will tell you that using milk or cream is a blasphemy not to be entertained, so in the interests of détente, this recipe is *sans* milk.

Take an eight-inch stainless steel omelette pan (for omelettes they actually work better than Teflon) and put it on near maximum. Then take the cubic equivalent of two tablespoons of unsalted butter and watch it melt. If you don't especially like the taste of butter, then use ordinary cooking olive oil (i.e. not virgin). Some recipes recommend bacon grease instead, and you make this by frying some bacon (no oil needed or wanted), and then removing the bacon.

Now break your eggs into a bowl, mixing until whites and yokes have become one, containing as much air as possible. And then pour into the frying pan, using a spatula to make sure it settles evenly. Season with a little salt and even less black pepper. Occasionally shake the pan so the eggs don't stick to the bottom.

When the surface of the omelette looks set, but is still wet on top, add your filling, on one side on the omelette. Using a spatula, fold the omelette over the toppings. Let set for 45 seconds, and then serve.

As for fillings, choose from cheese; oysters (cover the oysters in Parmesan cheese, fry in hot olive oil with sliced garlic); smoked salmon (lox) and cream cheese; poached haddock, Gruyère and crème fraîche; Stilton, shallots and parsley; tomato and Mozzarella, garnished with Parmesan; apple (Braeburn or Granny Smith), prosciutto, Cheddar and English mustard; roasted garlic and goat's cheese; Morbier cheese and walnuts; kippers and Swiss cheese; chorizo, rocket and cherry tomato. For a Spanish omelette, use onions and potato; if you're Nigel Slater you might also use parsley, mint and tarragon leaves, plus a tablespoon of flour, making it more like a tortilla.

Larousse Gastronomique is the world's greatest cookery encyclopedia (and therefore its best recipe manual), and in it you'll find foie gras omelette: chop some half-cooked goose foie gras into half-centimetre cubes. Put them into a deep plate which has been rubbed with garlic, sprinkled with freshly ground pepper, and turn the pieces so that they are covered with the pepper. Lightly beat the separated yolks and whites of your eggs, and mix by shaking the handle of the pan. Season with salt. When the eggs begin to set, add the foie gras cubes, then fold and cook until brown.*

---

*If there is no filling, you can always revert to making scrambled eggs. This is achieved by starting an omelette, then screwing up the omelette in some way (pan not hot enough, eggs not mixed well enough, eggs cooked too much, eggs burnt, etc), swiftly followed by a half-hearted shrug of the shoulders and the bare-faced lie that you were making scrambled eggs all along.

HOW TO COOK PERFECT PASTA

Always err on the side of caution. Unless you decide not to, of course

'A lot of people think that fresh pasta is superior to dried,' says Jamie Oliver. 'That's rubbish, it's just that they do different things. Dried pasta is generally made from flour and mostly water, which means that it lasts for ages and retains a fantastic bite which is great for seafood, oily and tomato sauces, whereas fresh pasta is silky and tender and suits being stuffed and served with creamy and buttery sauces.'

Which means that you should have no qualms about using dried pasta. In fact, for proper *al dente* pasta, dried is always best. *Al dente* means 'to the tooth' in Italian, and describes pasta (or in some cases, risotto) that is slightly undercooked, that still presents a little resistance when you bite into it. The pasta shouldn't be chalky or tough, just a little firm. The expression can also be applied to certain vegetables such as green beans, which are served while still retaining their crunchiness, but it's mostly used in connection with pasta.

To get perfect *al dente* pasta the pan must be removed from the heat and the pasta drained while it is still firm enough to bite into. You boil your water, having added a little salt and some olive oil, so the pasta doesn't stick together or to the pan, and then keep checking it so it doesn't get too soft (in the words of Nigel Slater, 'Cooked till tender but far from soft – in other words until it still has a bit of bite left in it'). Just about the only people who prefer soft pasta are children, so you need to monitor the pan carefully.

Don't be embarrassed if you occasionally fancy some good old-fashioned overcooked spaghetti. Aldo Buzzi felt the same way. 'Now and then I am overcome by a violent yearning for canteen cookery (be it school, barracks, office, hospital), for a plate of "back to basics" pasta,' he wrote, all those years ago. 'I dash into the nearest trattoria, sit down, and without even looking at the menu order a plate of Spaghetti Bolognese. I don't ask for it to be cooked to order, so I'm letting myself in for an overcooked portion; and I ask for Bolognese sauce, which I normally consider the very one to be avoided, because at that juncture it is precisely the sauce I want. I even want to shout to the waiter: "And take care it comes on a cold plate!" but there is no need, the plate will be icy.

'Once I've devoured the overcooked spaghetti in its nondescript sauce – with pleasure, I may add – the crisis is over. For a good while I shall revert to asking for spaghetti cooked to order, *al dente*, and make a fuss if that's not what I get.'

Alternatively, there are few more satisfying guilty pleasures than eating, fresh from the fridge, a cold plate of previously cooked pasta that was originally served only with tomato purée and black pepper. If you're feeling adventurous, throw it into a small pancake pan with some olive oil and fry it up.

Indulge yourself.

HOW TO DRINK COFFEE

Spruzzo di cioccalato?

In 21st-century society, knowing how to order your coffee is as important as knowing how to commission a suit. It's all very well thinking we live in a democratic, merito-cratic, metrosexual, mochaccino bubble, but when you're standing in the queue in Pret-à-Manger, wondering what coffee you might want to accompany your avocado, Gorgonzola and Nutella wrap, you can't just blithely ask for a cappuccino. It just doesn't work, sonny. Not after breakfast, anyway.

The cappuccino has inspired a smorgasbord of caffeine delights, from lattes and frapaccinos to the double mocha *fiordipanna* (with ice cream). But beware. If you want to drink like an Italian (instead of, say, walking like an Egyptian), then cappuccinos (or, more accurately, *cappucci*) are never drunk after 11 a.m. It stems from the principle that too much milk inside you after mid-morning will slow you down, which is why in most cafés in Italy you'll get a glass of cold water at the same time to dilute the milk in the stomach. (They do this in The Wolseley in London, too, although strangely they give you the water regardless of which type of coffee you've ordered.)

Any coffee drunk after this time should be espresso-based and should be knocked back standing up at the bar, barking into your mobile and speed-reading the paper. Drinking coffee is not a sedentary occupation in Italy; nor by rights should it be anywhere else. They won't tell you that in Starbucks, but then the Milanese and the Romans have never truly fallen in love with the Americanisation of their potent black brew. Proper coffee is not a leisurely activity, not something to be lingered over. In British country house hotels we still get asked if we want to 'take our coffee in the lounge'; in Italy you take it as you're paying the bill.

Take it straight and strong (*liscio*), or have a double espresso (*caffè oppio*), an extra strong espresso (*caffè ristretto*), or, if you're on your way home after a hard day worrying about which Barolo to drink tonight, then fire yourself up with a *caffè corretto* (with cognac or grappa).

They say that Milan is a city fuelled by ambition and coffee beans, but only the right sort of ambition and the right type of coffee beans.

Buon lavoro (good work).

HOW TO STOP EATING

Common sense and little-known tricks

I've often thought that if you want to stop eating so much and lose weight, then you should do exactly that: eat less food and start exercising more. Hello, anyone home? Sure, you can start a health regime and one of those weird, unsociable diets that will contort your working day and your social life so much that no one will ever want to spend any time with you – sure, you could do that. But why don't you just try eating less?

First you should cut out the cappuccinos and start drinking espresso (I'm already assuming you never take sugar in caffeinated drinks). If you have toast or cereal for breakfast, swap them for half a grapefruit: trust me, you get used to them. Then, cut out bread with lunch – just ask the waiter not to bring the bread basket. Don't drink at lunch (what's the point? You can't work after two drinks, and you know it). And start leaving things on your plate. Train yourself to leave at least two mouthfuls of everything on your plate (is having those two spoonfuls of mashed potato really going to make you feel so much better?) And don't snack between meals. If you have a business lunch every day, and if you're not going out in the evening, just skip a meal (it's not going to kill you). Your body's still running off what it got at lunchtime, anyway.

If you're feeling hungry, drink a third of a litre of water, as you could just be feeling a little dehydrated (the water will fill you up, too).

And if you're at home and you feel like diving into the fridge, go upstairs and brush your teeth instead; you'd be surprised how the taste of fluoride and mint can alleviate any hunger pangs. Then go and drink some peppermint tea. On no account eat pasta or heavy carbs after lunchtime, and try not to eat at all after nine. If you have low blood pressure, or your blood sugar level tends to drop dramatically, eat apples. And if you still feel an urgent need to eat, wait. Hunger pangs quickly pass.

Another trick is to buy smaller plates. In a lot of upscale restaurants you'll find thirteen-inch plates, while in America nearly all plates are eleven-inch. In Europe they tend to be nine-inch plates, and these are the ones I'd buy for home. After all, you feel full when your plate is empty.

If you're a normal, healthy, outgoing person, you're going to have nights where you drink your body weight in beer, when you eat a burger at midnight (and think about having another), and have a massive breakfast the next day because you've got such a hangover. But don't beat yourself up about it. Write the day off, and just try and be more careful tomorrow.

And when all else fails, appeal to your own vanity: if you let your waist expand you won't be able to get into that Prada suit; and I know for a fact it cost you a small fortune.

HOW TO ASK FOR THE BILL

'Some time this afternoon would be nice . . .'

One of the few irritating things about eating in restaurants is the time it takes to get the bill. Everything has gone according to plan – she's turned up broadly on time, laughed at most of your jokes, drunk at least one glass too many, and appears to have generally enjoyed your company (poor, deluded thing) – but you asked for the bill ten minutes ago, and not only has the waiter obviously been seconded to the Algarve, but the mood at the table is turning decidedly cool. You've exhausted the small talk, you can feel both of you getting a little edgy, and she's now thinking about going home instead of coming with you to the party. Where the hell's the waiter?

This is one of the reasons I have regular haunts that I use a lot both professionally and personally. If you use somewhere a lot, and the staff know who you are and what you like, a quick nod can usually facilitate a bill in the space of a minute or two.

But if you're on foreign soil – South London, perhaps, or just somewhere you don't normally go to – then you could be in for the long haul. There's no reason to expect the waiting staff in any restaurant to know your schedule, and they assume – quite rightly in many cases

– that their customers don't want to be rushed. But in your case they're wrong. You are a Big Swinging Dick (BSD for short, but not for long) and need to be back in the office, oh, at least twenty minutes ago. So you need matey boy over there to stop flirting with the two ugly girls from Wiltshire who came in for the second sitting, and come over here with your bill, pronto. Tonto.

What you should have done is asked for the bill when you were ordering the coffee. That way, if it doesn't come with your caffeine, you can ask again, just to make sure the waiter hasn't forgotten (and he may have done). He may be trying to turn your table and so will be unusually attentive, but as you've been fed and watered he's probably busying himself with a bit of new custom. So ask for the bill as early as is decent, and then chase him up for it. If it doesn't come in five minutes then you're quite within your rights to start asking every other waiter whose eye you can catch, or whose short-cut you can block by the judicious repositioning of a chair. Waiting staff hate this, as they all have designated areas, so this will help them to speed up the bill.

Then, when the bill does come, don't let him dart off, because he'll be gone for another ten minutes. Have your card ready and give it to him whilst the bill is still in his hand. Take a quick glance at it (is service included?) before letting him go. If he's the sort who isn't going to let you get away that easy, and turns on his heels, gently grab him by the elbow and give him your card.

Finally, when the credit card slip and your Amex are brought back, quickly sign the slip, pick up your card and vacate the premises. Gone are the days when you had to hang around waiting for your chap to see that you hadn't signed it Guy Fawkes or Frank Bruno. Protocol's different now, and the moment you get your card back, you can make for the door like a ghost.

If things get really silly, and you've been waiting for twenty minutes for someone to bring you the bill, then get up and walk towards the door – you'll be surprised how many of the staff will try and stop you. You've got the moral high ground now, and should say you've been trying to pay but that no one was taking any notice of you. This should do the trick. I've only attempted it a few times, but boy does it work. (It works especially well abroad, too, even more so if you can't speak the language.)

AFTERWORD

So there we are. At the end of the bar. I hope some of the above has helped you in some way, and maybe taught you a little about the whys and wherefores of modern etiquette. To my cost, I know there are many ways to be a man these days, and I hope some of the material here has proved to be useful.

As for myself, I learned to behave through trial and error. And mostly error, let me tell you. I learned from books, from records, from films, and from the things that real men did around me. Sometimes these men I knew, and other times – most times – they were the men I wanted to be. DeNiro. Bowie. Sinatra. As life lessons go, Sinatra probably taught me more than most, and any decent Frank biography will have a dozen or so *bons mots* you can take away and dwell upon. 'I think my real ambition is to pass on to others what I know,' he once said, a glass of Jack Daniel's in one hand, and a broad in the other. 'It took me a long, long time to learn what I now know, and I don't want that to die with me. I'd like to pass that on to younger people.' As his biographer Bill Zehme once said, he wasn't talking about song artistry. He meant life nuance, how-to stuff, the business of comporting oneself . . . the business of being a man. 'Be true to yourself,' he said. 'And stay away from dark thoughts.' Of course Sinatra is probably closer in spirit to the old ideas of being a man – ideas centred around the way you wore your hat, and the way you walked and talked. But the enduring thing about Frank – apart from all those songs, all those gorgeous, gorgeous songs – is the fact that he knew there was a code. A code for men. And while today that code is very different from the code that Frank lived by – that code is no less important.

You may, of course, disagree with me – and, of course, with Frank – and to those of you who do, I can only offer the following. Back in the day, whenever a reader wrote a letter to H.L. Mencken, the legendary editor of the *New Yorker*, he would always respond in the same way. Regardless of what the specifics of the letter were, he would always write back, 'Dear Sir [or Madam], You may be right. Sincerely yours . . .'

And the best of luck to you if you are. Swagger well . . .